MW01109960

Loving Immigrants
in America

Noviembre 2017

Diana,

gracias por la amatista.

Daniel

American Philosophy Series

Series Editor: John J. Kaag, University of Lowell

Advisory Board: Charlene Haddock Siegfried, Joe Margolis, Marilyn Fischer, Scott Pratt, Douglas Anderson, Erin McKenna, and Mark Johnson

The *American Philosophy Series* at Lexington Books features cutting-edge scholarship in the burgeoning field of American philosophy. Some of the volumes in this series are historically oriented and seek to reframe the American canon's primary figures: James, Peirce, Dewey, and DuBois, among others. But the intellectual history done in this series also aims to reclaim and discover figures (particularly women and minorities) who worked on the outskirts of the American philosophical tradition. Other volumes in this series address contemporary issues—cultural, political, psychological, educational—using the resources of classical American pragmatism and neo-pragmatism. Still others engage in the most current conceptual debates in philosophy, explaining how American philosophy can still make meaningful interventions in contemporary epistemology, metaphysics, and ethical theory.

Loving Immigrants in America: An Experiential Philosophy of Personal Interaction, by Daniel G. Campos

The Religious Dimension of Experience: Gabriel Marcel and American Philosophy, by David W. Rodick

Aesthetic Transcendentalism in Emerson, Peirce, and Nineteenth-Century American Landscape Painting, by Nicholas L. Guardiano

Richard J. Bernstein and the Expansion of American Philosophy: Thinking the Plural, edited by Marcia Morgan and Megan Craig

Peirce's Empiricism: Its Roots and Its Originality, by Aaron Wilson

Emerson's Metaphysics: A Song of Laws and Causes, by Joseph Urbas

Death and Finitude: Toward a Pragmatic Transcendental Anthropology of Human Limits and Mortality, by Sami Pihlström

Ethical Habits: A Peircean Perspective, by Aaron Massecar

The American Philosopher: Interviews on the Meaning of Life and Truth, by Phillip McReynolds

Recovering Integrity: Moral Thought in American Pragmatism, by Stuart Rosenbaum

Values, Valuations, and Axiological Norms in Richard Rorty's Neopragmatism: Studies, Polemics, Interpretations, by Krzysztof Piotr Skowronski

Loving Immigrants in America

An Experiential Philosophy of Personal Interaction

Daniel G. Campos

LEXINGTON BOOKS
Lanham • Boulder • New York • London

Published by Rowman & Littlefield
A wholly owned subsidiary of The Rowman & Littlefield Publishing Group, Inc.
4501 Forbes Boulevard, Suite 200, Lanham, Maryland 20706
www.rowman.com

Unit A, Whitacre Mews, 26-34 Stannary Street, London SE11 4AB

British Library Cataloguing in Publication Information Available

Library of Congress Cataloging-in-Publication Data

Names: Campos, Daniel (Central American Immigrant), author.
Title: Loving immigrants in America : an experiential philosophy of personal
   interaction / Daniel Campos.
Description: Lanham : Lexington, 2017. | Series: American philosophy series |
   Includes bibliographical references.
Identifiers: LCCN 2017026848 (print) | LCCN 2017032381 (ebook) | ISBN
   9781498547857 (Electronic) | ISBN 9781498547840 (cloth : alk. paper) |
   ISBN 9781498547864 (pbk. : alk. paper)
Subjects: LCSH: Philosophy, American—20th century. | United
   States—Civilization—20th century. | Philosophy, American—21st century.
   | United States—Civilization—21st century. | United States—Emigration
   and immigration. | Campos, Daniel (Central American Immigrant)
Classification: LCC B936 (ebook) | LCC B936 .C36 2017 (print) | DDC
   305.9/069120973—dc23
LC record available at https://lccn.loc.gov/2017026848

The paper used in this publication meets the minimum requirements of American National Standard for Information Sciences—Permanence of Paper for Printed Library Materials, ANSI/NISO Z39.48-1992.

Printed in the United States of America

A mis papás, Rodolfo y Liannette,
y mis hermanas, Anto y Xinia,
con amor
Loving Immigrants in America

Contents

Acknowledgments

Gracias is one of the most beautiful words in the Spanish language. I offer *gracias* to the very large community of family, friends, teachers, and students who have encouraged and nourished me over the course of so many years as an immigrant and an American saunterer. I owe *Loving Immigrants in America* to all of them.

My parents, Rodolfo and Liannette, my sisters Antonieta and Xinia, and my *abuelos, abuelas, tíos, tías, primos y primas*—those who are still living among us and those who still live in our hearts—have fostered the sense that I still have a home in Costa Rica and that has provided comfort and security in my attempt to make myself at home in the United States also and across America. My experience has been much less perilous than that of some of my immigrant friends because of them. They have also exemplified in their lives the active principle of resilient love that I have striven to develop in theory and practice. Philosophical sources aside, resilient love is really their living bequest to me.

My teachers Emily Grosholz and Douglas Anderson have also encouraged me to thrive over the years. As a student, they gave me freedom to grow in my own direction intellectually while drawing me back to philosophy as a starting point for explorations and experiments. Besides being excellent philosophers, Emily is a delightful poet and Doug is a singer-songwriter and sportsplayer. Both have been exemplary persons and good friends to me over the years.

My former teachers Mitchell Aboulafia and Catherine Kemp, and exemplary Latino philosopher Gregory Pappas, encouraged me and supported the writing of this book all along. They offered guidance in the conception and development of this book for publication. My editor, John Kaag, also nourished this project and opened doors where more conventional academic

ix

philosophers may have shut them. My colleague and friend, Lara Trout, read insightfully and critically several drafts of all the essays and alerted me to several of my phenomenological blind spots regarding other people's experiences in my descriptions and reflections. Critical readers will surely find still many blind spots and failures on my part to be sensible to the experiences of others; however, Lara kept me from making several gross errors in that regard. That aside, she was a most encouraging critic and friend all along. My colleagues and friends Amanda Hicks, Cesar Torres, Mariana Alessandri, Evgenia Cherkasova, and David O'Hara also provided very fruitful philosophical criticism and feedback over conversations and correspondence. I am thankful to all of them.

My Brazilian friends at the *Grupo Acadêmico de Estudos Cognitivos* at the Universidade Estadual Paulista in Marília, São Paulo, provided a friendly but critical environment in which to discuss the personal struggles and phenomenological and ethical principles at the heart of *Loving Immigrants in America*. I am grateful to professors Maria Eunice Quilici Gonzáles and Mariana Broens and their students for their caring support. Renata Silva Souza and Mariana Vitti were among the first persons to read a draft of my initial essays. Without their sensitive responses I may have quit on what I thought of as a secondary, eccentric project. Professor Susana de Castro and our co-researchers at the *Laboratório Antígona* of the Universidade Federal de Rio de Janeiro likewise offered a space for critical discussion and encouragement in the final stages of writing.

I struggled to narrate and describe experiences in order to write these essays. In the very early stages of writing, my Brooklyn friend Caron Levis—a playwright, picture-book author, and teacher of creative writing—generously read and criticized several drafts and guided me toward writing a bit less stiffly and sounding a bit less like an academic philosopher. All the roughness left in my style here is due to my own writing defects; Caron fostered the virtues. My friend Greg Cooper—an English teacher, actor, and documentary writer, among many other talents—carefully read and edited most of the essays, helping me with my many difficulties in writing in English. The better-written essays in this book are so mostly because of Greg's attentive editing. Jay Jankelewicz generously helped me with more technical matters of formatting files and endnotes.

I am also thankful to several former students at Brooklyn College. Certainly they inspired my writing. My friend Wilson Jachero created the bibliography and corrected several endnotes. Nwe Mar Win and Mrittika Deb discussed personally with me several of their own experiences as immigrants to the United States that gave me insight into the particularities of my own experience and a Latin American man. Sofia Ahsanuddin brought her political acumen and depth to our discussions of the need for loving resistance and solidarity between various immigrant and non-immigrant minorities in the United States. Nimra Asif acted as my research assistant and philosophical interlocutor. Besides, they all have been delightful friends in Brooklyn.

In that spirit, I am also thankful to several friends in America and Spain who over the years have in various ways helped me to live and write *Loving Immigrants in America*: Mandy Hardin, Brenda Beckloff, Jason Hiatt, Tiziana Cocchieri, Renato Salatiel, Leticia Ortega, Sonia Dios, Virginia Fernández Vallejo, Marisol García, Tami Aritomi, Niall Connolly, Clare McCarthy, Phil Peacock, Jen Smith, Moy Arburola, Jahel Palmero, and Carolina Murillo.

Institutionally I am thankful to Brooklyn College of the City University of New York for the sabbatical year 2012–2013 when this project emerged as central to my work and to the Wolfe Institute for the Humanities at our college for a Writing Fellowship in 2016 that freed me to complete the manuscript.

¡*Gracias a todos*!

Excerpts from A GOOD MAN IS HARD TO FIND AND OTHER STORIES by Flannery O'Connor. Copyright © 1953 by Flannery O'Connor. Copyright renewed © 1981 by Regina O'Connor. Used by permission from Houghton Mifflin Harcourt Publishing Company. All rights reserved.

Excerpts from "No Hearing" from COLLECTED POEMS by Robert Lowell. Copyright © 2003 by Harriet Lowell and Sheridan Lowell. Reprinted by permission of Farrar, Straus and Giroux.

Excerpts from "Sonny's Blues" by James Baldwin. © 1957, copyright renewed. Originally published in Partisan Review. Collected in GOING TO MEET THE MAN, published by Vintage Books. Used by arrangement with the James Baldwin State.

Additionally, grateful acknowledgment is made to the following for permission to reprint copyrighted material:

Aunt Lute Books, San Francisco, for passages from *Borderlands/La Frontera* by Gloria Anzaldúa.

Casey Black for lyrics from "Flowers" by Casey Black. Copyright © 2013 by Casey Black.

Niall Connolly for lyrics from "Calling Out for Rain" by Niall Connolly. Copyright © 2007 by c.u. records.

Philosophical Library, New York, for passages from *The Procession* by Khalil Gibran.

Sebastián López for lyrics from "Indocumentado" by Sebastián López. Copyright © by Sebastián López.

Chapter 1

Philosophical Prelude

Playfulness, Love, and Personal Growth

At once narrative and reflective, *Loving Immigrants in America* is a philosophical account of my experience as a Latin American immigrant to the United States. A series of interrelated personal essays together convey this experience of walking or sauntering, going on road trips, reading American literature in the South, playing association football (soccer or *fútbol*), churchgoing, and Latin dancing in the United States. This book's central motif is the caring saunterer, who is understood to be a person who makes him or herself at home anywhere, even as a Latino immigrant in the United States. The figure of the saunterer is taken from Henry David Thoreau's essay "Walking,"[1] but I reinterpret it to make it my own. Through the narrative essays I show the experience of trying to make myself at home affectively, socially, and intellectually in this country.

I hope to establish an open and earnest *philosophical* dialogue with critical readers interested in the problem of immigration in the United States today. I write as an American philosopher—in the continental sense of North, Central, and South America—whose reflections provide an accessible and provocative angle for the development of insight into the experiences of immigrants in the United States. Thus I bring philosophical reflection drawn from experience, in the broad American tradition, to bear on current issues—on the problems of people and not of philosophers, as John Dewey might put it.[2]

Since my essays speak directly to experiences we have in common as people, I hope they are apt for opening a thoughtful dialogue in which philosophy bears on life. I have in mind, for example, the lives of many of my students at Brooklyn College of the City University of New York. A large proportion of my students are immigrants or children of immigrants. Many others have immigrant ascendance. In our Brooklyn context, all are familiar, or at least acquainted, with the lives of immigrants and their communities. In fact, my

interactions with Brooklyn College students from Ecuador, Argentina, Myanmar, Mexico, Bangladesh, Peru, China, Uganda, Brazil, Colombia, Kazakh-
stan, Honduras, Yemen, Panama, Russia, and Guatemala—to mention only a
few examples—inform my writing in these essays. Our experiences are akin,
and what I have learned through personal interactions and relations with them
has helped me to reflect about my own experience since I first arrived in the
United States from Central America over twenty years ago.

All these experiences have shaped who I am as a person. Our personality
and our perspective emerge when our inner self interacts and even clashes
with the outer world. This is what American philosopher Charles Peirce calls
the category of resistance or reaction in experience. My sense of self as Latin
American and as immigrant has emerged clearly for me in my interactions—
harmonious or discordant—with US society and culture. My account is thus
deliberately perspectival—I aim to reflect personally, as a philosopher who is
a Latin American immigrant in the United States. I relate my perspective to
that of others, so that readers can learn with me as I write and hope for critical
interlocutors, but I strive not to universalize falsely my angle of vision into a
general theory of the immigrant's experience.

There are two conceptual threads that guide my perspective throughout the
essays. One of those threads is my understanding of my lived experience of
immigration as a process of "personal development" in the sense expounded
by Charles Peirce.[3] The experience of immigrating is lived at the level of (1)
affects, (2) relations to places and peoples, and (3) evolving aims, ends, and
purposes. My experience has been one of continuous personal evolution at
the levels of (1) affectivity—feeling, emotion, and sentiment—as a stranger
who wants to make himself at home in a new land; (2) specific relations
of trust and wariness, welcome and hostility, with people and places in the
United States, from the South to the North; and (3) the aims that I envision as
guiding my life here. I suggest that anyone who is receptive and attentive to
the commonality of human experience can empathize with immigrants once
they see their experience as one of search for personal well-being (affective,
material, and social), growth, and self-realization. The upshot is that these
reflections on immigrant experience can, in effect, enable philosophical
moments of insight for immigrants and nonimmigrants alike. Reading along
these lines can also provide a pedagogical platform for philosophical reflection on both human experience and immigration.[4]

A second conceptual thread throughout all the essays is twofold, namely,
(1) openness to the possibilities of novel experience and to establishing new
relations to others helps the immigrant to make him or herself at home in the
United States., and (2) corresponding openness and receptivity allow people
in the United States to welcome immigrants and help them to make themselves at home. When these conditions are deliberately and self-critically

cultivated by hosts and newcomers, the experience of an immigrant may be more conducive to personal development and evolution, rather than to being stunted in his or her personal growth. These themes are explicit in my essays. I show—narratively, not demonstratively—how these possibilities may be grasped and cultivated or curtailed and thwarted in our lives together in the United States. For example, while taking walks in small Southern towns, going on road trips, reading American literature, spending holidays with hosting families in Southern farms, or playing *fútbol* with friends in the United States, I have seized upon opportunities to make myself at home in this country and grow as a person. However, I have also experienced or witnessed xenophobia in "soccer" fields and subway cars, anti-immigrant prejudice in university cafeterias and in church pulpits and pews, and appalling ignorance in university classrooms and campuses that have threatened or even stunted the possibilities for meaningful connection and relation to places and people in the United States. Whether hosts and immigrants cultivate attitudes of openness or closure, receptivity or hostility, warm- or cold-heartedness, and whether they act upon those cultivated dispositions, has a crucial impact on how immigrants experience their lives in this country.

Regarding the writing style, I do not argue but narrate and reflect. There is a predominance of narrative content because I cannot argue others into understanding my experience; I can only convey and reflect upon it, so that a critical dialogue can ensue. In this sense, I aim for my style to approach William James's admonition, in his essay "The Moral Philosopher and the Moral Life," that "books upon ethics ... so far as they touch upon the moral life, must more and more ally themselves with a literature that is confessedly tentative and suggestive rather than dogmatic—I mean with novels and dramas of the deeper sort," because ethical inquiry is experimental, fallible, and ongoing through communal dialogue.[5]

Furthermore, I began writing *Loving Immigrants in America* in a spirit of playfulness. I wanted to explore important aspects of my various levels of experience as an immigrant to the United States through a freer, more spontaneous, and more intimate style of writing than academic philosophy usually allows. I began with variegated experimental essays; these evolved into a precariously stitched series of narratives, at some point they tended toward becoming a literary memoir, and finally they evolved into a coordinated series of personal essays marked by narrative and philosophical reflection. Throughout the writing process, I tried to preserve that spirit of playfulness. By playfulness I mean the original attitude that, according to María Lugones, turns a spontaneous activity into play, rather than the derivative attitude that results from rule-guided agonistic play, that is, from confrontation of skills and competences.[6] Positively, playfulness involves "openness to surprise, openness to being a fool, openness to self-construction or reconstruction and to construction and reconstruction of the 'worlds' we inhabit playfully, and thus openness to risk the ground that constructs us as oppressors or as being oppressed or as collaborating or colluding with oppression."[7] Negatively, playfulness involves "uncertainty, lack of self-importance, absence of rules or not taking rules as sacred, not worrying about competence, and lack of abandonment to a particular construction of oneself, others, and one's relation to them."[8] This attitude turned my writing, at crucial moments, into play. I needed the ludic attitude to carry me through the more deeply personal and sometimes painful aspects of my writing. I also needed it for balance. I did not want to belittle my experience, as it is worthy of being shared—like the experiences of every person—in its various layers. But I also did not want to overemphasize the gravity of my own experience in the face of the experiences of other immigrants I know intimately, people who have had much rougher paths to travel in their lives. I know I immigrated under very favorable conditions, much more favorable than many immigrants I know, love, and respect. Even so, in the spirit of American philosophy, I hope there is value in sharing my experience and in the philosophical reflections I can offer upon that experience, including a ludic strain in my approach. Because of the playfulness in the forthcoming essays, then I offer a prelude and not a prologue.

Writing *Loving Immigrants in America* also demanded love—*eros*, *philia*, and especially *agape*. It required the desire for truth, goodness, and beauty to be shared with and among actual or potential friends, and also the attitude of caring for and supporting our mutual growth. As I wrote, I sought to narrate some of my most intense experiences of feeling wary or welcome, rejected or accepted, discouraged or encouraged, and stunted or fostered in my personal growth as a Central American in the United States. I also reflected on my own dispositions and attitudes of being closed or open, hermetic or permeable, aloof or engaged, hateful or loving toward the land and people and society and culture in this country. I often grasped attitudes, dispositions, and sentiments—in others, but especially in myself—that pained or hurt me and required soothing and healing. Through writing I sought, perhaps, another kind of balance, akin to the *loving resistance* that Argentine immigrant María Lugones seeks in her own thinking and writing, theorizing and living.[9] Shifting emphasis, in writing I sought *resistant love* or even *resilient love*. For me, this loving attitude was nourished and clarified philosophically by Charles Peirce's understanding of *agape* as cherishing-love.[10] Cultivating agapic love had a dual function in my writing process. First, *agape* "at one and the same impulse [projects] creations into independency and [draws] them into harmony."[11] I had to nourish my own fallible attempts at writing experimentally, accepting my failures and not giving up on the experiment's possibilities but rather allowing my creation to become what it would and could become. The impulse to persist in the experiment came from my desire to converse with my American neighbors; that is, with those people whom I "live near, not locally perhaps, but in life and feeling."[12] I strove to engage them in order to understand and be understood by them, to cultivate caring relations with each other. Second, then, I felt and strove to enact agapic love as "the ardent impulse to fulfil another's highest impulse."[13] The agapistic gaze contemplates the possibilities for transformation, regeneration, and growth in what is hateful in oneself and in others. Contemplation is not sufficient, however; agape freely offers grace and actively fosters growth. Upon "recognizing germs of loveliness in the hateful," agape "gradually warms it into life, and makes it lovely."[14] As I wrote, I endeavored to apprehend, cherish, and foster possibilities for mutual encouragement and cooperative growth with my neighbors in America.

For its mixture of narrative and reflective style and its philosophical themes, this book is profoundly indebted to the tradition of W.E.B. Du Bois's *Souls of Black Folk*, Jane Addams's *Twenty Years at Hull-House*, John McDermott's *The Culture of Experience: Philosophical Essays in the American Grain*, María Lugones's *Pilgrimages/Peregrinajes*, and Douglas Anderson's *Philosophy Americana*. It can be related to other genres, such as memoirs or personal essays by immigrants. However, I have written this book from a philosopher's perspective. Another distinctive feature, I think, is that as a Latin American immigrant to the United States, I reflect on my experiences by appealing to US philosophy and literature; that is, the intellectual traditions of the country to which I immigrated have provided me with avenues for thought. I hope I have done justice to this tradition. I am deeply indebted to it—it has helped me become who I am as a person, teacher, writer, and friend in the United States today.

THE PERSONAL ESSAYS

I would prefer that interested readers discover the specific themes and narrative threads of my essays by going directly to them. Perhaps later they can return to this section of the prelude and compare their interpretations with my own sense of what I have written in the essays. However, I offer this summary.

Loving Immigrants in America consists of eleven intertwined essays. The first one, "An Inclination to Listen," sets the stage by contrasting my recent experiences of hostility and conflict as an immigrant in New York with my early experiences of being welcome in Arkansas, to a place and among people receptive to my presence and personal perspective. My initial openness to experiential possibilities and my drive to make myself at home affectively have been compromised by experiences of conflict, hatred, and xenophobia. Drawing from W.E.B. Du Bois's *Souls of Black Folk*, I suggest that I have peeked into mainstream Anglo-American culture from behind a veil. Just as Du Bois "lifts the veil" in order to make black experience visible to white people in the United States, so too as a Latino philosopher I make some of my experiences, most often lived in common with others, visible to those on the other side of the "veil." Then I propose that a dialogue between immigrants and United Statesians must be cultivated through a mutual inclination to listen. This is urgent and necessary in the United States. I do use the term "United Statesian" politically to designate US nationality because, throughout my essays, the term "American" is an honorific term designating those who are open to listening to others and willing to look at each other from either side of the veil anywhere in the Americas.

In the subsequent essays—"Southern Saunters," three on road trips, and four others on reading American literature—I convey various ways in which, when I arrived, I was open to the possibilities of personal experience that the United States and its people afforded me. Taking literal and metaphorical walks in Arkansas; going on road trips to Alabama, Kentucky, Oklahoma, Louisiana, and Ohio; and reading John Steinbeck, Henry David Thoreau, William Faulkner, Flannery O'Connor, Toni Morrison, and James Baldwin—doing all of this, I grew as a person because those contexts fostered growth. All those experiences involved mind, body and heart, even if walking and road-tripping emphasized the embodied aspect of exploring and searching for connections to new places and peoples, while reading literature in search for insight to understand my life in the South emphasized the intellectual aspect of immigrating to a new social, cultural, and interpersonal context.

However, there were always conflicts. Some of these were most evident on the football field. Thus the next essay—"Playing *Fútbol* in *la Yunai*" (*la Yunai* is how Central Americans refer to the United States)—introduces the violent clashes that immigrants can experience in the US. In my case, the clashes occurred most forcefully on "soccer" fields where open hostility to Latinos was unapologetically unleashed. As these conflicts opened wounds, I began to close myself off to the possibilities of relating to some people and places in the United States. I began to write "*gringos*" off. But "*gringos*" in this sense is a generalization ripe for hatred. What I needed to find, in Peirce's words, were "germs of loveliness in the hateful" and cultivate them. That is, I needed to adopt Peirce's ethical principle of "agapism"—the disposition to cultivate an effective love that cherishes the beloved persons, grasping and fostering their possibilities for growth toward their own ends and ideals.

Likewise, I experienced religious conflicts as a Christian churchgoer who witnessed moralizing hypocrisy and even hatred toward immigrants among Southern churchgoers. This is addressed in the essay "Churchgoing." To rescue my faith in a meaningful way, I needed to develop a secular understanding of the role of love and grace in human lives, so I could try to live by them—with contradictions and inconsistencies, but earnestly, without hypocrisy. Again, agapism—understood as a secular *ethical* principle for living well—provides a key for reflection. In "Finding a Loving Home among Friends," however, I convey how caring friendships grounded in reasonable and sensible affinities with people close to me counterbalanced my loss of interest in churchgoing. In cross-cultural friendships I have found an affective home in *la Yunai.*

Finally, during my time as a student in Arkansas and then in Pennsylvania, I had very little contact with Latin American people and culture for many years, except for connections with other students. This led to a sense of isolation, as if part of my personal identity had been severed because of a loss of tangible relationship to people from Latin America. So in "Dancing Out of the Labyrinth: From Solitude to Communion," I aim to describe how I have sought and where I have recovered, through Latin dancing, connections to people who share my cultural sensibility here in the United States. This is another agapistic search for relatedness. It is, as well, an escape from the labyrinth of solitude, as Octavio Paz would put it—that is, from a situation in which we are alienated from people who share our most intimate hopes, sentiments, ends, and ways of living and in which we feel these ways of living to be threatened. I aim to show why I cultivate these Latin American connections even as I try to remain a saunterer, equally at home in the United States and in Latin America. Latinos in the United States who want to remain Latin Americans can be persons who have a rich relationship with various peoples and places, with sensibilities, sentiments, hopes, aims, and purposes tied to the Americas, and to Americans, at large.

NOTES

1. Henry David Thoreau, "Walking" in *The Portable Thoreau,* ed. Carl Bode (New York: Penguin, 1982), 592–630.

2. John Dewey, "The Need for a Recovery of Philosophy," in *John Dewey: The Middle Works, 1899–1924,* ed. Jo Ann Boydston, vol. 10 (Carbondale and Edwardsville: Southern Illinois University Press, 1980 [1917]), 3–48.

3. C. S. Peirce, "The Law of Mind," in *The Essential Peirce: Selected Philosophical Writings,* eds. N. Houser and C. Kloesel, vol. 1 (Bloomington: Indiana University Press, 1992), 312–333.

4. I have developed this conceptual framework in my essay "Understanding Immigration as Lived Personal Experience," in Gregory Pappas, ed., *Pragmatism in the Americas* (New York: Fordham University Press, 2011), 245–261. However, in my experiential essays in this book, this conceptual structure is implicit, not explicit.

5. William James, "The Moral Philosopher and the Moral Life," in *Pragmatism and Other Writings*, ed. Giles Gun (New York: Penguin, 2000), 260.

6. María Lugones, *Pilgrimages/*Peregrinajes*: Theorizing Coalition against Multiple Oppressions* (Lanham, MD: Rowman and Littlefield, 2003), 93–96.

7. Ibid., 96.

8. Ibid.

9. Ibid., 19–20, 32–33. Lugones writes, for example, of being tender toward what is hateful to her, while remaining resistant, that is, thoughtfully responsive rather than reactionary.

10. See C. S. Peirce, "Evolutionary Love," in *The Essential Peirce: Selected Philosophical Writings*, vol. 1 (Bloomington: Indiana University Press, 1992), 352–371.

11. Ibid., 353.

12. Ibid., 354.

13. Ibid.

14. Ibid.

Chapter 2

An Inclination to Listen

We had been waiting a while on the cold platform in the subway station when the F train finally arrived. My hands and feet felt numb in the wintry New York City night, and I was eager to go home. Niall had played a gig at The Living Room in the Lower East Side, and I'd listened to his lyrics attentively as I drank a fine pint of Irish stout to go with the mellow guitar and soothing Irish voice:

It's like I'm trying to keep a storm at bay.
Quiet now, I cannot take this rest.
I fear I might have something stupid left to say,
and to bite my tongue and walk might be best.
There's a part of me that's calling out for rain
to wash me clean at this time of test.
If you got something, come on have your say;
but I have not found the right words yet.[1]

I wondered with whom he'd had that difficult conversation: How long did they stay silent after arguing? Did they find the right words to reconcile? But I did not ask after the gig. We just stayed with friends at the venue and listened to a couple other songwriters play and sing their own tunes.

So it had become quite late, and we were ready to get to Brooklyn. When we entered our subway car, we found it full of Bengali Muslims, Orthodox Jews, Mexicans, Central Americans, and Chinese, as well as Russians, Ukrainians, and white United Statesians. I stood at the end of the car, as I often like to do, watching people read, listen to music, talk, play with their phones, or sleep as they go home. Most people's faces seemed relaxed—only a few frowned wearily—but their eyes were glazed with tiredness, and their eyelids fell heavily. Some people, mostly working-class men but also women, were sleeping after the late shift at work. Everyone looked as if he or she just wanted to get home and be at peace.

At Bergen Street station, in a rich neighborhood of brownstone town-houses, the *gringos* began to exit the train. By the time we reached Park Slope at the 7th Avenue station, almost all of them had gotten off, leaving mostly Asians, Latinos, and Eastern Europeans on board. That was in the days before hipsters began to move to my neighborhood to gentrify it. At Church Avenue station all the Bengalis, Chinese, and Latinos got off, leaving only a Russian woman, Niall, a white guy, and me in the car. The woman was Caucasian. Niall is a redheaded, red-bearded, white, lightly freckled man from Cork. I have thinning brown hair, green eyes, and lighter skin that turns ghostly during winter. The *gringo*, a young guy in his early twenties wearing a hoodie, jeans, and work boots, looked at all of us, drew a quick inference based on ethnic stereotypes, and, guessing we were white folks who would agree with him, complained in a loud voice, "God, what the fuck is this? Where the hell am I? Isn't this the United States? Did you see all those people?" I looked at Niall, the woman looked at us, and we all decided to remain silent, as the guy continued to complain and curse.

I did not feel angry but appalled and sad for him. But I could see Niall's indignation growing in his hardening expression. Then, when we got off the subway in the very next station, the guy also stepped off while continuing to curse. Niall's indignation flared into anger, and he bumped the cursing man as we exited the station and walked downstairs from the elevated platform. The guy saw Niall carrying his guitar case on his back and yelled, "What is wrong with you, you hippie bitch?" Niall retorted, "That you are a xenophobic jerk." "A what?" he asked, as he caught up to us beneath the platform, by the Yemeni fruit and vegetable stand on the corner of Ditmas and McDonald Avenues. "A xenophobic jerk," Niall reaffirmed, stepping toward him. But to the *gringo*'s ears, Niall's Irish pronunciation sounded like "zehnophobic." Then he stepped forward, bringing his face almost nose to nose with Niall's, and said, "Can't you speak proper English?" As I saw the anger escalating into impending blows, I pulled Niall away and tugged him as we returned to our apartment. The guy taunted us, yelling obscenities, but Niall now knew it was not worth it. In the loud, angry confrontation there was no possibility of dialogue, no inclination to listen. The whole time, I felt weary for that *grin-guito*—weariness infused with tiredness and disgust and the dread of similar past encounters in *fútbol* fields and church pews and classrooms around *la Yunai*. I wanted nothing to do with that guy, did not want to listen to him, even as I guessed from his actions that his life—whatever the experiences that already had led him to hatred—may not have been easy but rather filled with economic and personal struggles.

And it pained me that I did not want to listen, that I had no inclination to engage, to find a way to make a conversation possible. For I recalled the opening verses from Robert Lowell's poem "No Hearing" that had informed my life, thought, and sensibility for years:

Belief in God is an inclination to listen,
but as we grow older and our freedom hardens
we hardly even want to hear ourselves ...
the silent universe our auditor—[2]

ARRIVING IN ARKANSAS

I first felt on my skin the sticky humidity of the Arkansas summer and breathed the muggy air, feeling its thickness fill my lungs, on a hot July day over twenty years ago. It was my first time not only in the South, but also in *la Yunai*—as the United States is often called in Central America, due to the way the English word "united" sounds to Spanish speakers. When I arrived in Arkansas, a group of young Central Americans were expecting me and the others. I had met Silvia along the way. She was from Honduras, and I recognized her as a traveling companion when I saw her crying and asking for directions at our airline's desk in the New Orleans airport. She had short, curled brown hair and brown eyes, and she was about my height and age. I guessed she was part of my cohort and had also been re-routed due to flight cancellations, so I approached her and asked if she was going to Little Rock. It must have been her first trip to *la Yunai* also and she seemed relieved to find that she was not stranded and alone. Eventually, we also ran into Angela, from Guatemala; Natalia and María, from Nicaragua; and Julio and Diana, from Panama. We arrived together in Little Rock, not knowing what to expect.

The warmth and camaraderie with which Miriam, Alonso, Manuel, and others greeted us, led us to the van, and drove us to our destination, a small town in Central Arkansas, surprised me. I had grown up in Costa Rica, and though I had had Nicaraguan and Panamanian friends there, I had never really been together with such a large group of Central Americans. The surprise was pleasant and a relief. When first meeting a group of people, I tend to be silent and observant. But I enjoyed listening to the conversation, trying to pinpoint the nuances of their different Spanish accents.

Miriam in particular was beautiful, with long black hair, dark eyes, and olive skin, and her Salvadoran accent was enchanting, so I listened to her quietly but attentively. "*¿Y vos estás bien, tan callado?*" she asked me. Her "s" at the end of "*vos*" was shortened, but not quite a "j" like that of Nicaraguans, who'd say "*voj*," and her "ll" sounded almost like an "i" when she wondered why I was so quiet, "*caliado.*" I responded that I just felt tired, though I really mostly felt curious and preferred to listen and observe. I focused on her smile and her words during that first van ride into the flatness of Central Arkansas.

It was highly unusual at that time to see so many Central Americans, or Latinos in general, together in Arkansas. Spanish was not commonly heard either. That much I had noticed right away from the glances people directed at us in the Little Rock airport as we chatted excitedly on our way out to the parking lot. They were not hostile or menacing, just perplexed or surprised looks. The circumstances that brought us together probably would have seemed unusual to the onlookers also: we were all students on full academic scholarships to a liberal arts college.

In my case, I came to the *Yunaited Estéits* a few days before I turned eighteen in order to study at the college. Though the scholarship provided a good academic opportunity, I came, in part, for the sake of adventure. I did not know it at the time, but I was a Thoreauvian saunterer. I was already a student at the University of Costa Rica, and it was unclear to me whether a US college, even a good one such as the college I was going to attend, would provide a better education—maybe, maybe not. However, the possibilities of living in a new culture, learning a new language, and seeing a new place in the world enticed me. So, when I was offered the scholarship, I accepted it, and soon afterward I packed a few clothes that filled half a duffel bag and flew to Arkansas. When Miriam and her friends picked us up at the Little Rock airport, I was carrying only that half-empty duffel bag and was ready to saunter.

Over the course of that first summer, I met many students from different places in the United States and the Americas, and I explored the campus and the small town where it was located. It was a time of discovery for me. I had a strong inclination to listen to anyone, to observe everything, and my freedom had not hardened—my mind, my heart, and my senses were fully open to the possibilities of experience that all people and all places could provide.

I wanted to start with the most important things, so on the day after I arrived I went to look for Miriam at her residence hall on the college campus to talk to her. She was happy not only to see me but to see me talking, she said, because I had been too quiet the previous night, and they had all wondered whether I was unhappy or unfriendly, not just tired, as I'd said. Costa Ricans sometimes have a bad reputation among Central Americans for being stuck-up, and I wondered if that was part of their suspicion. But I was eager to dispel any such notion, especially with her. And so I began to talk to her, and to all the others as well, and to forge a family of friends away from home.

I discovered the joy of long summer days. Costa Rica is too close to the Equator for the length of days to vary significantly throughout the year, and so summer days in Arkansas seemed blissfully eternal. The sun rose early, and dawn was the coolest time of day. By ten o'clock the heat was oppressive. If I walked outside, I would sweat profusely, and then, once inside, I would feel my clothes dry up and stick to my skin. But as the afternoon advanced and the sun began to settle on the west, a softer light would fall upon the world. I could sit under an oak tree and converse with friends or read a book as the late afternoon turned into evening. I could play some *fútbol* on the grass or throw a baseball with a mate like Julio and feel the joyful sweat of sporting. At dusk the big, bright sky would turn a darker and deeper shade of blue that spread from east to west. Then I could go to my dorm, take a shower, have dinner at the school cafeteria, and later walk to the movies at the only theater in town or go for frozen yogurt—a newly found joy—with my friends.

One weekend, I experienced two favorite cultural passions at once: going on a road trip and spending an afternoon at a baseball game. Julio, Manuel, and I joined a student trip to watch the Cardinals play in Saint Louis. We rose before dawn one Saturday, hopped in a van, and rode north, up the heart of Arkansas and into Missouri. Along the way we saw farms, woods, and a few small towns scattered here and there. It was an entirely new landscape for us. I observed the trees carefully—some evergreen and several deciduous species. Some were *robles*, I guessed, but I did not know the word "oaks." But most of the other trees I could not recognize, let alone name. There were no flowering *malinches*, *jacarandás*, or *cortez amarillos* in the farm fields, no sprawling *higuerones* for shade, no *jocotes* or *mangos* in fruit orchards, nor towering *ceibas* or *espaveles* rising above the canopy in the woods. Whereas I had been accustomed all my life to lushness and diversity, I saw along the road some comparative sparseness, even austerity, of species that gave its own character to the land. I could perceive but not name the beauty in this new landscape.

When we arrived in the city, we went directly to Busch Stadium. Julio was a full-blooded baseballer in good Panamanian style—he had grown up playing in the minor leagues in Chiriquí. Manuel had also played *béisbol* well in Nicaragua, where the sport is a national passion. I had only played baseball on the streets with the kids from my neighborhood in San José, and I had only learned some basic fielding and batting skills in high school physical education. I was mainly an enthusiastic fan of the sport. In San José we would play baseball on the street every October—that was the only time of the year when we could watch baseball since the so-called "World Series" was on television. We did not care or worry about the pretentiousness of calling a national championship the world championship; we simply enjoyed the sport, and every October it was time for baseball. (December, during the Tour of Costa Rica, was time for cycling, and the rest of the calendar was *fútbol*.) My grandfather, who had studied in the United States in the 1940s and learned to love baseball, was a Yankees fan, and so was my father. The earliest World

Series I could remember was a 1978 Yankee victory over the Dodgers, and so I was a Yankees fan also. But that day I was excited to see the Cardinals. I had watched them on television play three recent World Series, in 1982, 1985, and 1987, and I knew Ozzie Smith was a fine shortstop.

I bought a Saint Louis cap and cheered for the Cards. So did Manuel. Julio bought a New York Mets cap and supported the visiting team. But I was the one who got in trouble with the locals. We were on the highest bleachers with hard-core Cardinals fans. When the Mets came on the field, I started whistling loudly. In Costa Rican *fútbol* stadiums, whistling is an expression of disapproval and rejection. Anytime the visiting team steps into the pitch, the local fans whistle in disdain. So naturally I whistled against the Mets. But in Saint Louis the fans interpreted whistling as cheering. They did not like it one bit, and I started to get dirty looks. I was a bit puzzled. No adult said anything to me; they let their nasty glances speak for them. But an eleven- or twelve-year-old boy, blond and blue-eyed, looked at me and warned: "This is Cardinal territory." I knew I had to stop whistling, but I did not understand why. Only later I caught on to the fact that my whistling meant something different in this new context.

I do not remember who won the game—in my heart's memory it was the Cards. But we ate the traditional hotdog, drank a soda, and enjoyed a good, long afternoon at the baseball park. Afterwards, we walked to the Gateway Arch and stood on the western bank of the mighty Mississippi River, looking at Illinois on the opposite bank. It was larger than any river I had seen up to that point in my life, and its brown waters flowed quietly but powerfully. Since I was little, I had been drawn to geography and cartography. I would spend countless hours observing maps. I especially enjoyed studying the great, large rivers of the world and learning about their way of shaping human societies and cultures. Standing in front of the Mississippi, then, brought a quiet joy to my heart.

That very summer I had read some stories by Mark Twain, the Cervantes of Missouri and *Quijote* of the Mississippi. I stood watching the river flow for a long time, as the sun set and the large sky once again turned a deeper shade of blue, and I got a better experiential grasp of Twain's words from *Life on the Mississippi*:

> When I was a boy, there was but one permanent ambition among my comrades in our village on the west bank of the Mississippi River. That was, to be a steam-boatman. ... Once a day a cheap, gaudy packet arrived upward from St. Louis, and another downward from Keokuk. Before these events, the day was glorious with expectancy; after them, the day was a dead and empty thing. Not only the boys, but the whole village, felt this. After all these years I can picture that old time to myself now, just as it was then ... the great Mississippi, the majestic, the

magnificent Mississippi, rolling its mile-wide tide along, shining in the sun; the dense forest away on the other side.[3]

Contemplating the majestic river like young Samuel, I could feel the same hopeful expectation, the same yearning to navigate and explore. So far, I'd made it from San José to the Mississippi at Saint Louis. Riding back south to Arkansas late that night, I sat silently among my friends, recalling the sight of the river that sparked Twain's storytelling wit and imagination and allowing the fresh memory to enliven my joy.

My first roommate at the college was a redheaded guy from Little Rock who had all the habits and attitudes of a lawyer in the making: he studied, but not because he enjoyed it; he was straitlaced and charming to everyone; and he went to church on Sundays to be seen, but he loved "sinning." He was a political science major and an active, enthusiastic member of the College Republicans club on campus. I could see that he fancied himself on his way to being a politician. I found this mixture of social manners, religious form, and political aspiration a bit strange—a bit too conventional and old-fashioned for a young guy, a college student and pal. I could not yet see into the Bible Belt background from which these manners and forms emerged. But hey, having just arrived from Central America I probably seemed even stranger to him, so we passed no judgment on each other, and we got along well. He was interested in Costa Rica and asked me lots of questions about life there, especially about politics but also about girls. He liked listening to my accent, was observant of my grammatical mistakes, and helped me to improve my English at my request. He also got a kick out of teaching me to say "supercalifragilisticexpialidocious," even though my saying it was really quite atrocious. And so I felt that, though we were very different, we could be friends. Possibilities for human transaction are endless when you are open to them. I was still open to all of them at the time.

I have always had a romantic streak—I became passionate about Keats, Shelley, and the English romantics later in college—and I was especially open to the possibilities of the human heart. As to lovely Miriam, however, I soon learned that she had a boyfriend, David. The disappointment led me to brood a bit like an eighteen-year-old romantic. But I respected Miriam's choices, of course, and David turned out to be a very friendly guy, which helped my heart. About a year later, he in fact got me my first off-campus job in the United States, constructing new lockers in a local high school for a contractor who was short on labor. That job was illegal. However, it paid better than my on-campus job as an assistant janitor, for which I was *legally* paid *below* minimum wage. I never understood how that worked—the school could include me in its part-time payroll, but, as I was a foreign student on an F-1 visa, it could only pay me an hourly rate below minimum wage. Such on-campus work was also my only option for legal work. I may have been new to *la Yunai*, but I wasn't dumb—I could recognize unfairness. I was also a broke college student, and though my survival was not at stake and my needs were not dire, when David found me the construction job, I worked hard and took the cash. But that happened a year later, on my second summer, when I'd begun to see how US society and its economy worked. In those early days of my first summer in Arkansas, I was just finding my bearings in a new world. And my heart was open to all the people I might encounter and the relationships we could forge.

Of course, I was in the United States to study, so I enrolled in summer courses. I took swimming, though I already knew how to swim, because it was a source of pleasure in the overwhelming heat. With Angela, Julio, María, Silvia, Natalia, and the other new scholars, I also took English reading and composition—this was our time to improve our grasp on the language before the fall semester started. And thus I began to study college English and to love this language and its literature. Before I arrived, I had a decent grasp of the elements of English grammar from my schooling at home, but I had no fluency in speaking or writing. I had no sense of the ways of using the language creatively in formal or informal contexts, and I did not yet know the possibilities of playing with the language poetically.

Most crucially for survival purposes, I had no sense of slang. One evening, walking on campus along with Pam—a sweet southern girl I met on the last week of the summer—I crossed paths with two guys walking in the opposite direction. As I looked at them I heard one of them say, "What's up?" I did not understand what the question meant or that it was a greeting directed at me, so I walked past them. But I felt them stop and turn toward me, so I too turned. The guy spoke to me in a louder tone of voice and with a hint of irritation: "I said, 'What's up?'" I remained silent and puzzled, and this reaction increased his displeasure. Pam caught on to the reason for my perplexity at once and explained that I was from Costa Rica and did not know slang. He heard my accent when I confirmed this, and at once he was appeased. I had slighted his characteristic southern courtesy of greeting strangers, but he understood I meant no disrespect. Pam explained afterwards that "what's up?" was not to be interpreted literally as what's up above you. I laughed at myself, and in such small ways I began to learn to make the English language, as spoken in the South, a playful thing. Playful and sensual: I loved the way Pam's lips pouted at the end when she said "shampoo"—the gentle "sh" and the final "oo" so much softer than in the Spanish "*champú*," and her lips pouting as if inviting me to kiss her.

Endless possibilities of sense, of the heart, of the mind—when I arrived in *la Yunai*, I was open to all of them. And *la Yunai* itself was more open to the possibilities that people could offer, especially immigrants. The institutions themselves were friendlier to the foreigner: obtaining a student visa, a social security number, a bank account, and a driver's license was relatively simple. On my second or third day here, Alonso—another red-haired, freckled friend, but this one from Costa Rica—walked downtown with me, near the traditional courthouse, to obtain my social security card with my passport and student visa. A helpful lady with a lovely Arkansas accent helped me to do it quickly, and not for a moment did she look upon me with suspicion. But the institutional policies were mainly a reflection of the attitude of the people themselves. When I arrived in Arkansas, people knew little about Central- or Latin-Americans in general. Even, or perhaps especially, college students knew close to nothing about geography or history or languages in the Americas. But they were curious and inquisitive. Clerks at shops, barbers, bank-tellers, and fellow students would hear our accents and be interested to know where we were from, where our countries were located, what life was like there, what languages we spoke, what we ate, what music we listened or danced to. I experienced the same interactions when I took my first sauntering trips to Oklahoma, Texas, Louisiana, Mississippi, Alabama, Missouri, Tennessee, Kentucky, and eventually north to Ohio, Maryland, and New York. Over the course of twenty years, however, I've seen those possibilities for transaction—for conversation and learning and forging connections across American cultures—slowly closed off or curtailed in significant ways.

BROOKLYN

I am still in *la Yunai*, now teaching philosophy at a public college in Brooklyn. I live in an immigrant neighborhood. My next-door neighbors are a family of Albanians from Kosovo. A Polish couple live downstairs with their two young, lovely daughters. My landlord is Albanian—his name is Luftim but people call him "Jack." Our neighborhood is home to Russians, Ukrainians, Uzbeks, Poles, Mexicans, Guatemalans, Nicaraguans, Guyanese, Bengalis, and Yemenis. There are Orthodox Jews, Muslims, and Christians. My favorite fruit and vegetable shop is staffed by Mexicans and Turks. The former Ukrainian bakery is now a halal shop; the former kosher fish shop became an Uzbek restaurant. There are Yemeni, Dominican, Mexican, Guyanese, Bengali, Russian, and Polish convenience stores, where you can find little treats from the Middle East, Eastern Europe, the Caribbean, and Latin America—from Uruguayan *yerba mate*, Peruvian *aceitunas de botija*, and Colombian *arepas* to Turkish yogurt and Bengali delicacies that mystify me. My students at the college are Anglo- and African-American Brooklynites, Jewish- and Italian-Americans, as well as immigrants and children of immigrants from all over the world—from Azerbaijan to Spain, Nigeria to China,

Belarus to Uganda, Russia to Pakistan, Yemen to Myanmar—and from all over the Americas. They speak Portuguese, Spanish, French, Russian, Ukrainian, Polish, Urdu, Arabic dialects, Hebrew, Mandarin, Cantonese, Burmese, and many other languages, in addition to English. Through reading, teaching, observing, listening, and conversing, I am becoming rich in experiences. I love exploring this pluriverse of cultures and peoples.

As I discover these new worlds of possibility, experiences in the city sometimes remind me of some of the reasons why I came to forge meaningful relationships with the cultures and peoples of *la Yunai* and have stayed among them. Recently I went to an exhibit at the Whitney Museum on the blues culture that emerged in the South—deep in the Mississippi Delta—and has pervaded and shaped American culture. The exhibit took me right back to those early years of discovery—of studying mathematics and literature in Arkansas, going on road trips, and traveling to Beale Street in Memphis and to New Orleans and the Louisiana bayous to discover new literary, religious, and musical worlds. At the exhibit, I saw a portrait of James Baldwin by Beauford Delaney that moved me to the core. Delaney, a black child of Tennessee, portrayed his friend Baldwin in the soft brightness of pastel colors as a strong, beautiful, young, black man. Baldwin's forceful but serene expression surrounded by luminous color lit up my heart. I stood in front of the painting in awe as I remembered reading "Sonny's Blues" under an oak tree on the college campus's main lawn for an American short story class with Professor Long, an outstanding American teacher, so many years ago.

I had shared my affective commotion at reading about Sonny's tragic life with K—a lovely girl from Baton Rouge whose keen sensibility for literature attracted me—and I had discussed the story with Duane—an intelligent, serious southern gentleman with a passionate heart and conservative values in art and politics, who read literature insightfully but aspired to be a Navy pilot. We were all friends and could talk and be earnest as we tried to understand Sonny's experience.

In Baldwin's story, Sonny grows up in Harlem in the 1930s and 1940s, at a time when everything that surrounds black boys like him is hostile or threatening. His father dies, then his mother, while his older brother is at war and abandons him emotionally. Still a high school boy, Sonny remains in Harlem surrounded by drugs and violence. Under siege on all fronts, he tries to stay alive by playing jazz at the piano, and a story of emotional struggles, personal falls and redemptions, ensues. Later in life, during a still fragile period of reconciliation with his older brother, Sonny tells him what it feels like to be back in Harlem after being convicted and imprisoned for peddling and using heroin:

> It's terrible sometimes, inside … that's what's the trouble. You walk these streets, black and funky and cold, and there's not really a living ass to talk to,

and there's nothing shaking, and there's no way of getting it out—that storm inside. You can't talk it and you can't make love with it, and when you finally try to get with it and play it, you realize *nobody's* listening. So *you've* got to listen. You got to find a way to listen.[4]

K, Duane, and I had tried to listen, to understand, to empathize. In my case, I had *tried* to understand what it felt like to be Sonny, having lost a beloved friend to violence in San José and having fled to a different world in the South, with a silent torment inside of me. I had even tried to look up "Am I Blue" at the library's record collection. That was the tune Sonny played in the story's cathartic scene. But I did not know the artist, and no one could tell me who composed it. But I had found and listened to some of Charlie Parker's records, whom Sonny admired and whom I didn't know until reading Baldwin's story. I had wanted to grasp "what the blues were all about" for Sonny and his band leader, Creole, and the other players:

> They were not about anything very new. He and his boys up there were keeping it new, at the risk of ruin, destruction, madness and death, in order to find new ways to make us listen. For, while the tale of how we suffer, and how we are delighted, and how we may triumph is never new, it always must be heard. There isn't any other tale to tell, it's the only light we've got in all this darkness.[5]

At the piano, Sonny created new ways to make us listen to the story of our joys and sorrows, delights and sufferings, to our tales of love, loss, fall, and grace.

As I came out of my reminiscing trance in front of Delaney's portrait of Baldwin and walked out of the old Whitney Museum, I took the subway down to Union Square and headed straight for the Strand Bookstore, where I found a used copy of Baldwin's *Go Tell It on the Mountain*. The title had been on my reading list for sixteen years, and it was time to read about the black boy whose family had migrated from the South to the North, all of them carrying a world of grief, pain, and regret in their hearts. It was time to read the story of a sensitive boy growing up under the pressures of a confused religiosity meant to save him from perdition in the tempting world of Harlem.[6] I knew this to be a theme in my own experience in *la Yunai*. In the conservative religious world around the college campus and in the heart of the Bible Belt, I had felt in my soul the conflict between churchgoing, worldly living, and the search for genuine religious experience—a classical American theme that is enmeshed with my life in this land. In the days following the Whitney awakening, as I proceeded to read Baldwin and as I recalled the revival experience in front of Delaney's painting at the exhibit, I remembered the people with whom I have read literature, listened to music, gone to church, traveled, and lived my American life. Those people whom I love are the main reason I have stayed.

Sometimes, however, experiences in the city also trigger all the conflict and tension that has built up over twenty years in *la Yunai*—experiences such as the confrontation with the angry *gringuito* on a late-night train from Manhattan back to my Brooklyn neighborhood. In this city sprawled across islands just off the mainland, I continue to live my story in *la Yunai*, and I feel the increasing tension between love for and repulsion from it. I am all too aware that I have closed some possibilities of experience and have become indurated, like this country itself. Confrontations, rejections, and misunderstandings—ethnic slurs, cultural stereotypes, racial prejudice, threats of violence, ignorant contempt, systemic injustice, and even patronizing condescension—have a hardening effect on my heart. Nowadays, I hardly want to travel inland for dread of finding myself in an alienating context where these experiences are increasingly common. Meanwhile, United Statesian hipsters—waspy guys wearing their carefully chosen uniform of slim-cut jeans, flannel shirts, retro-looking glasses, and sneakers—are moving into my neighborhood, and I cringe upon seeing them and hearing them speak English in their characteristically banal way, with their shrill voices and self-involved smugness, thinking they're so unique and bragging because they once went to Argentina or Peru—they've "done" those countries already—and like to eat *empanadas* or *ceviche*. And yet they only hang out among themselves, checking each other's outfits for a different pattern in the flannel, say, and tell each other obnoxious stories of "ethnic" adventure. Their cultural explorations are not genuine expressions of interest in others, but only in themselves—their aim is the deliberate construction of a hip image.[7]

One late night I was walking from my neighborhood's subway station to the Turkish vegetable shop at Ditmas Avenue to buy fruit and bread for the following morning's breakfast. Two hipsters were walking behind me. We passed a group of Mexican men talking outside *El Pollo Rancherito*, another group of Azerbaijani men standing in a circle outside Old Baku, and some Russian men playing backgammon and drinking tea on sidewalk tables outside their small club. Women walked up and down the avenue, some with children. Outside Afsona, the Uzbek restaurant, several families gathered to talk on the sidewalk. Fathers and mothers were dressed up, and their young girls wore beautiful white dresses adorned with complex embroidery. Obviously they were chatting and saying their goodbyes after a birthday party. But as we approached them, one of the hipsters walking right behind me asked the other, "Is it safe to walk here at this hour?" The second responded, "I am not sure; I always feel so incongruous in this neighborhood." *Incongruous!* I wanted to turn around and say, "So why the heck did you move here? Couldn't mommy and daddy rent you a pad in a neighborhood where only hipsters hang out? You'd sure be *congruous* there!" But I stayed quiet and did my best to block them from my hearing and erase them from my thoughts. I do not mind hipsters when I am out and about the world; I just ignore them. But I don't talk to them in my neighborhood.

I silently fear my cold dismissal of them is because they remind me of a culture of which I have grown weary. Perhaps it is not just that they are hipsters—it may be that they are Anglo-Americans. I am loath to admit that I may be rejecting wholesale the culture of white Anglos—a culture that I sometimes harshly interpret as that of self-righteous, self-designated "Americans" who, no matter what their political leanings or religious views may be, always and at the core think of "their America" as exceptional, as some unique case of liberty and justice in cosmic history, and of immigrants as underdeveloped people who are blessed or fortunate to be here as passive recipients of "American" charity. A large proportion of *gringos* want to force them to go away, to "go home." Others think these "poor people" should stay and assimilate, under the guidance of either a self-sacrificing churchgoer or a condescending liberal.

A dreadful feeling of self-reproach, however, overcomes me when my thoughts lash out against an entire people, all of the white Anglos, in this way. I would be ashamed to reveal this harshness to my Anglo-American teachers or friends. I am aware, moreover, that my generalized characterization is unfair. I do not recognize any of my friends or former teachers or colleagues through it. And I shudder when I realize that this attitude may be a first step toward the kind of extremism of the *gringo* who wants to see no foreigner in his neighborhood or town and who thinks that immigrants are all the same, namely, pariahs in his "America." I do not want to walk along this path in my life.

LOVE AND HOPE

These feelings of mutual suspicion and rejection are real and have an effect on our world. I read nowadays of a preacher in Little Rock who lashes out against the immigrants and Muslims who are threatening "God's nation." Those church pews are full every Sunday with Christians who have forgotten the principle of *agape*—of love that cherishes the beloved, accepts their own ways of feeling, thinking, and being, and helps them along their own ways to achieving their own ends and purposes.[8] Meanwhile, I go about my living in Brooklyn, sharing experiences and cultivating relations with neighbors, students, and friends. But I no longer want to travel to visit *Gringolandia*, that vast heartland that *gringos* call "America." And I know that many United Statesians, some in those very church pews in my beloved South, would say, "Good riddance."

How did this happen? I think we might find insight by reflecting upon our *historias*, our stories and histories—insight into reasons that lie deeper in our hearts than wars and economic crises. Terrorist attacks, wars of retaliation, and financial crises that leave men and women—local and immigrant alike—unemployed and suffering throughout the land are only confounding factors which hide the causes of strife that lie buried in dark crevices within our hearts.

Since I arrived on that hot July day over twenty years ago, I have felt a strong drive, often a dire need, to explain myself and to interpret others, to understand them and to make myself understood, to try to connect with people whose background, cultural references, and life experiences are very different from my own. And I have wanted to make this connection a two-way affair, a dialogue. I have tried to listen, learn, and understand, but I also have yearned to be listened to and understood. This is, of course, a basic human drive. But it has taken strong cultural connotations for me, initially as a foreign student and then as an immigrant to the United States. I have wanted to know this country, its people, and its culture, but I have also wanted to share my people, my culture and my own experiences with my friends, peers, and students here.

It has not been easy. The pressures of assimilation and acculturation in this society are sometimes enormous, and often what deviates from the mainstream is ignored or misunderstood, if not openly rejected. On the whole, though, I think I have come to understand a bit about life, people, and culture in *la Yunai*, and this culture and these people have come to shape who I am, even as I have continued to cultivate my living bond to Latin American culture. I have sought, sometimes consciously and often nonconsciously, ways to adapt and to evolve while cultivating a continuous link to my place and culture of origin, a link that continues to be vital and thriving.

This process has been rather silent, however, and difficult to explain to United Statesians, even when they are openly receptive to my friendship. The fact is that our interactions take place in a largely Anglo-American setting, and the structuring force of cultural context is difficult to overcome. Our conversations are in English, and our points of common cultural and experiential reference are most often linked to the United States. The very ways of social and personal interaction—with whom I relate and how, where we gather, what we say, what we don't say, what we express or hide— are dictated by Anglo social, cultural, and economic norms.[9]

Keeping in mind social, historical, and personal differences, but appealing to the commonalities of human experience and sentiment, I often think of W.E.B. Du Bois's metaphor of the Veil in *The Souls of Black Folk* to understand this situation. Describing a boyhood experience in which a white schoolmate in Tennessee refused, with a disdainful glance, to exchange visiting cards with him, a black boy, Du Bois writes: "[I]t dawned upon me with a certain suddenness that I was different from the others; or like, may-hap, in heart and life and longing, but shut out from their world by a vast veil."[10] This Veil divided the world of whites and blacks in Du Bois's United States—especially, but not only, in the South. African-Americans could see through the Veil into the lives of white Anglo-Americans, and they could understand their norms, ways, privileges, and culture. At any rate, they were forced to accept them or pay the consequences. But they could not trespass the Veil and partake of the white world as equals. And whites could not even see through the Veil into the other side, into the ways, norms, struggles, aims, and culture of African-Americans. The Veil blinded them to the hope, strife, and toil of African-American life. Beyond the Veil, there was nothing worth seeing or caring about. Du Bois, however, masterfully revealed the presence of the Veil and explained its operations with the hope that lucid minds with open hearts could see through it in both directions.

The Veil metaphor is helpful to understand the current situation of many immigrants in *la Yunai*—those who are able to adapt so as to function in mainstream socioeconomic life while knowing they are not, and do not want to be, United Statesians, and those who do not have the opportunities and resources to escape their socioeconomic and cultural marginalization. In *la Yunai* we all need to see through the various veils that obstruct clarity of vision and limpidity of mind and heart.

As for me, I certainly have not suffered like Du Bois, his black predecessors and contemporaries, or most of *my* immigrant predecessors or contemporaries. Still I feel that I have not been able to convey to most of my friends, colleagues, or acquaintances this process of immigrating as I have lived, experienced, and witnessed it. I have seen through the Veil into their world, but they have not seen into mine. And I feel that now, more than ever, we are in need of sympathy and mutual understanding.

The history of American philosophy, in its reflective responsiveness to experience, can help us along the way toward raising mutual affective sympathy. Jane Addams often writes of the life of immigrants in Chicago in the early twentieth century for this purpose. She writes, for instance, of a young Italian girl, Angelina, who seemed to be ashamed of her immigrant mother until she learned that her mother was "the best stick-spindle spinner in America."[11] Addams then tried to explain to Angelina that her mother's

whole life had been spent in a secluded spot under the rule of traditional and narrowly localized observances, until her very religion clung to local sanctities,—to the shrine before which she had always prayed, to the pavement and vaults of the low vaulted church,—and then suddenly she was torn from it all and literally put out to sea, straight away from the solid habits of her religious and domestic life, and she now walked timidly but with poignant sensibility upon a new and strange shore.[12]

Addams is in fact concerned with eliciting the daughter's sympathy for her mother's life as an immigrant. This possibility of raising affective sympathy that leads to mutual understanding makes it worthwhile, I think, to attempt to describe the personal experiences of immigrants in order to reflect about them.[13]

As I wrote above, I feel that we are in need of sympathy and mutual understanding. And I deliberately say that I *feel* it. I do not merely *think* it, in the sense in which one may hold an intellectual belief on the basis of observed facts and events. I *feel* it in my flesh and bones, because my emotions, personal relations to people and places, and life-guiding ideals are intricately enmeshed with a people and a country in cultural turmoil over the future place of immigrants—including Latinos—and their cultures in this nation.

I did not always feel this way in this country. Perhaps telling a part of my story, and the related stories of others, might help me strike up vital conversations with friends past, present, and future. Perhaps through dialogue I can open my heart, smooth its sharp edges, and turn my imagination to possibilities of experience that seem now closed off or lost. I may regain a bit of my lost freedom—that freedom to explore all cultures, to listen to all people, to learn from all contexts, to grow and evolve. And perhaps these conversations might help others, in the way that reflection upon simple stories and humble testimonies helps us all be more sympathetic—to "feel-with" one another and expand our grasp on the wide array of human experiences. I hope we can still be inclined to listen.

Brooklyn, New York
2009–2016

NOTES

1. Niall Connolly, "Calling Out for Rain" in *The Future Tense* (c.u. records, 2007), compact disc.

2. Robert Lowell, "No Hearing 3" in *Collected Poems*, eds. Frank Bidart and David Gewanter (New York: Farrar, Straus and Giroux, 2003), 638.

3. Mark Twain, *Life on the Mississippi* (New York: Oxford University Press, 1996), 62–64.

4. James Baldwin, "Sonny's Blues," in *Going to Meet the Man: Stories* (New York: Vintage, 1995), 133.

5. Ibid, 139.

6. James Baldwin, *Go Tell It on the Mountain* (New York: Bantam Dell, 1980).

7. In terms of María Lugones's philosophy, they are not loving and playful "world"-travelers but rather imperialist conquerors, no matter how liberal they think they are. That is, they do not aim to experience other people's "worlds"—environing contexts with their own characteristic ways of cultural, social, and economic living—from within other people's grounds and perspectives, but only see those "worlds" from their own conquering gaze and in order to make themselves "cooler" and more "hip" in the opinion of their peers. See María Lugones, "Playfulness, 'World'-Traveling, and Loving Perception" in *Pilgrimages/*Peregrinajes*: Theorizing Coalition against Multiple Oppressions* (Lanham, MD: Rowman and Littlefield, 2003), 77–100.

8. For this philosophical concept of *agape*, see C. S. Peirce, "Evolutionary Love," in *The Essential Peirce: Selected Philosophical Writings*, vol. 1 (Bloomington: Indiana University Press, 1992), 352–371.

9. Again in terms of Argentine philosopher-immigrant María Lugones, I travel lovingly to my friends' "world"—where they are normatively and habitually "at ease," that is, where they agree with the rules and know what to expect and how to act to achieve their goals—in order to interact with them. But I would like my friends to know how this travel feels and the risks, adaptations, gains, and losses that it involves. And I would like to invite them to travel to my "worlds" in *la Yunai* and Central America, to try to experience my ground and perspective, my ways of living and being in those "worlds," while I am helping them along the road. See Lugones, "Playfulness, 'World'-Traveling, and Loving Perception," in *Pilgrimages/*Peregrinajes.

10. W. E. B. Du Bois, *The Souls of Black Folk*, ed. Brent Hayes Edwards (Oxford: Oxford University Press, 2007), 8.

11. Jane Addams, *Twenty Years at Hull-House*, ed. Victoria Bissell Brown (Boston: Bedford St. Martin's, 1999), 141.

12. Ibid.

13. Philosophically experienced readers will observe also that Addams writes of the woman's disruption of habits, poignant sensibility, and overall affective experience in American pragmatist terms.

Chapter 3

Southern Saunters

My first southern saunters were short walks in a small Arkansas town. The college campus where I lived and studied was located on the south edge of town, but that still was only a few blocks from the main commercial avenue and within walking distance of the town center and its quaint southern courthouse. This architectural gem was situated in a square surrounded by a pharmacy, a jewelry store, other family-owned shops, an old movie theater, and some government offices. Even though the town had only the small population of ten thousand people, the residential areas were spread out, and hardly anybody walked. Everyone drove everywhere. Except for some poor students, no one even seemed to bike, much less walk anywhere. I must have seemed eccentric, then, while taking random walks around town when I got tired of the routine of going to class, eating at the cafeteria, studying at the library, and hanging out at the college campus.

There was one time in particular when I realized just how strange I must have appeared to others. On Friday and Saturday nights, the local kids, probably from the high school but also those that didn't go away for college, would cruise around town in their pick-up trucks and cars. They would drive in a single file from east to west on the main avenue to arrive at the square downtown and then go around the courthouse, return to Race Avenue, and drive eastward. They would pack the cars full of friends and cruise around town for hours, checking out each other's cars, trucks, boyfriends, and girlfriends. One Saturday night, bored and tired of campus and with nowhere to go, I decided to take one of my random walks. I started north to reach Race Avenue and then headed west toward the courthouse, walking against the traffic cruising eastward. Some kids would stare at me with perplexed looks as they drove by. I was the only pedestrian walking along the avenue for several blocks. A guy and a girl in one car even rolled their window down and said something to me, but I could not understand it, so I continued on my way.

Taking a leisurely stroll seemed normal to me. In my native San José people walked everywhere, and I was used to getting around on foot and by bus. Given the absence of public transportation in my new Arkansas town, I just walked. When I arrived at the courthouse, I decided to sit on a nearby sidewalk bench. I had nothing to do, so that place was as good as any for me to relax and watch cars cruise around before choosing an alternate route to return to campus. It was amusing to observe the young people from town sit in a traffic jam for the sake of seeing others and being seen riding their hot wheels. The cruisers stared at me, and I at them, without judging each other, but rather in a reciprocal act of anthropological observation. Eventually, the car with the couple who had rolled down the window to talk to me looped back around. The traffic around the courthouse was particularly slow, so they stopped and again rolled the window down. My bench was under a street lamp in front of the main entrance, so they could see me well.

"What are you doing?" the girl in the back seat asked me.
"Nothing. Just out for a walk," I answered.
"Why?" she asked, now perplexed.
"Just because. And you?"
"We're cruising around."
"Why?"

They looked at each other. The girl answered, "I dunno. It's fun, I guess." They laughed, told me to have fun, and waved good-bye as they drove away. They probably thought I was strange, but that was fine with me. I was enjoying myself.

I had never wondered why I walked. It just came naturally. In Henry David Thoreau's sauntering spirit, I never really had a definite destination when I set out for a stroll.[1] The point was just to walk and follow my fancy and my whim. I often headed west, and I often ended up at the courthouse. I thought the building was a small architectural wonder in the otherwise plain town. It was built shortly after the Civil War and then expanded at the beginning of the twentieth century in neoclassical style. It had arched stone entrances facing all four directions. The main entrance faced west, with three arches creating a portico under a balcony. The balcony had white wooden railings and Ionic columns supporting a plain frieze and Doric cornice. A graceful cupola, with crystal windows and four clocks facing each cardinal point, supported a flagpole and crowned the courthouse. All around the building there was a perfect symmetry of windows and red semi-columns with white Ionic capitals. The grounds were beautifully landscaped, especially with cypress trees. The beauty of the courthouse drew me toward it when I set out on walks.

Perhaps I was trying to make myself at home by seeking a familiar experience. In Costa Rica, most cities and towns are laid out in the characteristic

Spanish colonial style, with a square or *plaza* surrounded by a church, a municipal building, and the houses of important families that over time were replaced by restaurants, *cafés*, and shops. Though some elements of the urban design had been lost over time as towns grew and evolved, when I left for Arkansas, one could still experience the centrality of the square, park, or *plaza*, certainly in small towns but even in old quarters of larger cities. It was a place to watch people, meet friends, run errands, and, for Catholics, go to church. So it seemed strange to me that in this Arkansas town the central square with its courthouse would be deserted on nights or weekends, when the county did not conduct its official business. All the same, I was drawn to it, as if trying to find something—some connection to place and people—that I had left behind at home. Perhaps I was trying to be *sans terre* in a liberating way, in the way of one who makes his home wherever his travels take him.

For over the course of my years in *la Yunai*, I have become a saunterer in my own way. Henry Thoreau writes of saunterers as those who in their walks travel to the metaphorical *Sainte Terre*, the Holy Land, so that a saunterer is a Holy-Lander, one who seeks his or her spiritual home.[2] He also writes of them as persons "*sans terre*, without land or home, but equally at home everywhere. For this is the secret of successful sauntering."[3] Thoreau prefers the first sense of being a saunterer. I have in some measure become the second, aiming to be equally at home in various lands. At any rate, when I first stepped on Arkansan soil, I did so in the spirit of a Walker: "We should go forth in the shortest walk, perchance, in the spirit of undying adventure, never to return, prepared to send back our embalmed hearts only as relics to our desolate kingdoms."[4] I arrived as a free man, ready for a walk, ready to chart new outward and inward terrains, without predetermined destinations, without prohibitions or warnings against geographical, cultural, or spiritual trespassing. Ahead of me lay the walk of life:

> We would fain take that walk, never yet taken by us through the actual world, which is perfectly symbolical of the path which we love to travel in the interior and ideal world; and sometimes, no doubt, we find it difficult to choose our direction, because it does not yet exist in our idea.[5]

I was simply following my instincts, my inclinations, and the dispositions felt in my gut.

THE OZARK MOUNTAINS

Sometimes my saunters were not literal walks but daytrips with friends. These would require a car and usually a predefined destination, but they were animated by the same sense of adventure, of freedom from fixed purpose, of allowing the day to bring what it may, as my walks around town. They were days for sauntering in the sense of wondering, musing, and wandering in spirit. My favorite daytrips were to the Ozark Mountains. On Saturdays during the summer and early fall, one group of friends or another would travel north to Greers Ferry Lake, a dam reservoir at the foot of Round Mountain into and out of which the Little Red River flows. Usually we would go to the beach and rocky cliffs near the small town of Heber Springs, but sometimes we would go to other areas of the shore where the cliffs were higher for diving into the water and where we could camp.

On a Saturday morning during my first Arkansas summer, Manuel and María, my new friends from Nicaragua, asked me to go with them to the lake. María's roommate, a nice girl from the South, had a car and drove us to the lakeshore in Heber Springs. It was a hot, sunny day with clear blue skies. The lake's water clearly reflected the surrounding woods of deciduous and evergreen trees and invited us to dive from the cliffs and swim. The water was fresh, cool, and calm. Swimming was easy and relaxing—there was no need to resist any currents, and you could simply float for long periods of time. This sensation was new to me. In Costa Rica I had swum in many beaches, both on the Pacific and Caribbean coasts, and in many rivers, but never in a lake. In the sea, whether swimming or snorkeling on rocky points, I had always had to be mindful of tides; in rivers, of whirlpools; in both, of strong currents. But here, in this lake, swimming in the smooth, tranquil water felt delicious and effortless. I swam into the lake to observe the cliffs and woods from a distance with ease and felt nearly no resistance. My friends and I spent the day on the lake playing, diving, swimming, drying and tanning in the sun, and talking about our experiences in our home countries and in *la Yunai*.

María was a senior, and throughout her years at college she had traveled to more than thirty states, following the paths of her own saunters, some of which she recounted for us. She had traveled around the South and Southwest, up North, and out West. Sometimes she rode with roommates to visit their homes; other times she took long distance buses for days to visit friends; occasionally she flew to places she wanted to visit on her own. During some spring breaks she had gone on missionary trips with other students to nearby states. As she told her stories, she flashed an easy smile that emphasized her high cheekbones and also twinkled in her chestnut-brown, almond-shaped eyes. Short, athletically built with powerful shoulders and legs, curly-haired, round-faced, and cinnamon-skinned, I gathered she was an animated and courageous explorer. Being a woman and a Latina, she sauntered in *la Yunai* at greater risk than I ever would, and in that conversation she blazed a trail in my mind, a walking path that I should follow. Manuel was a quiet guy, a bit rough in his manner and more interested in swimming and sporting than talking. As for me, that first time swimming in a tranquil lake already brought the discovery of a new sensation and heralded experiences yet to be lived.

I did not have to wait long to return to the lake. On the week before the fall term began at the college, I met Pam, a lively girl from Fort Smith with a great sense of humor, a generous laugh to go along with it, and a lovely native accent. After we met at an activity for incoming freshmen, we started to spend time together, mainly walking around campus or sitting on the swings or on the grass in the main lawn, occasionally going for frozen yogurt in town. Pam, her best friend Matt who was also a freshman from Fort Smith, and a couple other students invited me to go with them on a Saturday in late September. The summer was coming to an end, but the leaves were still green, and the Arkansas heat made the prospect of a swim in the lake very enticing. This time I found myself on the shore of Greers Ferry speaking in English with a group of native Arkansans. Most of the time, I was simply attempting to follow the conversation, often trying to decipher their accent and particular ways of enunciating words like "mountain" by dropping the vowel sounds almost entirely, whereas my tendency as a Spanish speaker would have been to pronounce each vowel distinctly—not to say "*mantn*" but rather "*ma-un-ta-in.*"

When listening to the conversation without being able to say anything began to tire me, I got on with diving and swimming. Matt and I dove several times from higher and higher positions in the rock formations. A couple of dives were probably acts of madness, as they involved running and jumping off the cliffs at just the necessary distance to avoid hitting the rocks below the water surface. But for us, sporting in nature was a shared act of joyful freedom.

Matt, though, out-dared, or rather, out-sported me. Swimming and diving near the rock formations, we found a narrow, underwater tunnel probably only five meters in length. Matt swiftly dove, swam into and through the tunnel holding his breath, and came out of it on the other side. The tunnel was not much wider than his broad frame. I was smaller and leaner than Matt but did not dare follow him. I feared getting stuck. To this day, I do not understand why, and I regret not having gone into the tunnel. I had done similar things, perhaps even more difficult because of the tides, while snorkeling into rocky underwater caves in Costa Rica. This time, however, I hesitated. At that lake, in that moment, there was an unrepeatable possibility of playful experience— a chance to swim into the tunnel and let the sunlight guide me to the other side—but I let it slip away. The sight of Matt, however, diving through the tunnel and coming out on the other side, where the bright sunlight greeted him as victor, struck me with its beauty. He moved with grace and force, his strokes short and precise to fit within the narrow tunnel, his long dirty-blond hair floating and shinning like golden algae lit by the sunlight. The scene remained vivid in my memory for a year, before I returned to the lake again.

Very late in the following summer I sauntered to the lake with some friends I had made during my freshman year at college. My friend Tibor—who was the son of Hungarian immigrants to the Northeast and had come to study in the South—invited me. His roommate owned a pick-up truck and drove us. Along with a couple others, I rode in the truck's bed. The day was sunny but not blistering hot, and the wind was refreshing, so the ride felt pleasant as we drove on the winding road, along farms and woods, to Heber Springs. The day at the lake once again consisted of swimming, diving, horsing around, joking, and talking. My fluency in English had improved, so now I would participate in the conversation occasionally, though still I most enjoyed listening to others while lying on the flat rocks of the cliffs and looking toward the blue sky.

Tibor was a particularly interesting guy. I think he was a bit older than the rest of us—perhaps he'd done something other than studying between high school and college—and at any rate he had a more mature disposition than most *gringo* kids, who even to me often seemed a bit too infantile to be university students. He was athletic, of intelligent conversation, and observant of the people around him. Perhaps because his parents were immigrants, he had a keen cultural sensibility and had cultivated friendships with several Central American scholars in the college, including my *chapina* friend Cecilia, who had a crush on him for his good looks and sense of humor. Though we were not intimate friends and did not converse a lot, I enjoyed his presence and felt that he had a similar sensibility to mine.

After a day of glorious swimming, on the ride back a state trooper caught us speeding with his radar. Our driver, however, decided to flee. He had received a speeding ticket just the day before, also near the lake. This time, he took the chance that the trooper would take a while to turn around in the road to chase us and probably didn't have time to see the plate's number. So he decided he would race away. We all lay with our backs flat on the bed, and he floored the accelerator. To a crew with better judgment, this would've seemed foolish and dangerous. But none of us had better judgment. I thought it was exciting, which, come to think of it, put me in the same childish category as the infantile *gringos* I was just trashing. I was looking at electric poles and tree tops whiz by in a blur, feeling the motion of the truck. Nirvana was then the hottest band in the land, *Nevermind* was revolutionizing the music scene, and in my mind I listened to Kurt Cobain sing "Breed," expressing carelessness, fear, and a desire to flee.[6] Our driver, however, did not outrace the cop. After probably five minutes of chasing, he caught up to us. Our friend pretended he hadn't seen the trooper behind us because of the winding road. I thought we were in trouble—the truck would be impounded, our friend arrested, and we'd have to walk back for days. But the cop was merciful with us; after a grave speech, pronounced in the tone of a fire and brimstone preacher, he wrote a speeding ticket and let us get on our way. We arrived home safely, having returned from the holy land of a summer day's joy.

Over my four years of college in Arkansas, Greers Ferry Lake became one of the destinations that, in one way or another, pulled and attracted me. Part of what led me there was a craving for natural beauty and for the sight of mountains rising from the earth and giving boundaries to the horizon. San José, in Costa Rica's Central Valley, is a city surrounded by the mountains of a volcanic *cordillera*. If you tire of the city, you can raise your eyes and refresh your sense of sight and your mind—in almost every direction you can see rows of lush mountains, the shape of *cordillera*'s spine, accentuated by high peaks, drawing the contours of the horizon. Almost anywhere in the city, the possibility of seeing the mountains rise to the sky is present, or not far. I did not discover how important the sight of those mountains was to my senses and my mind until I lived in Central Arkansas, where the ground initially seemed completely flat—I only learned to perceive its subtle undulation over time—and the horizon too distant. Without mountains, I sometimes felt without sensual and emotional bearings, whether I was aware of it or not. So I was drawn to that beautiful lake in the midst of the Ozarks as one who tries to make his home—in my case, among mountains—wherever he might be.

The richness of sensual experience that the lake made possible also drew me toward it. I sought the possibility of total immersion not only in the lake in the midst of cliffs and woods but in the sensuality of the moment—the feel of cool water on skin touched by the summer sunrays, the soft sound of my swimming movements in the water, the smell and taste of fresh waters flowing in from the Little Red River.[7] Thoreau writes: "When we walk we naturally go to the fields and woods. ... Of course, it is of no use to direct our steps to the woods, if they do not carry us thither. I am alarmed when it happens that I have walked a mile into the woods bodily, without getting there in spirit. ... But it sometimes happens that I cannot easily shake off the village. The thought of some work will run in my head, and I am not where my body is; I am out of my senses. In my walks I would fain return to my senses."[8] Swimming, playing and sporting in the lake, I returned to my senses, resting from any thoughts of school and any concerns of life on campus amidst a culture to which I was foreign. My inward footsteps led me to the lake to swim and, in this sense, I was walking. Sometimes my friends might accompany me in spirit, other times only bodily, but I at least was walking.

Sometimes, though, a friend would lead me, spontaneously and unintentionally, into a walk. One weekend in the spring of my sophomore year, I went camping with a large group of friends in the woods near the shore of the lake. It was perhaps early April already, and the weather was warm enough to camp. We arrived at the campsite already in the afternoon and set up our tents. I was sharing one with Adrian—a tall, dark-skinned, dark-haired guy from Hazard, Kentucky—and Tim—a big Texan from San Antonio with a hearty laugh and a sensible heart—who had become good friends of mine. Tibor, his buddy Mark, and others were there as well. Soon after we set up camp, we walked down to the lake's shore. The day was overcast, and we couldn't see the sun; the thick clouds threatened to rain.

We were not planning to swim because we thought the water might be too cold. So we stood in front of the lake, talking and looking across it into the distant woods on the other side. There was no one else at the campsite, though there was a cabin for guards nearby. Then Tibor decided to swim. Suddenly, without hesitation, he took off his t-shirt, shoes, and shorts and ran into the water saying, "Guys, I'm going skinny-dipping." Adrian, Mark, and I decided to jump in nude as well, even as I thought, "What does 'skinny-dipping' mean?" Some guys followed, but most of the others, including Tim, stayed dry on the ground, unwilling to swim or afraid the guards might come or the cops we had seen earlier might drive by. Though I was following Tibor, the act came spontaneously. It felt like the natural flow of events. I had never gone skinny-dipping; I did not even know there was a term in English specifically referring to swimming nude. I didn't care. Unburdened by clothes or worries, I just jumped in to feel the cold water on my goose-bumped skin. My breath shortened, my heart beat hard against my breast, and I felt joy.

As I was swimming, Larry, Adrian, and others stepped out of the water and took off hiking naked through the woods. Tim and others walked back to the campsite. I stayed in the water awhile. I was suddenly all alone, and the stillness of the water was soothing. I could hear the guys running through the woods and screaming. As it was turning dark and the clouds thickened even more, I came out of the water, put my dry clothes on my wet skin, and walked to camp. I greeted Tim, who offered me a Dr. Pepper, his favorite soda. Some of the guys were beginning to light the grill. As we were talking, a patrol car drove by slowly, the cops checking us out. Tim was worried the cops might spot our friends somewhere up the road. I felt relaxed beyond all care. Eventually, when it was already dark, we heard them walking toward us talking. They had eventually had the good sense of putting their clothes on during the course of the hike. When the cops spotted them, they were walking back to camp.

Our plan was to grill, make a campfire, and talk. But soon after dark, a thunderstorm unleashed itself, and the rain started pouring. We had to run to our tents. The rain kept coming down all night. Tim, Adrian, and I were stuck inside a tent that was really too small for the three of us. And the water was leaking in, slowly soaking our sleeping bags, our clothes, and our skins. I started feeling cold and stayed cold until dawn, when the rain finally stopped. It was a miserable night for all of us. All our gear was wet, and the day looked to be overcast again. We had a quick breakfast and drove back to the college. But we had had our walk. Tibor seized the possibility first—just like Matt had a couple years earlier by swimming through the underwater tunnel—but I did not let it escape this time.

FREEDOM TO SEIZE POSSIBILITIES

Seizing the possibilities that appear spontaneously—this is crucial to the art of walking. When the possibility of sauntering presents itself, one must be attentive, open, and ready to actualize it. The condition for this attitude of attentive readiness is a form of inner freedom. Thoreau makes a strong statement when he describes this condition as follows: "If you are ready to leave father and mother, and brother and sister, and wife and child and friends, and never see them again; if you have paid your debts, and made your will, and settled all your affairs, and are a free man; then you are ready for a walk."[9] Being a free person in this way is difficult; perhaps it is most plausible when one is young and privileged to have few material responsibilities.[10] Afterward, walkers must be mindful and careful to preserve this condition, at least in spirit, for I interpret Thoreau to be recommending that the saunterer be untethered by *inner* chains resulting from banal material ambitions or possessive personal relations. I do not interpret him to be suggesting, naively, that people should or could ignore their legitimate material needs or their loving responsibilities to others. For me, this is Thoreau's point—among my responsibilities and occupations, I must preserve my freedom to saunter, to wander and go forth in "the spirit of undying adventure."

In my privileged case, during my college years this freedom existed so naturally as to be nonconscious. Fostered by my parents and siblings—one of their most valuable legacies—such inner freedom allowed me to seize the opportunity to study in a foreign land. I did not need to be free *from* my family, from my bonds and responsibilities to them; rather, their non-possessive, agapic love—the sort of love that sets the beloved free to grow and encourages their development toward their own life goals[11]—fostered and sustained my freedom to saunter. Those local Arkansas adventures, alone or with fellow saunterers, were but a manifestation of the walk of life that I'd begun. In Thoreau's words again, the freewheeling experiences at Greers Ferry Lake in the midst of the Ozark Mountains were "perfectly symbolical of the path which [I] love to travel in the interior and ideal world." Countries, borders, and nationalities had no place or meaning in this inward path—they placed no mental or spiritual constraint on the requisite inner freedom to travel along it. The South, which at that time seemed so distant from my native Costa Rica, was as good a territory and context for respectful sauntering as any in this world.

OKLAHOMA

Gradually my symbolical "walks" took the form of trips in the South. These trips were not, strictly speaking, Thoreauvian walks, since they were not walks in the natural wilderness in search of inner wildness. Rather, I took them in the nomadic, exploratory spirit of the friendly saunterer. During the spring break of my sophomore year, I took one such memorable trip. Though it may seem far from a "wild" trip in today's colloquial sense of "wildness" among United Statesians, it was meaningful and revelatory to a young foreigner in the South. I went with a group of fellow students on a missionary trip to Oklahoma. The majority of students at the college I attended were members of a church born of the Restoration Movement in the old American frontier. The college in fact identified itself with that denomination. It was common, then, for groups of students to organize themselves to visit churches during school breaks and help them in their missions throughout the United States and abroad. To travel abroad, students had to raise their own money, but spring break trips in the country were financed by the local churches. Being a foreign student with no money and facing the prospect of being locked out of my residence hall for a week—and feeling eager to see another state—I signed up for a missionary trip to a small Oklahoma town.

Though my motivations for the trip were not holy, they were not hypocritical either. Uncharacteristically for a Costa Rican at the time, I did not grow up as a Catholic but as an Evangelical Christian. My mother converted from Catholicism when I was four or five years old, and she raised me to follow her evangelical church. In a sense, I grew up with two Sunday morning religions. At 10:00 am I would attend Sunday school at my mother's church, where I learned stories from the Old and New Testaments. At 10:55 am exactly, with my mother's permission but to the dismay of most other churchgoers, I would run away from the service and dash home, in time to watch the Sunday morning professional *fútbol* matches with my father on television. So I developed a degree of respectful but detached familiarity with the doctrines and missions of evangelical churches in a Catholic country. Signing up to help the mission of a small church in a small town in Oklahoma, then, did not betray my conscience or deceive my fellow missionary students or *Okie* hosts. Though in my heart I did not believe that the souls of wretched sinners needed to be saved by preaching to them the true gospel, I did think that the church could help some people by providing a loving community. With my conscience perfectly at ease, then, and wanting to see new places and meet new people, I got on the road. Among my companions were my friends Carolyn, a blond, blue-eyed, witty girl from Walla Walla, Washington, and Luis, my Afro-Costa Rican friend, a fantastic *futbolista* who had played in Costa Rica's professional first-division league.

Soon after we crossed the state border into Oklahoma on Interstate 40, we stopped at a service station and diner in Sallisaw. The town's name was significant to me because I had just read and been moved to the core by John Steinbeck's *The Grapes of Wrath*, and its story of suffering migrant *Okies* passed through Sallisaw. Most of the others, including Luis and Carolyn, wanted to have a bite to eat. I had no money but pretended I wasn't hungry, so I walked up a small hill behind the station. It was a sunny and pleasant spring afternoon, and from the hill there was a clear view of the surrounding area. I stood there a while, thinking how different that world seemed from the one Steinbeck described in his novel: "To the red country and part of the gray country of Oklahoma, the last rains came gently, and they did not cut the scarred earth."[12] But the rains stopped, and the "surface of the earth crusted, a thin hard crust, and as the sky became pale, so the earth became pale, pink in the red country, and white in the gray country."[13] Sixty years earlier there had been great suffering here during the Dust Bowl, but now everything seemed peaceful.

My reveries were soon halted when it was time to join my friends, who had come out of the diner and were ready to get on the road again. I do not remember the name of the small town to which we drove, where the church was located. It was Eastern Oklahoma, not too far perhaps from Tulsa. I have looked at maps carefully, trying to remember its name and exact location, but I cannot. The town was tiny, sure, but perhaps the main reason I cannot remember its name is that I stayed in a farm along with Luis. It was a large, beautiful farm with a comfortable family house, a stable for horses, a large barn, a pond, and large fields of hay—a quintessential southern farm, unlike any family farm I had ever seen in Costa Rica. There were tractors, machinery, and large pick-up trucks to transport products and supplies, but the heart of the farm was the family that owned it and made it productive. These *Okies*, our hosts, worked hard but did not suffer as those of the past, whose stories were depicted in *The Grapes of Wrath*.

Jerry and Phyllis, a couple in their late forties or early fifties, had two daughters—Stephanie, a teenager, and Linda in her early twenties—and a son, Steve. He was a man in his late twenties who worked with his father on the farm. They were all native *Okies*—kind, friendly, churchgoing people who received us with warmth and thankfulness and shared with us their way of life. Over the course of that week, when we were not helping the church in its evangelical mission, Luis and I discovered with our host family a new social and cultural world. Jerry was tall, thick, white, and his short dirty-blond hair, parted on the left side, was graying. He was kind but quiet, perhaps a bit shy. Along with his son, he showed us the farm and took us fishing to the pond, just to spend time together. Steve, in turn, was a mixture of farmer and cowboy. He wore a black, wide rodeo-brimmed hat, button-up long sleeve shirts, tight blue jeans, metal buckle belts, and black leather boots. He loved to ride horses, and he cared deeply for them. He rode gracefully, with firmness and elegance.

One afternoon, Steve and Jerry asked us if we wanted to ride a horse. Luis and I accepted. The young man saddled up his horse and gave us instructions and a demonstration on how to ride. I knew my limitations as a city slicker, though, and as I had very rarely ridden horses before, I rode prudently, and rather timorously. But they celebrated my riding anyway. Phyllis took several photographs of me and had them developed at the local store. I was wearing glasses, a white t-shirt, faded light-blue jeans, and white canvas shoes. In one of them I wore a black hat with a rancher brim; on the back of the picture Phyllis wrote "Cowboy" in quotation marks. In another, I am standing by the brown horse caressing its neck and holding the reins, and she wrote, "Preparing for the ride." Then I appear on horseback, awkwardly hunched and slightly off-balance because my feet are not firmly planted on the stirrups: "Hi-Ho Colter Away." In yet another picture I am trying to pull the reins to my *right* with my *left* hand, because with my right hand I am holding on to the saddle's horn, but the horse is going straight; "Trying to make a right turn," she wrote. In the final photograph of the sequence, the fine brown horse is still and seems to be waiting for me to give an order with the reins; a smiling "cowboy" and a powerful, intelligent stallion look at the camera. "Daniel Campos stopped to pose for a picture," Phyllis recorded. But I am sure it was the bored horse who decided to stop. I must have seemed so passive to them, but I like to fool myself into thinking that she perceived my pensive bent. At any rate, she sure had quiet fun at the expense of my riding.

In contrast to me, Luis jumped on horseback as bravely as he might charge up the *fútbol* field dribbling opponents. But this was a fine horse, well trained to obey a firm hand and not accustomed to inexperienced riders. Luis made a mistake with the reins, pulling them back, and the horse obeyed by backing-up right into the sidewall of the stable. Luis fell off the horse, hitting the ground hard. Our friend Steve immediately ran to get a hold of the reins and calm the horse. Luis got up, startled but fine, as the young cowboy rode his horse away, toward the pond down the hill, to appease it. The rest of the week Luis and I, urban kids from San José, restricted our wild adventures to fishing in the pond.

I felt most thankful to discover Phyllis's life and character. She was a few years younger than her husband. Loving wife and mother, she ran the household with wisdom and practicality. She also cooked delicious, hearty meals and baked a wickedly delicious peach-cobbler. I had never tried it in my life. But one afternoon, as Luis and I talked to her in the kitchen, she offered us some freshly baked cobbler with coffee. She cut through the thick crust with one of her sharp kitchen knives and served us generous slices of cobbler on a country-style plate—white with blue flowers around the rim, as if bluebonnets on a snow field—and poured coffee in matching cups. I had been eating and drinking from the generic, cheap plates and cups from the campus cafeteria for so long that these details warmed me up inside. We sat at the wooden kitchen table by the window, looking out to the hay fields and the stable. The coffee, as usual in the United States, then and now, was awful, but the cobbler, prepared with fresh peaches, was a divine revelation—a veritable piece of heaven descended upon the South and given as a blessing to its people. I had never tasted such delicious peaches or cobbler, and that sensual discovery alone would have made for a memorable trip. I had come to convert the heathens, but instead I had received a taste of the divine.

As Luis and I ate our cobbler and politely sipped the coffee, Phyllis started to ask us about our lives and stories from Costa Rica and Latin America— where in Costa Rica we'd grown up, what landscapes we could see, what life and people were like there, what foods we ate, what music we listened to, did we dance, had we been to other countries? During a pause in conversation, she placed her small white hands gently on the table and looked out the window—her hazel eyes searching for the horizon, and her light-brown, permed hair glistening in the sunlight. Then she confided that she had never been outside the state of Oklahoma, not even to Arkansas or Texas. She had always wanted to travel, but she married young and moved to live with her husband, who did not like to be away from the farm, even now when the children could look after it. And of all the places in the world, she most wanted to see Rio de Janeiro, Brazil, especially during *Carnaval*. This good country woman, loving wife and mother, and devout Christian from rural Oklahoma longed to see the *Cidade Maravilhosa*—the Marvelous City—during its famous pagan carnival in the days immediately prior to Ash Wednesday, a day of holy significance to Catholics. I thought that behind her mild demeanor there must have been fire burning in the core of her kind heart.

When I reflect upon that experience, it seems distant but significant. What made these conversations between two Central American college students and a homemaker from Oklahoma possible? My romantic streak tells me that although Phyllis's loving heart kept her at home all her life, her spirit was free to roam, wander, and explore. She was a walker living in an *Okie* farm and sauntering in her mind. We discovered a woman full of wanderlust, and she found two people to take her on an adventure. She traveled by talking to us.

In a recent conversation, however, my friend Lara Trout— an American philosopher—helped me to see the nuance in Phyllis's story. As much as, or even more than her loving heart, established social norms and restrictions on her freedom had kept her from sauntering. My freedom to roam—like Thoreau's own—was informed by male and, to an extent, economic privilege. While I sauntered I was not transgressing roles prepared in advance for me by society, was not in danger of sexual assault, and was not dependent on the authorization or financial support of parents or a husband. I was a broke student but not tied down by poverty or family responsibilities or gender roles. Phyllis did not enjoy that freedom. She had married young, moved to her husband's farm, and raised a family. She never had the option to saunter free of cares or expectations, even for a few college years.

Yet, in spite of the deep gap in our life experiences and freedoms, Phyllis found a way to relate to Luis and me and to let us participate in her life, even if only for a little while. She led us along the way to a meaningful connection. We got a glimpse of her passionate heart and even tasted heaven by eating the peach-cobbler she had baked for us.

Perhaps in an offering of thankfulness, throughout that week I tried to persuade people to come closer to heaven or at least go to church on Sundays. I did not succeed in persuading a single person. I suppose I didn't really try all that hard. My missionary partner Lisa and I walked around the neighborhoods in town, approaching people's homes to invite them to church without annoying or insistent proselytism. We'd knock on a front door, and someone, usually a woman, would open it cautiously, eyeing us up and down. We both wore cotton t-shirts, jeans, and canvas shoes, smiled, and looked like good ole' college kids. Lisa, a sweet Southern girl of vivacious, green eyes and long, brown, curled hair, who had a timid but enchanting smile, spoke every time while I listened. She would explain we were in town inviting people to our local congregation, and I would hand the woman a flier with the times and topics for each meeting of the missionary campaign. The woman would accept our fliers politely, explain she already attended a church, and quickly close the door. We were already walking in the streets of heaven on earth, everyone saved and living in the kingdom come. And yet Lisa seemed to approach each home with optimism.

Only once do I remember a woman's inviting us into her home—a simple, small, ranch-style house. In her late thirties or early forties, white, red-headed, and too wrinkled on her forehead and around her eyes for her age, she lived alone and seemed rather wearied. She sat at her worn-out armchair and smoked while we spoke. Because of her age and her being home in the midafternoon, I wondered if she was unemployed or perhaps had a late-shift job at a restaurant or supermarket. Initially she seemed interested to ask where we had come from and why. A visit from a couple of college kids was perhaps a welcome break from her routine. But eventually she let on that she had divorced recently and was looking for a new congregation, somewhere where she'd feel welcome and not judged. She asked us if our church thought of itself as having the only true Christian doctrine, as she disliked that attitude from her previous one. Lisa and I looked at each other, knowing full well that our denomination did think of itself as the only true restoration of the first-century Christian church, according to its strict reading of the New Testament. I did not have the heart to tell our hostess that our denomination would disappoint her hopes. Lisa, however, did have the integrity to admit it, and soon afterward our conversation ended. Yet we had been welcomed, for a little while, into a home where another woman had shared a bit of her life with two young students interested in her story. I did not have the experience required to empathize with deep understanding, but I listened with care, as I had listened to Phyllis, even if I had nothing to say.

When the week ended, and it was time to return to the foreign land of Arkansas, Oklahoma and her *Okies* had left a mark in my heart, like the imprinted map of a territory discovered by an explorer. I returned to the college campus, my courses and books, and my friends, but the kindness of our host family and the zest for vital experience of their loving mother remained vivid in my mind for months.

ALABAMA

Another trip to the heart of the South had come earlier that sophomore year during Christmas break. I worked as an assistant janitor in a building on campus. My plan was to work during the break to save money for a study abroad trip to Italy the following autumn. That required many hours of payroll work because, as a foreign student, I could work only on campus, and the hourly pay rate was well below minimum wage. The residence hall would be closed, but Tibor, who shared a house off campus with several roommates, offered to let me stay in his room while he and his roommates were away visiting their families.

I did not mind spending the break working. However, the prospect of spending the time before Christmas Eve and New Year's Day alone did not appeal to me. While I was growing up in Costa Rica, those were my favorite days of the year. In December the rainy season ended, the skies remained clear in the afternoon, and there were pleasant, cool breezes sweeping in from the onset of winter in the Northern Hemisphere. The school year ended by mid-December, and students would have the prospect of the entire summer— or dry season—ahead of them. Every day there would be a chance for a *mejenga*—an informal *fútbol* match on the street—or a long bike ride to emulate the cyclists of the *Vuelta a Costa Rica*. In the evenings my friends, guys and girls from the neighborhood, would gather on the street corner to talk. Friends and families began to plan holiday festivities, and the pace of work relaxed. Most families—really the women in most families—would prepare several dozen *tamales*, the traditional food for the holiday season, according to the family recipe. It was customary to exchange *tamales* among families, so that one could try several varieties and twists in ingredients and flavor. I loved sharing a *piña*—or pair—of steaming *tamales* with a cup of black coffee during the midafternoon coffee break that all people would share at home or at work, taking the moment to talk, joke, or converse.

As *Noche Buena* approached, the preparations would intensify for the celebrations. My mother would usually prepare a *pierna de cerdo* and a batch of delicious Christmas cakes. In Costa Rica, most families celebrate Christmas Eve rather than Christmas Day by dining together and often staying up late, except for the children who go to sleep expecting gifts from *San Nicolás*—if they are privileged enough, as the middle-class kids from my neighborhood were. In the case of my family, my parents, my two sisters, and I would customarily dine together at home. Sometimes an uncle's family or my maternal grandparents would come to dine with us as well. On Christmas Day, children would go out to play on the street with their friends, excited to show and share their new toys. We would go to my paternal grandparents' home for lunch with our extended family—*abuelos* Enrique and Dora, three uncles, their wives, and six cousins—and then to my maternal grandparents' home for late afternoon coffee with my *abuelos* Hernán and Luz, one aunt and two uncles, their spouses, and, over the course of the years, seven cousins. Both sets of grandparents lived within a couple of kilometers from our house, so these visits were accomplished by walking together from one place to the next. These moments of playing, talking, joking, and sharing with our family seemed like a natural part of life to me.

The days between Christmas and New Year's usually consisted of more gatherings for coffee and *tamales* or for *rompope*—eggnog—with even more extended family—great aunts, second cousins, and so on—or friends. In San José people would go to the *Festejos populares*—or "popular festivals"—for eating, dancing, or watching the *Corridas de toros a la tica*—the Costa Rican-style bullfighting, in which improvised bullfighters dressed in extravagant clothes would jump all together into the bullring to be chased by a succession of charging bulls. I was not so keen on going to the *festejos,* except occasionally with friends, but liked to watch with my father the *corridas de toros* on television and listen to the narration by comedians. I preferred to play *fútbol* and spend time with friends in my neighborhood, go cycling, or go away to the beach for a few days if possible.

The festivities would culminate with a family party on New Year's Eve consisting of glorious dining and dancing together, usually listening to Tony Camargo's version of *"El año viejo"* in order to thank the Old Year for the good things it brought us.[14] One of the parties I remember most vividly was celebrated at my house. I must have been eight or nine, because my younger sister Xinia could already walk. My maternal great-grandparents, Manuel and Cristina, were still alive and came to the party. They danced together in our living room for hours. Manuel Quirós and Cristina Loaiza, who usually hosted very large social gatherings in their ample home designed for such occasions by Manuel, always loved to dance. Many of their daughters were there—my grandmother Luz and her sisters Daisy, Carmen, Nelly, and Lilí. My grandfather Hernán, my uncles, cousins, and close friends of the family dined with us and then danced to the music of *La Sonora Santanera, Billo's Caracas Boys*, Beny Moré, and other great classics of my grandparents' and parents' time. The evening pulsated with joy and happiness. Even Xinia, who had been put to sleep, got up, put on my father's shoes—she loved wearing other people's shoes from the moment she could walk—and came to the dance floor. That *Noche Vieja* truly brought us "*cosas muy buenas, cosas muy bonitas.*"

My first Christmas Eve in Arkansas was very different. After six months in *la Yunai*, I did not have money to buy a plane ticket home, and the residence hall would be closed for the entire break. A family of friends from Houston, however, invited me to spend the break with them. Calvin and Linda had been missionaries in Costa Rica, and during their years there had struck a close friendship with my mother and even my father, who was not a church-goer. When I arrived in Arkansas they were living in Texas with their three children—Michelle was my age—and took care of me in various ways. For Christmas, they offered to pick me up at the college on the twenty-fourth on their way to Northern Arkansas, where Calvin's father lived. We would spend Christmas Eve and Day in Arkansas and drive back to Houston to spend New Year's there. Though I could not go home, the plan seemed interesting. I'd see more of Arkansas and then Houston, and I would spend time with friends.

As soon as final examinations ended, most students left town, and the residence halls closed. A friend of mine who lived in on-campus apartments left me his keys so I could stay in his pad for a few days until my friends came to pick me up. I spent those quiet days reading the war memoirs of José Figueres, one of the main statesmen of the twentieth century in Costa Rica and the leader of the 1948 revolution that founded the Second Republic and definitively abolished the army.[15] My father had mailed me the book, and I took it up immediately, perhaps homesick and definitely needing a break from reading in English after my first semester in college. I would also take my usual walks around campus and town, now more solitary since the students had left. I missed the *café con tamales* in Costa Rica, the mild December weather, and the conversations and gatherings with family and friends. But I had enjoyed those quiet days, reading and walking at leisure, just as much.

Then, starting on the morning of December 24, a major ice storm swept down the heart of Arkansas into Texas, right over Interstate 30. My friends, the Henrys, were caught in the storm. They made some progress into Arkansas but in the midafternoon had to give up and stop at a roadside motel. The thick sheets of ice made driving too dangerous. I had seen ice pellets and freezing rain fall all day but did not realize the magnitude of the problem until Calvin called, late in the afternoon when I was expecting them, to say they would not make it. At that point, it became clear I would be spending the first Christmas Eve away from Costa Rica alone. Worse still, in the nearby supermarket, Piggly Wiggly, I had bought just enough groceries for those few days, but now there were none left except for a can of instant soup.

The sun set, darkness came, ice continued to fall, and it was impossible to walk even a block, let alone to the grocery store. Calling home internationally was prohibitively expensive, and at any rate I did not have a calling card and did not feel I could use my friend's phone line without his permission. My family expected me to be with Calvin and his family, so they were not planning on calling me. They had no way of knowing I was still in the apartment.

Christmas Eve came. I warmed a can of instant soup on the stove and ate it. Irremediably alone, I picked up my book, read until I finished it, and went to sleep. I woke up and had no breakfast and no more books to read. Midafternoon on Christmas Day, when my friends finally arrived, I was starving and bored. As we drove north, there still was ice everywhere. A cold, lonely Christmas had come and gone.

After this experience, I did not want to spend the holidays alone during my sophomore year. Yet, I needed to get to work soon after New Year's Day, when most students would still be away for a couple more weeks. Then *Beffy* Heffington saved me for the season. She worked at the college's library and also needed to return soon after New Year. She invited me to spend the holidays with her family in Pine Bluff, so that we could return to campus together. I happily accepted her invitation.

Pine Bluff is a relatively large town south of Little Rock, between the mighty Arkansas River to the north and the Bayou Bartholomew River to the south. It sits in the midst of large tracts of farmland. As *Beffy* drove south of Little Rock approaching her home, I gazed into the distance observing the largest rice fields I had ever seen. In the northwestern Costa Rican province of Guanacaste I had seen rice fields, but the farmland did not stretch as far into the horizon as it did here. The land itself was extremely flat, even more so than in Central Arkansas, with no discernible undulation even to the keen eye. Rice, rice, rice; cotton, cotton, cotton—farm crops extended as far as I could see. I felt as if I were entering the heart of the agricultural South—mechanized and industrialized, of course, but the agricultural South nonetheless.

As we drove, I did not know my friend by the name of *Beffy* yet. But she called her little sister *Heffy*, and so *Heffy* called her *Beffy*, I learned as soon as I met her sister, a high school senior, at their home. *Heffy* and *Beffy* were two sweet, caring, fun-loving Southern girls. They were from Georgia but had recently moved with their parents to Pine Bluff, Arkansas, where their father accepted a position as a public librarian. They were a loving family that lived modestly on a librarian's salary, their father said. In fact, from our very first conversations their parents were open about their lives and inquisitive about mine. Years earlier they had survived in more modest, even difficult, conditions as students, and when their daughters were little they had struggled at times. To describe some of those struggles, at the dinner table one evening they confessed that they often had eaten only rice and beans. In Costa Rica, the typical daily meal at most homes consists of rice, beans, some vegetables, fried plantains, cassava or *yuca*, and perhaps some meat. It had never occurred to me to think of rice and beans as a poor person's meal, since it is the basis of a Central American diet for rich and poor people alike, but in the context of the United States it made sense. Being a studious and somewhat bookish *muchacho*, at any rate, I found Mr. Heffington's vocation as librarian to be admirable regardless of its unfair pay, and most importantly, I felt at home in the midst of their loving family life. I had found a nice refuge for *Noche Buena* and *Noche Vieja*.

To my surprise and delight, however, we would not spend the holidays in Pine Bluff. Instead we would drive into the heart of Alabama to visit *Beffy*'s aunt at her farm near Danville. We must have driven south on 65 and then east on 82, crossing the Mississippi River and cutting through the Magnolia State into Sweet Home Alabama, but I do not remember the ride. Perhaps we drove at night? Southern landscapes attracted my attention so much that I cannot explain this gap in my memory. The only other possible explanation I can muster is that during those holidays I was engrossed reading Ernest Hemingway's *The Sun Also Rises*, and I may have read during the whole trip.[16] As a sophomore, I still read literature in English slowly and deliberately, but I read with passion. And so I spent several days entranced by the lives of Hemingway's characters' feasting and suffering quietly during the summer *san fermines* in Pamplona, a long way off in time and space from winter in Alabama. In fact, much of my joy during those unlikely holidays in rural Alabama resulted from the chance to read quietly in a warm farmhouse. Some members of *Beffy*'s extended family were puzzled that I spent so much time reading during a school break, but she understood me, as did her father, and they explained that, as a mathematics major, I did not have as much time to read during the school term, and this was my chance to immerse myself in American literature. They let me be happy in my quiet way of being.

Not all of my joy consisted in silent reading, however. I could have read alone had I stayed at the college town. Instead, I would emerge from contemplating the quiet desperation in the lives of Jake Barnes and Lady Brett Ashley to a much different life, a festive family life in an Alabama farm. I thoroughly enjoyed this large family reunion for *Noche Buena*, Christmas

Day, and the anticipation of the New Year. The family members gathered at the farm house's heart: a single large room where *Beffy*'s aunt had arranged three separate settings—a living room of comfy couches and armchairs, a fireplace we could approach after a walk around the farm, and a dining room where the large wooden table always offered comfort food and festive sweets. Aunts, uncles, and cousins would move from one space to the next, and their conversations would change—American football or politics in the living room where the TV set played the sports channel or newscasts; cold weather, fog, or fresh country air near the fireplace; religion and the lives of friends and family members around food in the dining room. In the kitchen, of course, more intimate conversations happened, mostly between women—I was not let in to hear them, nor were most other men.

In the open spaces, however, I loved to listen to the conversations and to talk to all of the family members, especially *Beffy*'s aunt. She was in her early fifties, I guessed, and lived alone, and loved her beautiful farm, with its well-groomed grounds and pastures. It seemed to me that not much farming was actually happening, and that perhaps she just liked a quiet place to live. It was a lovely setting for short, pensive walks, even if the thinking took place through a dialogue with a fellow walker, like Aunt Heffington, and not inner monologue. She smoked and had a raspy voice to go with her mellifluous accent. One foggy afternoon, we stepped out into the humid cold of southern winter and took a walk around the farm. She told me nothing of her past life or of her future; she just pointed out present details—the reflection of evergreens on the pond, the recently painted shed, the well-kept fence. I thought of present order and grace and stillness.

Danville itself is but a hamlet in Morgan County in Northern Alabama, not far from the Appalachian Mountains though still in flat terrain. Thus the farm, located in the vicinity of this tiny rural village, seemed like a peaceful refuge in the midst of nearby lakes, creeks, and a national forest. It probably was a quiet place most of the year. During the holidays, however, the family made it festive, and *Beffy*'s aunt felt glad for that as well.

And so the festive days passed—everyone waking up in his or her own time, having a hearty southern breakfast, preparing meals, watching some sports on television, talking about politics or the church or affairs of the family. The life of the church was important to them, but they were not fanatical, just honestly faithful. I had a hunch that Aunt Heffington had a more rebellious, wilder edge, and had walked and lived along that edge, but I couldn't explain exactly why. Perhaps it was her direct, penetrating gaze or her slightly sardonic smile and sarcastic sense of humor. *Heffy* also seemed to me to be a bit more mischievous than *Beffy*, flirtatious and perhaps even a bit rebellious, a bit more of a "bad" girl but only relative to her "good" sister. She had short, dyed red hair, a beautiful round face, creamy-white skin, provocative brown eyes, and a wry smile. Her gaze also was penetrating but more playful than her aunt's, and she laughed often. Both *Auntie* and *Heffy* took special care of me, and my heart was delighted. They checked on me, whether I was comfortable or hungry or sleepy. They brought me food, brewed me coffee, sought me out to talk or walk—they *cared* for me, in the way that Phyllis had in her Oklahoma farm, with generosity that reminded me of my mother, my sisters, and my grandmothers. They cared for me in ways for which I gave my wholehearted thankfulness, knowing that even my courteousness and disposition to help could not reciprocate the grace they offered me. I found myself in the midst of a loving family for the *fiestas*, observing and listening and discovering their familial way of being. This care and love I carried in my heart as the Heffingtons drove back to Pine Bluff and, later, as *Beffy* drove us back to our college and our work—hers at the library, mine as an assistant janitor.

LOVING RELATIONS

Since then I have experienced this kind of welcoming love with several friends over the years. *Philia* and *agape* are possible loves for foreigners, for immigrants, to be experienced in the midst of American families and friends. I came to grasp this fully, to comprehend it, with *Beffy* and her family in a farm in rural Alabama. Sauntering had led me to experience with them love freely given and enjoyed.

This kind of connection gradually emerged as a central purpose, an end or *telos*, of my first personal and cultural saunters in the South. For I have been writing about symbolical saunters, and one of their features is that they begin as open-ended explorations with no predetermined direction. Instead, in the course of attentive sauntering, a destination, an end, a *telos*, gradually emerges.

What emerged for me as purpose was the search for and cultivation of possibilities for experiencing meaningful human transactions in different languages and across cultural differences through play, sports, travel, food, literature, and conversation. I sought to establish relations of mutual understanding and love with people no matter what their culture or place of origin in the world—relations based on *philia, eros,* and *agape*, according to context and persons. I perhaps sensed instinctively that such relations were the key to being equally at home everywhere, even in *la Yunai*. More than an immigrant, at that time I still felt myself to be a sojourner in this country, but I wanted my sojourn to be imbued with the meaning found in earnest, sincere connections with the people and places that life brought to my experience.

NOTES

1. Henry David Thoreau, "Walking," in *The Portable Thoreau*, ed. Carl Bode (New York: Viking, 1964), 592–630.
2. Ibid., 592–593.
3. Ibid., 593.
4. Ibid.
5. Ibid., 602–603.
6. Listen to Curt Kobain, "Breed" in Nirvana, *Nevermind* (DGC Records, 1991), compact disc.
7. Henry Bugbee writes of experiences of "immersion" such as swamping, building a damn, and rowing in *The Inward Morning* (Athens, GA: The University of Georgia Press, 1999), 42–54. By "immersion" Bugbee means "a mode of living in the present with complete absorption; one has the sense of being comprehended and sustained in a universal situation. The absorption is not a matter of shrunken or congealed attention, not a narrowing down or an exclusion. One is himself absorbed into a situation, or by it, and the present which is lived in does not seem accurately conceivable as a discrete moment in a series. The present in question seems to expand itself extensively into temporal and spatial distances," 51–52.
8. Thoreau, "Walking," 597–598.
9. Ibid., 593.
10. I recognize that external constraints such as poverty, oppression, and risk of violence can severely constrain the possibility of actually sauntering. I do not aim to ignore the gravity of such constraints. I rather aim to emphasize the inner freedom required for sauntering, while acknowledging that having the inner *and* outer freedom to actually saunter is a privilege. Argentine immigrant-philosopher María Lugones analyzes and responds to situations of oppression in which oppressors would consider "walking" by the oppressed as trespassing. For the oppressed, trespassing into such contexts involves risk of psychological, physical, political, economic, and sexual violence. I think, for example, of some of my students at Brooklyn College who are undocumented immigrants brought to *la Yunai* as children. They study earnestly but live in the shadows, hiding their immigration status to avoid any chance of denunciation. After graduation, they find economic and social roadblocks everywhere. Meanwhile, I have heard "wasps" from upstate New York, Irish and Italian descendants from the city agitate to the effect that these kids should not have access to learning in public schools or legal work afterwards. Gloria Anzaldúa, in turn, describes the perilous situation of various ethnic groups in the borderlands: "Gringos in the U.S. Southwest consider the inhabitants of the borderlands transgressors, aliens—whether they possess documents or not, whether they're Chicanos, Indians or Blacks. Do not enter, trespassers will be raped, maimed, strangled, gassed, shot. The only 'legitimate' inhabitants are those in power, the whites and those who align themselves with whites, Tension grips the inhabitants of the borderlands like a virus. Ambivalence and unrest reside there and death is no stranger." *Borderlands/*La Frontera: *The New Mestiza*, 4th ed. (San Francisco, CA: Aunt Lute Books, 2012), 25–26. For reasons such as these, María Lugones does not recommend carefree sauntering to the oppressed, but

rather prudent and adaptable "world"-traveling or tactical-strategic "streetwalking" as forms of resistance. See María Lugones, *Pilgrimages/*Peregrinajes*: Theorizing Coalition against Multiple Oppressions* (Lanham, MD: Rowman and Littlefield, 2003), 77–100 and 207–237.

11. See C. S. Peirce, "Evolutionary Love," in *The Essential Peirce: Selected Philosophical Writings*, eds. N. Houser and C. Kloesel, vol. 1 (Bloomington: Indiana University Press, 1992), 352–371.

12. John Steinbeck, *The Grapes of Wrath* (New York: Viking, 1986), 3

13. Ibid.

14. Listen to Crescencio Salcedo, "El año viejo" in Tony Camargo, *El año viejo* (RCA Records, 1996), compact disc. Mexican singer Camargo first recorded this song, composed by Colombian songwriter Crescencio Salcedo, in 1953.

15. José Figueres, *El espíritu del 48* (San José, Costa Rica: Editorial Costa Rica, 1987).

16. Ernest Hemingway, *The Sun Also Rises* (New York: Scribner, 2006).

Chapter 4

Road Trips

The Mason-Dixon Line and Beyond

My road trips, even during college when I'd already come to the *Yunaited Estéits*, did not consist of searches for meaning in booze, drugs, rock and roll, and good-looking women to seduce. In that sense, I'm no Sal Paradise or Easy Rider. During a childhood road trip in Costa Rica with my father, though, I did manage to get him in trouble because of good-looking women wearing bikinis.

I must have been about seven years old. We were traveling on a dirt road in a double-cabin pick-up truck, courtesy of the Coca-Cola Company, for which my father worked as an accountant. He was on a business trip to make inventory of soft-drink products in the company's distribution centers in the province of Guanacaste. It was Sunday, however, and the center in the city of Liberia was closed, so we headed to a nearby beach—either Hermosa or Panamá in Bahía Culebra. My father was driving, his work buddy Pintura was in the front seat, and I in the back. *Mi Tata*, my dad, had big, broad hands with protruding veins—with the left hand he held the steering wheel, with the right one the gearshift. In the rearview mirror I could see his short, curly brown hair parted on the left side, honey-golden eyes, light skin, and prominent, straight nose like his mother's. He was good-looking like her, especially when he thought of something mischievous to say and his eyes lit up and he smiled before he said it. He was not tall but rather strong-framed, with a broad back, thick shoulders, thin and fit torso, wiry legs, and big, long-toed feet.

As we made our way along the dirt road toward Playa Hermosa and Playa Panamá that veered off from the paved road to the more popular Playas del Coco, we passed a group of beach-bound, hitchhiking women. They were young and pretty, wearing shorts and see-through blouses that showed their bikini tops. My father, who was courteous and still a young man in his early thirties, stopped. He and Pintura offered the women a ride. I saw my opportunity for riding in the open air and immediately volunteered to hop out of the cabin and into the truck's bed. My father agreed. So I hopped on the wooden bed, and the women slid into the back seat. The rest of the time my father drove gently, and I enjoyed the ride, feeling the salty breeze cool my skin under the sun climbing up in the sky. When we got to the beach, my bed-riding adventure was over, but I was excited. The women thanked us and went their way, and my father, Pintura, and I spent the day sitting in the shade under the bowing almond trees, playing in the sand and swimming in the sea.

That was all fine and innocent. When we returned to San José, though, my mother asked me about the trip. And I was still so excited about my ride on the truck's bed that I told her all about it—how there were women hitchhiking and we picked them up and as a result I got to ride in truck's open bed exposed to the *intemperie*—to the wind and the sun and the smell of salt and life. She did not say anything to me. And I never heard another word about it.

Decades later, however, when I was an adult, my mother recalled the story in a family conversation at home. Only then did I discover that she had become so furious at the situation that she scolded my dad, asking him how he could be so irresponsible as to send me riding on the truck's open bed just to give a ride to some young, bikini-clad women. I'd never realized I'd ratted on my dad! The whole thing had been so innocent that I had told the story naively and earnestly. Of course, though riding on truck beds was common and not illegal in Costa Rica then, my mom saw the danger. And it added salt to the wound to know that my danger had been for the sake of giving a ride to some young women, even if offering rides to hitchhikers was also common and safe in Guanacaste. My father and Pintura had offered the ride to the women and not, say, to a group of farm workers.

On the other hand, *mi Tata* was always so careful with me, but never overprotective, that I don't think he saw any harm in a gentle truck-bed ride on a marginal back road. Perhaps he did not strike the Aristotelian mean virtue of prudence and just erred on the side of temerity rather than timidity. At any rate, I am still here to tell the story, and I am glad to have a story to tell. The unexpected joy I felt at riding in an open truck-bed on a faraway dirt road, and the long-lasting affective memory of that simple joy, shaped my later road-tripping experiences. I am still just a boy riding, exposed to the elements, in Culebra Bay. My father no longer drives me, but he sent me on my way, and I claim my part in the American road-tripping tradition.

KENTUCKY ON A MOTORCYCLE

Road trips, like Thoreauvian saunters, are explorations of experiential possibilities while on the move; unlike saunters, however, they do begin with a destination in mind, however vague, revisable, or negotiable it may be. As we saunter, our destination gradually emerges; in road-tripping, we explore and experiment with ways of getting to our destination.

One such experiment took place on a motorcycle with my friend Adrian. On one of my first road trips in *la Yunai*, we rode his bike from our college in Central Arkansas through the heart of Tennessee and into the mountains of Kentucky to the "city" of Hazard—a small town, the seat of Perry County, which sits in an isolated valley near the Virginia border. We were on break from school, and Adrian invited me to visit his mother's home. I took the chance to travel with a buddy into the uncharted depths of Kentucky.

It must have been summer—or a very hot spring or early fall—because we decided to travel at night in order to avoid the heat and blistering sun during the day. We took off in the late afternoon, rode eastward on the gently undulated terrain, and a couple hours later crossed the bridge over the mighty Mississippi into Memphis. As the sun descended we headed north toward Jackson and then Nashville. By the time we got across the Tennessee-Kentucky border, the darkness of night had deepened. As we sped forward, I mainly saw the glowing paint of the lines marking the road ahead and bugs—dozens, hundreds, thousands of bugs fluttering in the bright beam of our headlight, some of them crashing into the shields of our bike and helmets.

As we rode, I was surprised by how cold one could feel on a summer night in a speeding bike. I had inadequate gear and very little previous experience riding. I had learned to drive a motorcycle two or three years earlier, during a high school vacation, on a Yamaha for motocross that a friend of mine used to ride over the dirt roads near the fishing village of Brasilito on Costa Rica's Pacific coast. But riding on a dirt road in Costa Rica and cruising over interstates and state highways in the southern United States were very different experiences. I did not prepare well for road conditions.

Besides, as Adrian was driving, I felt a bit uncomfortable huddling too close to him, and so I kept my body at a distance from his back and my legs open wide, away from the bike's seat. As the natural consequence of my unwise scruples, the cold wind castigated my chest, inner thighs, and genitals. By the time we stopped for gas after midnight at a station somewhere past Bowling Green, as I descended from the bike, I told Adrian, "Man, my balls are freezing!" He burst out laughing: "Close your legs, dimwit." I had no option but to surrender to the dictates of need and practicality, and for the rest of the ride I did keep my body huddled. When we arrived in Hazard, in the dark and quiet of early morning well before dawn, I was still cold, but my testicles had not fallen off by the side of the road.

It hadn't been a joyful ride, but it was a memorable experience. Though the ride was cold, long, and uncomfortable, the sight of the smooth road emerging before us in the dark and the feel of cooling air turned into wind by our movement made me feel that if I endured those hours of riding something good would come of it.

The good that came of it was the time with Adrian, his mother, and his sister Heather—who'd also come home from college—at their home. Though with personal and financial difficulties, I surmise, Adrian and Heather's mother had raised them with care on her own in a small Kentucky town. The house was humble; the living was simple; the care was palpable. Adrian had been a rebellious teenager, who'd broken the social rules of conservative southern churchgoers and even experimented with drugs—of the varieties that grow off the soil, not the ones produced in laboratories. Even in college he continued to rebel against the rules of a conservative system that did not allow students the freedom of choosing how to live and experiment with possibilities. But his rebellion was not against his mother. He was caring and careful with her. For her part, during our visit she was happy to have both of her children home and to receive me as one more of them. Our best moments of that trip were spent in her kitchen and dining room, talking with her. One evening, she prepared a feast—roasted potatoes, grilled pork chops, corn on the cob, and diverse green leafs, all served together to make a beautiful plate—and we sat on the spare wooden table to eat together. She looked at her children lovingly, her eyes tender with joy at their presence, and spoke of their childhoods spent playing and roaming in rural Kentucky.

As for Hazard, there was not much to see. There, as anywhere, it was the people—my hosts—that mattered most. But the winding roads in the nearby Cumberland Mountains, a stretch of the legendary Appalachians, provided the stage for joyful motorcycle rides, and the mountains themselves were quiet and peaceful. At one juncture we stopped at a bridge and saw the forest enveloping and hugging the course of the Kentucky River, the green lushness contrasting with the muddy brown waters. At Buckhorn Lake, a reservoir on the north fork of the Kentucky, people could camp, fish, and swim in brown while seeing the greens of the woods and the blue of the sky. I was surprised by the brownness and asked Adrian about it; he in turn was surprised when I said most mountain rivers in Costa Rica flow on beds of rock and the water is crystalline.

Adrian may have known the winding roads we covered, or perhaps he was exploring. As for me, those rides in the Appalachians composed the real road trip. We did not travel over many miles of asphalt, but I had the sense of being deep in the heart of *la Yunai*, at least, in one of its many hearts—in this case, in the land of coal-mining folk who no longer mined much, though the water still smelled of sulfur, perhaps from chemical reactions with minerals in the soil. Even the smell of water, at any rate, let me know I was in a different world. As we rode back to Arkansas, retracing our route through Kentucky and Tennessee on the bike, I felt privileged to have experienced that distant world of miners, forests, and muddy waters in the Cumberland Plateau and its nearby mountains.

I realized, though, that I was not much of a bike rider. I certainly was no Easy Rider, as I'd confirm on my way to New Orleans later. Yet in a semiconscious, mostly instinctive way, I knew I wanted to see *la Yunai* on the road. After a few saunters and road trips in the South, I also knew I wanted to cross the Mason-Dixon line into the North.

CROSSING THE MASON-DIXON LINE

The chance to cross the imaginary cultural line dividing the land of Dixie from the Union's North came during another spring break. The road trip to Ohio, though, involved no Kerouacian frenzy; it was a temperate and earnest missionary trip, purportedly to help convert Yankee heathens to "Religious Truths" that were well known in the Bible Belt. I'd been on a missionary trip to Oklahoma a year earlier, only to find that everyone already knew those Religious Truths, within the dogmatic confines of their own partisan denomination, of course. My devout peers hoped, I guess, that beyond the Mason-Dixon line there were veritable heathens in need of conversion. As for me, I again needed a place to go while the residence halls were closed, and I took the chance to go meet and talk to some of those heathen Yankees in their own land. Carolyn, my beloved friend from Walla Walla, and Luis, *mi compa tico*, also needed a place to go and came along again. Carolyn may have believed in the mission; Luis, like me, had his own personal mission of surviving the break without money in an enjoyable way. The local church of Middletown, Ohio, would pay for gas and lodging and feed us during our missionary break.

Our group took off early in the morning in a pilgrims' caravan of two cars. We weaved our way east and north in Arkansas and entered briefly the southeastern heel of Missouri before crossing the Mississippi River eastward into Tennessee. It was an unremarkable stretch of Interstate 155, but the Mississippi, as always, seemed majestic to me. We then cut through the northwestern corner of Tennessee and drove into Kentucky, edging Paducah and continuing toward Louisville. We drove over the bluegrass region of central Kentucky in good spirits, chatting at times, silently looking out the window over the rolling pastures at other moments. Carolyn sat next to me, her noon-sky blue eyes observing the landscape. I loved my friend, and that made the trip more joyful.

Because of Adrian, his mom and sister, the Cumberland Mountains, and the memory of muddy river waters flowing silently past green forests, I'd come to love Kentucky also. Seeing now actual bluegrass country pleased my heart. If we were playing music on the car's stereo, however, it must not have been bluegrass. Perhaps it was rock 'n' roll, though I doubt it. It likely would have been Acapella—a choral group of righteous white guys who sang gospel songs. All of my missionary friends loved it because our denomination's doctrine did not allow religious songs and hymns to be sung with instrumental accompaniment. All praise needed to come from our hearts, souls, and vocal chords. A good gospel song for this trip, sung a cappella, would have been "Travelin' Shoes." It would have encouraged us to convince heathens that it is better to be Christians—traveling shoes ready for when death comes knocking at the door—than sinners, liars, or gamblers, unprepared for the summons of the Black Herald.[1] Oh Lordy! Forget living lovingly and well; what matters is to be ready to die. Inspired by this, we could tell those Yankees that if death came a knockin,' they better be ready to put on their travelin' shoes and go. I must say, though, that those gospel lyrics were catchy, and those white guys did a good job at singing harmonies to create a hit tune of sorts—a good one to keep you happy as you travel over bluegrass country, for instance.

Be it talkin,' thinkin,' lookin,' or listenin' and singin' along—at any rate travelin'—we eventually we made it past Louisville into the northernmost edge of Kentucky and crossed the Mason-Dixon line just south of Cincinnati. Though we crossed the Ohio River as it flowed toward the mighty Mississippi, nothing really changed geographically. Beyond Cincinnati there were more rolling hills of grass—as blue as any other green grass, as far as I could tell. But I felt something had happened in my internal mapping of *la Yunai*. I'd crossed a historical and cultural boundary and wondered what it would be like on the other side. I was in the North.

Some changes were noticeable. For one, there were more African-Americans driving near Cinci than anywhere in Kentucky. For another, the city did seem a bit more industrial, even if it also seemed run down by hard economic times. Other changes were gradual. Beyond Cincinnati, the landscape was still rural—we saw many farms by the side of the road, and just like in Kentucky, their barns were painted black. Had sarcasm crept into my heart, I would'a wondered if the farmers had listened to the Rolling Stones' song "Paint It Black" and, upon looking at their red barns, had decided to paint them black, like their hearts, like the sun.[2] But then, if death came a knockin,' maybe they would'a been found to be sinners in the company of sinners. Sarcasm hadn't crept in yet, though—I just found the black barns to be odd, attractive, mystifying, and beautiful and thought of the hard work of farmers to paint them black.

Soon we left the barns behind us and arrived in Middletown, a small city just south of Dayton. Here the land and the people did feel different from the

South. The people of the church welcomed us with joy. It was a small con-gregation, and, unlike in the South, they seemed to be in the cultural minority. I was still in the conservative United States, no doubt, but the conservatism seemed less religious and more socioeconomic. That mattered very little to me though—the churchgoing people were warm and welcoming.

Luis and I stayed together with a local family—the Kinsers; father, mother, daughter, and son—and our time with them was the best part of the road trip. During that week of missionary a knockin' on sinners' doors, I failed to convince even a single person to visit our church, let alone get any to put on their travelin' shoes before death came a callin.' Okay, I didn't try to tell anyone our "Truth," but still I failed initially to get any conversation going. Most people just wanted us to go away. I realized that missions were not a good way to start a conversation there. Yet, the trip gave us the chance to stay with a warm family, happy to have us visit them and share our stories with them. Were it not for our will to travel and their will to host us, they may have never met any Central Americans, and we may never have known the lives of middle-class churchgoers in southwestern Ohio.

One evening, mid-week, during a break from the missionary campaign, we all sat down at the dinner table to share a meal and spend time together. We passed the dishes around the large wooden table, served ourselves a banquet cooked by Mrs. Kinser, and ate with delight. Luis and I offered thanks for the meal, a break from cafeteria food on campus, as if it were a gift from heaven. I learned about their quotidian lives as they shared them with each other while dining. The family went to church on Wednesday nights and Sunday mornings. The rest of the week, every one of them had a different schedule. Mr. Kinser, the local preacher, spent his time meeting with members of the congregation to exhort or help them in their difficulties, organizing church activities, solving practical issues, studying the Bible for his lessons and ser-mons, and actually teaching and preaching. In his mid-fifties, he was tall and thin, with a clean-shaven round face, very dark and thick eyebrows, and dark hair graying on the sides. Soft-spoken and affable, he lived his faith sincerely, loving his family, educating his children, caring for the people of his congre-gation. Mrs. Kinser had a job in a local bank or store to earn income and make their family's ends meet. Sadly, my memory of her has dulled beyond the possibility of description, and I wonder why that is. Perhaps she was so busy all the time, going from home to work and coming back to her chores, that I had no chance, or failed, to actually regard her as we talked? I have pictures of us at their home, but she is in none of them. Did she take them all? Or was she away working, or home but in the kitchen when I took them? I know she held the household together, but I cannot remember her. Laura, their daugh-ter, studied in a local community college. She was a sophomore taking as many general studies courses as possible on cheap tuition before transferring to a more expensive school to earn her degree. Her long, blond hair rose up in a puffy perm well above her forehead before falling down more gracefully upon her shoulders. She had a perfectly symmetric oval face, green eyes, high cheekbones, straight nose, and a wide, easy smile. He brother, John, also oval-faced but dirty blond, stood a couple of inches taller than his father. Broad-shouldered and wiry, he had the build of a safety or corner back that could play for the local high school's football team. He seemed focused on graduating and making it to college.

At various moments during dinner, I thought consciously of the fact that I was in a place a long ways from San José, in a household very different from my own. I even thought of my mother's home-cooked meals with fondness and nostalgia. And yet we were just folks a talkin' and getting to know each other. No mysteries and no complications in the guise of politics, culture, or religion either. It turned out Yankees were just people.

Even the Yankee heathens were just people. A few were aggressive to fend us off when we approached to invite them to a church service. Most listened politely at their doorstep, took our brochure, and put it on the table or threw it in the trash as soon as they shut the door. But eventually one woman did want to chat. An elderly lady, who lived alone, invited us in to have a cup of tea and talk. I really was not particularly interested in telling her anything about religion. I was instinctively—albeit not philo-sophically—aware that I had no wisdom, that I knew no infallible Truth, that everyone is looking for their own way to happiness, and that we tell each other stories about how to get there. I just wondered about her, about her life alone in that big house. Was she an old spinster? A widow? Or was her wild husband on his way to a jazz festival in New Orleans or Chicago? Did she have children? Grandchildren? Did they visit? I don't recall the answers, if I ever found them out. I do remember her loneliness, however. She just wanted a conversation about anything, and religion was some-thing to talk about. My partner was enthusiastic about the topic—she did believe in our mission—and so we did that. I would've rather asked about life, loneliness, and the search for a flash of happiness in brief moments of conversation and personal transaction. But, oh Lordy, religion was more important.

Middletown, though, did have a quite different feel from, say, Sallisaw, Oklahoma or Hazard, Kentucky. People, though kind, were more sober. There were fewer churches. And the land seemed utterly flat, not even undu-lating a bit. Being in the vicinity of Dayton, it also seemed to be on the edges of the industrialized regions of Central and Northern Ohio, and the working- and service-class neighborhoods had a suburban rather than a rural aspect. Truth is, I preferred the homely feel of the small towns of the south to the blahness of a midsize town just north of Dixie's border.

As we started to drive back to Arkansas after a Sunday church service, I knew I'd miss our hosts—I even corresponded a few times with our host father-turned-friend—but I was not thinking of the land left behind. I rather looked forward to returning to the South, driving again over bluegrass country, before cutting the corners of Tennessee and Missouri into Arkansas.

GUANACASTE

A missionary road trip from Arkansas to Ohio was not the wild stuff of spring break trips further down to South Padre Island in the Gulf of Mexico or west to ski in New Mexico. Friends offered those options to me, but I could not afford them. I needed a trip with lodging, gas, and food paid for and covered, and that is the trip I took.

But my road-tripping experiences back in Costa Rica had not begun as teenage searches for freedom and partying anyway. They began in my childhood as explorations of land and culture with my father, who often took me on his business trips around the country, and especially to the Pacific province of Guanacaste. Though he worked for the Coca-Cola Company in San José, where we lived and the main cola bottling plant was located, he often had to travel to the distribution centers around the country to make careful inventory of the cola products. When I was about four years old he started taking me along on his trips, and our traveling together continued during breaks throughout my first years of elementary school.

I waited for those trips with a sense of wonder and impending adventure. They'd take place in a Datsun or Toyota pick-up truck. The company always sent my father along with one of his workmates—Pata, Chompipe, or Pintura—all of whom I only ever knew by their nicknames. My father often drove, and I would sit in the middle, expecting to see the roadscape open and change in front of us along the way.

We'd take off from San José in various directions according to the destination, usually toward the Pacific coast. When we were bound for the northwestern province of Guanacaste, we'd drive west out of the city and then northwest toward Alajuela and beyond on the Pan-American Highway. The mythical highway was really a two-lane road shared by cars, passenger buses, small and large trucks, and eighteen-wheelers—for which Costa Ricans use the Anglicism *trailers*—hauling cargo to and from other Central American countries. We gradually ascended the *Panamericana* from the green Central Valley to the mountains of the Cordillera Central, edging the small towns of Atenas, Grecia, Sarchí, Naranjo, and Palmares, until reaching the highest point on the road just north of San Ramón. Usually my father and Pata would stop for a midmorning cup of steaming black coffee with a *pastel de carne* or an *empanada de pollo* at the traditional roadside restaurant La Colina, from which there was a nice view of the nearby mountains and one could breathe the cooler air of the cordillera. As a young schoolboy, even that relatively short trip to San Ramón in company of grown men already represented a journey of adventure and discovery, and it was exciting to imagine the impending descent from the mountains to the Pacific lowlands and eventually to the beaches of Guanacaste.

Indeed, as soon as they'd drunk their *yodo*—as brewed coffee is called in our slang—we'd continue our trip, winding our way down the curves of the Cambronero incline. I sat on the edge of my seat, as we wound down the sharp curves and steep slopes of Cambronero, surrounded by forested mountain slopes on the left and deep gorges on the right. From some points on the road, we could see in the distance the Pacific Ocean, blue and glistening under the sun. When we finally ended the slow descent through Cambronero, I'd be relieved. Then a rush of exhilaration would overcome me, as I would feel the lowland heat on my skin and experience the truck's acceleration to 80 or 90 kilometers per hour on the long, level straight stretch of Macacona before entering the town of Esparza. Sometimes we would stop again at a roadside restaurant to drink a *fresco de fruta*—a smoothie—and look at the sea in the distance from the viewing point in the backyard. Now we were really near the Pacific, the beloved ocean of my childhood and youth.

A few kilometers further down we would cross the bridge over the Río Barranca, the first major river one crosses on the lowlands as one travels northwest, toward Guanacaste and Nicaragua. At the riverbank under the bridge, there were always people swimming, enjoying the cool, pristine waters as they roared down over a bed of rock from the cordillera toward the littoral. On my father's business trips there was no time to stop. But on our family's trips along with uncles, aunts, and cousins, we often stopped there to swim and have a picnic consisting usually of corn tortillas, *frijoles molidos* (mashed black beans), and salted boiled eggs. So as we would drive by the Barranca River, I was always a bit envious of the people who had time that day to stop and have a swim.

The business of corporations anywhere does not stop for a child's swim, though, so we'd keep going northwest on the *Panamericana* toward Guanacaste. Along the way beyond the Barranca River bridge toward the intersections with roads to Miramar and Sardinal, the geography, flora, and socioeconomic landscape began to shift dramatically. We were now in the Pacific lowlands, but not yet in the pampas or plains. The terrain undulated perceptively as we rode up and down the hills, eroded remnants of ancient mountains. The road presented long, sloping straight stretches, ideal for accelerating and enjoying the ride. The trees were now typical of the tropical dry forest. *Malinches* and *higuerones* (giant figs) grew by the side of the road, their large boughs overarching the asphalt and offering a pleasant shade even in the heat of noon or early afternoon. The *fincas* by the highway still were mostly agricultural, farms rather than ranches.

As we drove past the Sardinal intersection, where tourists today veer off the *Panamericana* and drive up the broken dirt road toward the cloud forest wonderland of Monteverde, we could begin to see more clearly the Cordillera de Tilarán to the east. Its peaks rose higher and higher, one behind the other, their colors shifting from bright green to dark- to light-blue according to their distance from the highway. We also crossed many rivers whose waters, overflowing during the rainy season and scarce during the dry one, run down from the cordilleras over broken, rocky beds toward the Gulf of Nicoya or the Tempisque River.

My father always liked to point out the geographical landmarks along our journeys; it was from him that I learned to observe the terrain and pay attention to natural landmarks to know just where it is that I am standing—or riding, flying, or navigating—in the world. It is important to know just where one is and stands. And so over the many joyful trips, we memorized together the order of the many rivers we crossed along the way to Liberia, Guanacaste. We knew the rivers, their location and their features, by heart. As soon as we crossed over one, we predicted the next one a few kilometers ahead. We could recite them in order, not only the major ones but also the minor ones, even the creeks, in between. These rivers would mark the stages of our road trip. The Río Seco dwindled to a minor stream running on a mighty bed during dry season. The Aranjuez was powerful and mighty. The Guacimal was the last one in the province of Puntarenas before arriving at the Río Lagarto, which marked the border with the province of Guanacaste. Whenever we crossed the iron bridge over the Lagarto, I experienced the sheer joy of returning to my beloved Guanacaste and somehow felt that I was where my heart belonged. There was no noticeable difference—the dry tropical vegetation and the contours of the land remained the same, but inwardly there was a shift from longing and hope to homecoming and fulfillment.

My thoughts would then turn to the rivers, volcanoes, towns, and beaches coming ahead. First came the town of Cañas and its eponymous river. My father would say each time that this was the hometown of Carlos Alvarado, the *tico* cyclist who'd won the *Vuelta a Costa Rica* by riding over mountains and plains throughout our country faster than anyone and thus had become one of my most admired sportsmen. By the time we crossed the bridge over the Corobicí, and certainly after the Río Tenorio, my father would point toward the volcanoes of the Cordillera de Guanacaste in the east. The perfect cone of the Arenal hid behind nearer mountains, but the Miravalles and Tenorio were visible from the highway. Though their peaks, rising about 2000 meters above sea level, were usually covered by clouds, one could distinguish their massive mountainsides towering over the nearby *serranías*. And occasionally, if we were blessed by a confabulation of the winds and the dry season, the clouds lifted, and we could see perfectly the contours of the cordillera and the tall peaks of its volcanoes, painted in deep, dark blue against the lighter blue of a glorious summer sky. My heart would then over-flow with the joy of a child overtaken by sensing the beauty of the world in the company of a loving father.

Later came the Bagaces River with its corresponding city founded exactly at the midpoint between Cañas and Liberia. My father would then explain that Bagaces was equidistant from both of the other main cities in this stretch of the *Panamericana* because its position marked exactly a day's journey on horseback from either of them. In the good ole' days, the *sabaneros* (cow-boys and farm hands from the *sabana guanacasteca* or plains) would ride their horses between those towns herding cattle or looking for work at the *fincas* and haciendas of the region. The journey from Cañas to Bagaces and from Bagaces to Liberia or vice versa would each last a day on horseback. As I heard this story, I'd try to imagine what Guanacaste was like in those days of *trochas* (horse and oxcart paths) when horseback was the best way to travel.

As these conversations with my father and the ensuing reveries unfolded, we'd approach the city of Liberia, known as *la ciudad blanca* because of the off-white color of dirt in the region. This was, at the time, my favorite city in the entire, though small, world I then knew. We'd check into one of the hotels near the Coca-Cola distribution center. All of them had names alluding to cattle ranching or oxcart transport, the traditional activities of the region—Las Espuelas, La Ronda, Boyeros. My favorite was Las Espuelas (the spurs), built in the architectural style of a traditional Spanish hacienda or ranch house from Guanacaste—a flat-stone fence, large front gardens landscaped with cactuses and *sábilas*, flat-stone façades, tiled roofs overhanging ample front corridors, and large interior patios.

We adapted to the easygoing rhythm of Liberia. The climate was hot, and there was no air conditioning, so the good ole' evolutionary method of adapting your activities to the environing conditions prevailed. Rise early and start working soon. When the heat begins to roast you, go to lunch. Then find a shaded place, hopefully with a breeze, and take a long nap. Get up at midafternoon and work a couple more hours as the heat subsides. Don't work long hours—life is short, and it's best to enjoy food, drink, and the presence of your loved ones. So be done by 6 pm and enjoy the warm evening. When my father's workday was over, it was time for swimming in the hotel's pool before dinner. A feeling of quiet joy overcame us as the sun set, the sky grew a darker shade of blue, and the stars began to glow in the wide sky over the pampas.

The greatest pleasure of those road trips, however, came when my father's work was complete and the weekend arrived. We did not head for hikes in the forests, however. He hadn't grown up hiking or hunting in them, but rather swimming and fishing in the ocean, and we headed straight for any of the many pristine beaches of Guanacaste. Most were undeveloped. In those that were populated at all, you could find only humble houses making up fishing villages, and perhaps a few cabins for tourists or vacation homes for *josefinos* or *cartagos*, that is, for people from the present or former capital cities, and more generally from the Central Valley, of the country. The architecture was simple, even for the vacation homes—two-storied wood structures with wide doors and many windows for the breeze to flow through, a balcony upstairs and an open terrace downstairs for relaxing in hammocks or rocking chairs, and in the yards as many trees for shade—*higuerones*, *almendros*, and *palmeras*—as possible. There was no air conditioning, and here people also did what intelligent species do—adapt to environing conditions. The architectural aim, at any rate, was not luxury but well-adapted and simple comfort. The fishermen's houses were humbler and smaller but equally practical.

As we made our way toward those beaches—especially from Liberia to Playas del Coco—my father would tell me stories of his own trips with his father, brothers, uncles, and cousins during his childhood and youth. Purportedly they were fishing trips, but much of the action took place in jeeps on Guanacaste's dirt roads. It was tough to make it from San José all the way to the Guanacaste coastline, especially beyond Liberia. My grandfather and his brothers started visiting Playas del Coco in the 1950s, when it was still a remote fishing village, and some local entrepreneurs like Ricardo Barrera, whom they befriended, offered a few basic services such as lodging in simple cabins, eating homemade food, and renting out their *pangas* for fishing. My grandfather and my granduncles would travel in jeeps over rough dirt roads— the time of travel on horseback was already passing, the empty iceboxes— meant to be filled with their catch—rattling on the roof. As soon as my uncle Yique, my father, his younger brothers Beto and Chino, and their cousins turned five or six years old, they would become part of the fishing expedition. Preparations took weeks, and the road trip was long and tough. But eventually they'd be in front of the mighty Pacific, looking at its blue waters, listening to the waves breaking, drinking their beers or shots, and preparing their rods and gear for fishing. My father always took great delight in telling me, however, that my grandfather and granduncles came up empty-handed most of the time and had to settle for buying home-cooked fish from Barrera's restaurant and returning to San José with the empty iceboxes still rattling on the jeeps' roofs.

The fact is that my father was no fisherman at heart. My uncles Beto and Chino really inherited the passion from my grandfather. When Beto became a physician he used his money to buy fine fishing gear and go on fishing trips.

Chino used his job as a government engineer to ask to be appointed to remote locations of the country, where he could purportedly help to build roads but really spent as much time as possible fishing or snorkeling. My dad, to the contrary, liked the youthful fishing trips for the chance to be on the road and then at the beach, swimming in the ocean and probably, as he grew up, talking to girls, whether they were local or on vacation with their families in the 1960s, when roads improved, finer cabins were built in Playas del Coco, and national tourism began to grow.

He never told me about any such girls. I was too young. But I can imagine him liking a *morenita* during his adolescence, talking to her, perhaps even singing some verses from Hector Zúñiga's "*Amor de Temporada*," the classic Costa Rican *pasillo*: "*Morena de mi vida, te vengo a contar mis penas ... .*"³ It tells the story of a guy who meets a girl on a summer day at the beach in Playas del Coco. While listening to the sound of *marimbas* and guitars, as the fishing boats sway in the water, he sees her singing and approaches her. They draw closer and closer and, as the moon rises, he kisses her. It is an ardent, loving kiss. Perhaps my dad even kissed the teenage *morenita* before she broke his heart, as the lyrics go on to finish the story. Of course, later he would really meet *la morena de su vida*, my mother. But who knows if he did not have an innocent *amor de temporada* in Playas del Coco.

The seeds of all of these *historias*—family histories and imagined stories—were planted in my mind and heart during my own road trips with my father, listening to him tell stories on the way to Playas del Coco. Eventually we had the shared story that got him into trouble for picking up some hitchhiking women and taking them to a beach in Bahía Culebra, Guanacaste. There were others, like the business trips beyond Liberia to Nicoya, the old colonial city and provincial capital with its ancient church. *Mi Nicoya querida* seemed so distant and hot, but it was the capital of the province dearest to my heart and the gateway to Playa Sámara, another undeveloped jewel on the remote ocean side of the Nicoya Peninsula. Only rarely could we make it to Sámara. From Nicoya we had to drive westward amid more cattle ranches, up and down and through seemingly innumerable *cerros*, until in the last descent, after a sharp curve, the view would open up, and the blue ocean would appear in sharp contrast with the white beach. When the sea appeared in front of us like a mystical vision, I felt a childish joy that shall never die but will be lived and relieved, imagined, remembered, and interpreted in my heart and mind for years and years.

For this is the point. The experiences during those road trips with my father nurtured my sauntering and exploring spirit and inspired stories that I tell time and again, to myself and others, in order to weave threads of continuity with later moments *en mi historia*. I had learned from my father to go on trips, seeking out new places to feel their character and meet the people who live there. His loving guidance gave me the confidence to go forth "in the spirit of undying adventure," as Thoreau might put it.[4] This disposition to explore while on the road is the meaningful legacy of all the trips on which he took me along—his bequest to me from all his own experiences on the road, traveling with uncles and cousins on rock and dirt roads all over Costa Rica, to the Pacific coast, to the northern lowlands, and southeast over the massive Cerro de la Muerte to the fertile Valle del General. My father's youthful trips and my travels with him, all those stories heard or lived, imbue with meaning my own later experiences undergone on road trips in *la Yunai*—trips in which I sought to explore the land of Dixie and beyond, and meet the people that shaped that land and made it endearing.

NOTES

1. Listen to Keith Lancaster, "Travelin' Shoes" in Acappella, *Travelin' Shoes* (Clifty Records, 1985), audiocassette.

2. Listen to Keith Richards and Mick Jagger, "Paint it Black" in The Rolling Stones, *Aftermath* (London Records, 1966), 33 1/3 rpm.

3. See Hector Zúñiga, "Amor de Temporada" in *Lo que se canta en Costa Rica*, 12th ed., ed. J. Daniel Zúñiga Zeledón (San José, Costa Rica: Imprenta Universal, 1980), 129–130.

4. Henry David Thoreau, "Walking," in *The Portable Thoreau*, ed. Carl Bode (New York: Viking, 1964), 593.

Chapter 5

Americans on the Road

Kerouac, Anderson, and Guevara

Many years after my first road trips in *la Yunai*—even after later road trips in South America, from Argentina and Uruguay to and through Brazil and back to the Southern Cone—I tried to understand what such trips meant to a variety of American peoples, their cultures, social imaginations and self-understandings. Looking for clues, I turned to Jack Kerouac's *On the Road*.[1] When I was in college, several United Statesian friends who were hungry for experiments in travel and life, with some of whom I'd backpacked through Europe, had read it. After college, throughout the years of graduate school interspersed with dreadful incursions into the world of business, seemingly omnipresent cultural references kept the book in view. Eventually, after I'd found my way and my vocation in life, my own students, who were also eager for living experiments, recommended the novel to me. So, when I finally turned to it, seeking to understand some of my own experiences in light of my broad American context and culture, I expected to undergo a veritable epiphany—an enlightening revelation as to the significance of experience—as I had sometimes underwent while reading great American literature.

All I experienced, however, was disappointment. Perhaps I'd become too hardened to care, or worse, too hostile to *gringo* experiences to give a damn about what I interpreted to be the white boy angst of a bunch of idiots on the road. It did not help that the protagonist narrator, Sal Paradise, was a hipster. I was living in Brooklyn, and hordes of gosh darn hipsters, or worse, hipster wannabes, were gradually invading and gentrifying my neighborhood of Eastern European, Central Asian, Latin American, and Bengali immigrants. The early pages of *On the Road* were then a painful read about a hipster traveling westward, without sense or reason, in his very own *gringolandia*. I only became interested when he fell in love, or became infatuated, with a Mexican migrant and went to live with her in a tent to work picking cotton on a plantation. He at least seemed to show a sensibility beyond his hipster's egocentrism. However, he always had a way out—to call his auntie and ask for money to return to New York—that was not available to her. She had no way out; she was stuck in the hard-going way of the migrant worker. And in fact, Sal did take his ticket out of migrant farm work and went home with his auntie's dollars—jackass—while his girlfriend stayed by the side of Sal's road, caring for her son while being harassed by her own family.[2]

It was only half way through the darn book that Sal Paradise made it clear that he was lost, in movement and on the go, but without direction. After hurting his woman and becoming lost in the midst of an absurd party, in the emotional quagmire of his New York, he writes: "This is the night, what it does to you. I had nothing to offer anybody except my own confusion."[3] "Maybe one needs to read the novel when one's twenty," I wrote in my journal. I could understand being lost, the despair of lostness, but not his deliberate abandonment of a search for direction.

I did not abandon the book, though; I kept reading. As the narrative progresses, Paradise gives some signs of reflection in the midst of his frantic confusion. The most significant, for me, is the following: "All my life I'd had white ambitions; that was why I'd abandoned a good woman like Terry in the San Joaquin Valley."[4] Growing impatient in my self-righteousness I thought, "Really, Sal? I couldn't tell you were a self-involved jerk. And for goodness' sake, her name is Teresa, not Terry." But I also welcomed his admission and began to get the sense that the narrator—perhaps Kerouac's faithful and earnest portrait of himself—was aware of some of his own flaws and not afraid to display them.

The ambivalent attitude—both the character's and my own as reader—continued throughout. In his final trip to Mexico, Sal thinks to himself while observing some indigenous Mexicans by the side of the Pan-American Highway: "They were great, grave Indians and they were the source of mankind and the fathers of it. ... As essential as rocks in the desert are they in the desert of 'history.'"[5] But almost immediately he narrates a frenzied binge of booze, weed, and sex with prostitutes in a small town where he and his dumbass hipster friends become a spectacle for the townspeople. Weed, booze, and sex—fine, go right ahead and have your fill, but why don't you take your binges to *gringolandia*, jackass?

For me Sal's ambivalent attitude tended, overall, not toward insightful search but toward emptiness. There are some reflective passages, as when Sal sees indigenous women not *on* but *by the side of* the road: "They had come down from the back mountains ... to hold forth their hands for something they thought civilization could offer, and they never dreamed the sadness and the poor broken delusion of it."[6] The "Beats" on the road, however, did not seem to offer anything to fill up the emptiness of that delusion.

I did not want to give up on Kerouac's "Beats" though. In the end, the sense that Paradise and the rest of Kerouac's characters do search for something on the road did emerge for me. They search for IT. In the words of Dean Moriarty and Salvatore Paradise after *an* experience in a concert: "'Now, man, that alto man last night had IT—he held it once he found it; I've never seen a guy who could hold so long.' I wanted to know what 'IT' meant. 'Ah well'—Dean laughed—'now you're asking impon-de-ra-bles—ahem … .'"[7] The description that follows is of an ineffable experience—a saxophonist had expressed what all in the audience know and feel without being able to say it, and the experience does not seem to be in time but in an eternal present.

Upon reading this, I was left wondering if this experience of apprehending something imponderable and ineffable could be called a trance or a mystical experience. I also wondered if the apprehension was transformative or simply ephemeral. The book ended, and I did not know very well what to make of Paradise, Moriarty, and the Beats' experiences on the road. Were they simply dated, culturally narrow, pseudo-poetic, self-indulgent *gringo* wanderings, or was there some enduring American significance in them?

Before I started hurling any stones, I turned to the Americana philosophy of Douglas Anderson in search of clues. And this time, a culturally engaged philosopher in the American grain did illuminate my search. According to Anderson, American experiences on the road, such as some of those *sought* by Kerouac's Paradise, may be *sensibly mystical*.[8] They are *sensible* in involving not only organic sensitivity but also perceptual awareness, engagement, immersion in concrete situations, and receptivity to the pervading, unifying qualities of an experience—qualities sensibly felt as heartbreak, despair, joy, elation, tranquility, or melancholy. They are *mystical* in the sense of being partially ineffable—in as much as qualitative experience may not be reduced to propositions and verbal explanations but may only be partially captured by them. They are mystical also in the sense of being transformative by requiring reflection, interpretation, and elaboration of their meaning in thought and action. The experience undergone by Paradise and Moriarty at the concert is thus sensibly mystical. Sal and Dean are aware, receptive, immersed, and open to living a situation that raptures both their organic sensitivity—to sounds and visual images, for instance—and their sensible heart, a heart eager for felt connection and mutual understanding through the language of music. Though the experience was not immediately transformative, years later Sal, as he writes, is struggling but still trying to work out the meaning of *that* experience.

Some of their experiences together on the open road also hold forth the potential for transformation, for the consummation of the possibilities of the sensibly mystical American road trip. In Anderson's words, "Our road experiences are not meant to be final, to end questing or questioning; they are meant to lead forth and to illuminate new dimensions of our habits of existence. In Thoreau's way of thinking, they are ways for staying alive and awake."[9]

As I pondered this, the problem for me continued to be that Sal's experience was not transformative of his actions so as to prevent some significant emotional damage to self and others. In spite of the experiences undergone together, Sal in the end abandons Dean, as he'd abandoned Teresa after having *his* experience with a *mexicanita* in the agricultural fields from which *he* could always escape. And both Sal and Dean do not constrain their experiences to contexts that involve only other willing *gringo* hipsters, but they take their binges to trample different ethical sensibilities all over Mexican towns. As Anderson acknowledges, male *gringo* experiences on the road can fail to be transformative and instead be quite harmful to self and others—witness the guy with the car wrecking the woman's life in Tracy Chapman's "Fast Car."[10] Perhaps Natalie Merchant with her 10,000 Maniacs is trying to get at something similar when she asks: "Hey, Jack, now for the tricky part: when you were the brightest star, who were the shadows? Of the San Francisco beat boys you were the favorite."[11] My difficulty was with Sal, not Jack, but Merchant's question frames mine: Who were the shadows in the *inferno* that Salvatore Paradise left in his wake?

Other male American experiences on the road discussed by Anderson seemed to me more understandable and less harmful ethically. As this New England milling-town boy turned philosopher puts it,

> We in the United States engage in an initiation into a life of quiet desperation in our twenties. If we have not already become laborers, the end of college will bring us to the cusp of a world in which we risk falling asleep for the rest of our lives. This is the time of life in which Herbert Marcuse's *One Dimensional Man* makes sense to everyone, not just contemporary leftists. Young folks have a good sense of the impending flatness of life. They gradually begin to see that it's all around them. Experiences of qualitative immediacy—or mysticism—remind us of the reality of possibility, and thus they become the places of potential conversion. We can accept the "facts" and resign ourselves; we can, as Thoreau suggests, "come to die and discover that [we] had not lived." Or we can seek a conversion of spirit that will give us a heading toward experimental lives, lives that "live deep and suck out all the marrow of life."[12]

For a *latinoamericano* trying to understand Kerouac's Sal and his Beats and other *gringos* on the road, this passage came as a flash of insight. I remembered my college friend Carolyn, with whom I took a few road trips and later backpacked through Europe. We were listening to John Mellencamp's song "Jack and Diane" somewhere—Arkansas? Oklahoma? Ohio? Italy?—and I told her I did not think the chorus was right: "Oh yeah, life goes on long after the thrill of livin' is gone."[13] It made no experiential sense to me. We were on the move, meeting people, seeing places, seeing the possibility of a thrilling life opening up before us. But she looked at me with her clear blue eyes and said she thought Mellencamp was right, that life goes on long after the thrill of living is gone. How could that be? I attributed the view to the good ole' mentality of the churchgoing folk around me, as in Mellencamp's song: "Let the Bible belt come and save my soul. Hold on to sixteen as long as you can"[14] Perhaps Carolyn was talking about the dreadful life of grown women and men according to the stern dictates of Bible Belt's cultural prejudices—no longer sixteen, no longer young, no longer thrilled or thrilling, at twenty-three they must be churchgoing and married or else they are a failure.

Anderson showed me this dread as one form of the general fear of many United Statesians as they come of age. Their popular music, across generations, reflects it. But it also reflects the possibility not to give up the thrill, not to give up on life, even in the ordinary lives of the Jacks and Dianes of the Bible Belt, the heartland, the rust belt, and every corner of *la Yunai*. Anderson points to the lyrics of Springsteen's "Born to Run" and "Racing in the Street."[15]

The guys who come home tired from work but wash up and go racing on the road are the ones who do not give up on the thrill of living. For Anderson, they try to stay awake to the possibilities of experience, even in their ordinary lives: "Wherever one is, however one lives, the question is about staying 'alive' to the lives we're already in. The road, the car, the movement are, both rhetorically and literally, modes of keeping ourselves awake."[16] I thought of Tom Petty's "Mary Jane's Last Dance," a bit closer to my own school days, singing: "I don't know, but I've been told, you never slow down, you never grow old."[17]

In this way, Anderson helped me understand the deep feeling of American despair and contradiction that animated Kerouac's writing in *On the Road* and elsewhere. He writes,

> What the Beats learned as they sought a 1950s version of the frontier experience was that there was nowhere left to go. The old Turneresque anarchy of the American west was by this time almost completely fenced in. San Francisco led only back to New York, and vice versa. … Acid, together with a host of other pharmaceuticals, became gateways to the last American frontier: the internal roads and highways.[18]

It was this despair at the closure of life in *la Yunai* that led to the damage inside and around Sal. The despair cripples the transformative possibilities of his experiences on the road. These fail to illuminate and enrich future experience and thus fall short of what Anderson calls an American sensible mysticism: "Consummation without closure, but with promise of even richer consummation, is our inheritance and, perhaps, our bequest. Though to bequeath it, we must in some fashion live it. Somehow we must remain in the street and on the road."[19] They must remain there in an open, attentive, receptive attitude toward the possibilities of experience.

Seeing Kerouac's motivations and themes through Anderson's lens provided a perspective from which to understand the iconic American author's characters:

> In *On the Road* the dialectic of doing and undergoing is alive and well in a series of cross-country journeys that leave us—and the protagonists—weary and confused. But Kerouac, despite the brooding, the loss, and the emptiness, sees in his America a source of enlightenment bound simply to the acceptance of what happens. … [H]e acknowledges the risk we take in being and acting, and shows a willingness to live with the consequences.[20]

The dialectic of doing and undergoing, of acting and reflecting, is a feature of American sensible mysticism that gets taken up on the road by Kerouac in all its possibility, hope, and tragic failure and loss.

Was my initial reading of Kerouac's *On the Road* too narrow and damning? I think so, as I failed to see what motivated the characters' despair and lostness and thus to understand Kerouac's point. I also failed to appreciate that Paradise needed forgiveness and that I was not anyone to grant or take away that grace. Would Teresa forgive Sal and offer grace? I can never know, but I think grace is always possible, and, when it is truly given, it is freely offered. Perhaps my narrow reading was a reflection of my own state of defensiveness and even outright hostility to hipsters invading "my" immigrant neighborhood in Brooklyn as I read the book. Subsequent understanding does not prevent me from reflecting ethically about Sal's actions, but it does keep me from hurling any stones, lest a rock be hurled back to crush me.

Still, my personal quest was for understanding my own American experiences on the road, and Kerouac did not help me. I lived in a different world than he, and the animating spirit and aims of my experiences were different from his. Perhaps these experiences were to some extent sensibly mystical—for instance, the motorcycle ride to the Cumberland Plateau, the eponymous mountains, and the north fork of the Kentucky River was shot through with a sense of exploration and immersion in the heart of Appalachia that led me to reflect upon and interpret the experience throughout the years that followed.

For me, however, *my* experiences on American roads seem now more overtly to have been about the search for connection with people and places, with personscapes and landscapes in which I could, for a while at least, feel at home. This is the road-tripping spirit that my father cultivated and fostered in me.

In literature I found a bit more affinity with Ernesto "Che" Guevara's *Diarios de Motocicleta* than with Kerouac's *On the Road.* Though Guevara did not have Kerouac's gift for writing, I felt greater resonance with his youthful exploration and awakening to social reality in South America—though not with his proto-military observations and reflections—in the months that led up to my own trip to Uruguay, Argentina, and Brazil after finishing my philosophy degree. Ernesto and his friend, Alberto Granado, ride their motorcycle, *La Poderosa*, from Buenos Aires, south and west across Argentina, and over the Andes into Chile in search of adventure on the road. When their *motocicleta* dies eventually, they continue on foot, on the bed of trucks, by bus, by boat, and even on a raft into Peru and beyond. But they also aim to see our continent—José Martí's *Nuestra América*—in all its natural beauty, human joyfulness, and profound social injustice. Guevara, in particular, seems to have a social sensibility from the start. He is open and receptive.

He in fact opens his published version of the diaries with a description of the changes he underwent during his journey that resounds with Anderson's sensible mysticism. Introducing the diaries he edited for publication, he writes of himself as a character that was at once receptive to the possibility of experience on the road and actively transformed by it: "The person who wrote these notes passed away the moment his feet touched Argentine soil again. The person who reorganizes and polishes them, me, is no longer, at least I am not the person I once was. All this wandering around "Our America with a capital A" [*Mayúscula América*] has changed me more than I thought."[21]

However, his receptivity also strikes me as having been overly constrained from the get go by his theoretical lens. He did not become a Marxist—even one along the lines of José Carlos Mariátegui's unorthodox Marxist interpretations of Peruvian reality[22]—on the road. He was, or wanted to be, one as soon as he mounted *La Poderosa*. This could have been fine—Marx, Mariátegui and others did and do still help us understand some aspects of our social reality in Latin America. And Latin American Marxism has often been more animated by moral sentiments than by theoretical concepts— namely by indignation at social injustice and solidarity with the poor and the dispossessed. This is the pervasive sentiment in the poetry of Chilean Pablo Neruda or Costa Rican Jorge Debravo.[23] But Guevara's theoretical attitude seems often to lead him to stand at a distance from the people and places he encounters, as if gazing at them from the heights of knowledge and through the lens of theory. Thus, even as he spends a cold night with a couple of Chilean migrant laborers on their way to a copper mine, he writes of the man as being a communist based on an instinct devoid of theoretical understanding:

Apart from whether collectivism, the "communist vermin," is a danger to decent life, the communism gnawing at his entrails was no more than a natural long-ing for something better, a protest against persistent hunger transformed into a love for this strange doctrine, whose essence he could never grasp but whose translation, "bread for the poor," was something which he understood and, more importantly, filled him with hope.[24]

For Guevara the theorist, Marxist doctrine seems to grasp truth essentially, while the man's instinct leads him to accept it by a natural desire devoid of understanding. The working man merely feels; the educated theorist knows but cannot explain to him who cannot understand.

This same theoretical aloofness creeps up when he writes as a physician and observes the hygienic habits of indigenous peoples in the Andean region of Cuzco. Describing a train ride in which the indigenous *Quechuas* must travel in a third-class wagon apt for cattle rather than human beings, his observations are not sympathetic but rather clinical and critical:

> In these types of trains there are third-class carriages "reserved" for the local Indians: they're like the cattle transportation wagons they use in Argentina, except that the smell of cow shit is ever more pleasant than the human version. The somewhat animal-like concept the indigenous people have of modesty and hygiene means that irrespective of gender or age they do their business by the roadside, the women cleaning themselves with their skirts, the men not bother-ing at all, and then carry on as before.[25]

The young Che, in some ways so committed to social justice, is not above equating the *Quechuas* to animals regarding hygiene and decency. In these passages, his commitment to justice seems to be more animated by theory than by human sympathy. This is the same Che who also fills his journal with observations of the military fortifications of the Incas and what they may reveal about their military strategies. This is the Che whose fraternal heart is corrupted by a military mind. It is not surprising, then, that he did not think of indigenous liberation as a process that could be carried out peacefully by *Quechuas*, *Aymaras*, and other native American peoples themselves over the course of a political struggle, but as an armed revolution that needed to be led by *mestizos* enlightened by theory. This is already the Che of the *Diaries* with whom I do not identify in trying to understand my American road trips.

I do sympathize, however, with the sentiment of thanksgiving he expresses on a toast during his twenty-fourth birthday, as he also gives his farewell to his Peruvian friends:

> In our presently precarious state as travelers, we only have recourse to words and I would now like to use them to express my thanks, and those of my

traveling compañero, to all of the staff of the colony who, almost without knowing us, have given us this beautiful demonstration of their affection, celebrating
my birthday as if it were an intimate celebration for one of your own.[26]

This is the youthful man who is capable of developing bonds with, and
expressing his affection for, the people he encounters on the road. This attitude of thanksgiving animates the political ideal of Latin American unity
that follows with something close to agapistic sentiment, that is, a loving
sentiment of solidarity and affinity that guides one's conduct toward his or
her neighbors:

Although our insignificance means we can't be spokespeople for such a noble
cause, we believe, and after this journey more firmly than ever, that the division
of [Latin] America into unstable and illusory nations is completely fictional.
We constitute a single mestizo race, which from Mexico to the Magellan Straits
bears notable ethnographical similarities. And so, in an attempt to rid myself
of the weight of smallminded provincialism, I propose a toast to Peru and to a
United Latin America.[27]

Taking away the ethno-racial component, this sentiment may still animate
the road trips and commitment to unity and social justice of Latin American
idealists today.

As for me, I could understand this sentiment of yearning for unifying bonds
to people and places as one of the animating principles behind my early road
trips, even in the *Yunaited Estéits*. This sentiment pervaded my initial search
for connection with various peoples and lands within *la Yunai*, thus extend-
ing my understanding of myself as an American beyond my sense of being
Latin American. As long as this sentiment thrived, I was not closed to the
possibility of establishing and fostering meaningful connections to persons
and regions in *la Yunai* so as to feel at home here, even while on the road.
In fact, the feeling of deepening connection grew and evolved as I began to
travel to the depths of the Louisiana *bayous* with K.

NOTES

1. Jack Kerouac, *On the Road* (New York: Penguin, 1976).
2. Based on Jack Kerouac's personal diaries, Linda Alcoff presents a critical,
but more nuanced, interpretation of the author's own racial attitudes and habits of
racialized perception of self and others. For Alcoff, Kerouac was ahead of his time in
being aware of racialized, nonwhite others, of his own racialized whiteness, and the
chasms that such socially constructed, culturally contextualized, but effectively real
racialization could bring about. He even lamented the vacuousness and sadness of his

own white ambitions. But he could not escape his habitual white gaze that led him to perceive nonwhite others as exotic, emotional, happy, and true-minded simply by virtue of his projections of their lived experience. See Linda Martín Alcoff, "Toward a Phenomenology of Racial Embodiment," in Robert Bernasconi, ed., *Race* (Oxford: Blackwell, 2001), 267–283, especially 273–274.

    3. Kerouac, *On the Road*, 126.

    4. Ibid., 180.

    5. Ibid., 280.

    6. Ibid., 298.

    7. Ibid., 207.

    8. Douglas R. Anderson, *Philosophy Americana: Making Philosophy at Home in American Culture* (New York: Fordham University Press, 2006), 129–154.

    9. Ibid., 143.

    10. Listen to Tracey Chapman, "Fast Car" in *Tracy Chapman* (Elektra, 1988), compact disc.

    11. Robert Buck and Natalie Merchant, "Hey Jack Kerouac" in 10,000 Maniacs, *In My Tribe* (Elektra, 1987), compact disc.

    12. Anderson, *Philosophy Americana*, 143.

    13. John Mellencamp, "Jack and Diane" in *American Fool* (Riva, 1982), 33 1/3 rpm.

    14. Ibid.

    15. Listen to Bruce Springsteen, "Racing in the Street" in *Darkness on the Edge of Town* (Columbia, 1978), 33 1/3 rpm. Lyrics quoted in Anderson, *Philosophy Americana*, 144.

    16. Anderson, *Philosophy Americana*, 144.

    17. Thomas Petty, "Mary Jane's Last Dance" in Tom Petty and the Heartbreakers, *Greatest Hits* (MCA, 1993), compact disc.

    18. Anderson, *Philosophy Americana*, 147.

    19. Ibid., 153.

    20. Ibid., 230–231.

    21. Ernesto Guevara, *Motorcycle Diaries: Notes on a Latin American Journey* (New York: Ocean Press, 2003), 32.

    22. José Carlos Mariátegui, *Seven Interpretive Essays on Peruvian Reality*, trans. Marjory Urquidi (Austin, TX: University of Texas Press, 1988).

    23. See, for instance, Pablo Neruda, *Canto General*, trans. Jack Schmitt (Berkeley: University of California Press, 1991), and Jorge Debravo, *Antología Mayor* (San José, Costa Rica: Editorial Costa Rica, 1986).

    24. Guevara, *Motorcycle Diaries*, 78.

    25. Ibid., 116.

    26. Ibid., 148.

    27. Ibid., 149.

Chapter 6

Down on the Bayou

I thought K was cool from the moment I met her. She loved literature and had an intelligent sensibility for reading it; listened to alternative rock, folk, and blues; and drove well and fast. Her father had repaired and given her a sweet Audi coupe that she controlled with mastery and grace. The coupe was green like her eyes—her favorite color, old, and had a lot of miles, but they kept it well, and she knew how to squeeze out of it all the driving and riding pleasure it could provide on highways and country roads.

Carolyn, who was her suitemate in the residence hall, had introduced us during our sophomore year. About a year into our friendship, during a break after summer school before the fall semester started, she invited Carolyn and me to go to her family's home in Baton Rouge. The plan was also to see and explore New Orleans, the Louisiana bayou, and the mighty Mississippi near its delta. It was a chance, then, to get on the road with two friends I loved and go to the land of Cajuns and creoles and blacks and *gringos*, blues and jazz, bayous and lakes, and the muddy river delta.

One fine morning in K's cool Audi, we went on the road. We drove south, crossing over the Arkansas River at Little Rock and then further south to Pine Bluff. That was the stretch of the trip I had covered before, on a Christmas break with my friend Beffy. But K drove it faster. The flat, agricultural lands south of Pine Bluff to Monticello and over the Louisiana border still seemed familiar. From Southern Arkansas into Northern Louisiana there was no noticeable change in landscape or personscape—rice fields, a few small towns with gas stations, roadside restaurants, convenience stores, and good ole' Southerners. We were still west of the Mississippi. But as we gradually approached the river and began to drive by and between bayous, the feel and look of the land began to change. The trees were lusher and thicker; the humidity became more intense, fragrant, and sticky; the land seemed wet.

When we crossed over the river at Natchez and entered the state of Mississippi, I felt I was in a different world, a different South—K's South of blues and bayous. She also seemed to feel at home driving down that winding state road over the undulating land, controlling her Audi along the curves and straights, accelerating, breaking, and steering with ease and coolness. I liked looking at her green eyes piercing the road and her cute, white hands holding the wheel. As we entered Louisiana again and approached Baton Rouge, she grew more excited about her homecoming and I about the new experiential possibilities.

Our excitement was tempered, though, by the fact that Carolyn was grieving the death of her father. Just a couple of months earlier, the relatively young man still in his fifties had died of cancer. She was trying to enjoy a trip with her friends, but the pain of loss was also acute. Perhaps with us she felt she could just be as she was and feel just what she felt. That ambivalence of feelings marked by expectant homecoming, eager exploration, sincere solidarity, moving sympathy, and silent grief set the mood for the road trip. To be in Southern Louisiana with them brought me a quiet, tempered joy.

Once in K's home, her parents made us feel at ease—Carolyn had been there before—and we were free to roam. Baton Rouge seemed at first glance just another mid-sized southern city surrounded by interstates and suburbs. At least it may have seemed that way when we drove into their suburban neighborhood right off of an interstate exit. But just a bit more exploration revealed something different, as it would to me over the years. Though the sprawling urban design was typical of a city dominated by the automobile, the lushness of the bayou could be seen everywhere, as in the oak trees covered by Spanish moss or in the beautiful magnolia trees around the city and on the state university's campus. The many restaurants and cafés let us know also that we'd arrived in a different culinary culture. Cajun restaurants—both fancy and humble—and a couple Louisiana-French style cafés were unlike anything I'd seen in Arkansas. At a little roadside shack under a highway overpass, one could stop to have Cajun-style red beans and rice. The decrepit joint looked like it could crumble at any moment, and it served only red beans and rice. But it was the best in the world, or close to the best, at the only thing it did—the bowls, full of that simple, poor-man's dish, were hearty, and the carefully balanced seasonings filled the palate with flavorful delight. The bowls cost one buck. At a local coffee house one could drink *café au lait* accompanied with legitimate *beignets* without needing a trip to New Orleans' French Quarter. Both the shack and the café were frequented by students from the university. Elsewhere one could try *gumbo, andouille* sausage, crawfish *étouffée*, boiled crawfish, and the rest of the fare. Even the Tex-Mex joints in Baton Rouge had a distinctive Louisiana style and flavor to them.

As one entered the old downtown near the riverbank, a different world emerged—that of the impoverished urban people, whites and blacks, hidden under the social rug, living in houses in disrepair, often without a car to drive even to basic jobs in the suburban *gringo* world of business and commerce. The State Capitol—Huey P. Long's legendary but real hall of power and Robert Penn Warren's fictional but truth-resembling site of political intrigue and malaise[1]—overlooked the mighty Mississippi, its tower rising above the tiny, insignificant homes and lives of the poor. As they seemed trapped in a forgotten downtown, their poverty appeared to be more dreadful than that of the simple fishermen of the bayou. But I would come to understand that fully only over the years that followed, as I learned to interpret what I saw in Louisiana's Acadia and in *la Yunai*.

During that first trip, as we explored the drylands and wetlands beyond Baton Rouge, a fascinating world of contrasts was beginning to emerge. Our main mission was to make it to the Big Easy. I was anticipating the city's scene of the old Spanish and French colonial worlds mixed with the jazz of Afro-Americans. I did not anticipate, however, the astounding natural beauty on the stretch of Interstate 10 that runs over bayous and swamps just north-east of the Mississippi River and southwest of Lake Maurepas until it reaches the shore of Lake Pontchartrain and then continues roughly along the shore, between Laplace and Kenner. That wetland of trees rising from the shallow water, everywhere covered in Spanish moss; of aquatic plants; of waterfowl flying, fishing, or basking in the sun; of still, dark water surfaces reflecting the sun like opaque mirrors enraptured me. I'd never seen a wetland such as this, nor a highway running right through it, raised on concrete stilts, on which a cool driver in a fast car could speed while listening to rock or the blues.

And that was just on the way. Then New Orleans appeared, first its sub-urbs, then Metairie, and eventually its heart, the old French town surrounded by levees on a sharp bend of the Mississippi. Once there, we decided to saunter. We had no plan, no specific list of things to see. I was happy just to be there with them. K knew the city, especially since she'd lived in Laplace prior to Baton Rouge. For Carolyn and me, it provided a whole new place for exploring and walking. We started at Jackson Square, and at once I felt I was not only in a new land, but at home. The urban layout in and around the square reminded me of any Spanish colonial town in Costa Rica, even though the surrounding architecture and garden landscaping was more elaborate and richer than that of any town from the poorest and most secluded province in Central America during the colonial period. *I* might have called the square a *plaza*, though it was a French garden surrounded by a wrought-iron fence and its nineteenth-century monument honoring a general from the US civil war and not, say, from the Spanish American *guerras de independencia*. It idealized Jackson, and not Bolívar, San Martín or Artigas, riding the bronze horse. At the head of the *plaza jardín*, however, stood the Catholic Saint Louis Cathedral and on its sides the *Cabildo*—or Spanish town hall—and the Presbytère or rectory. I admired the chromatic simplicity of the cathedral's three-layered white façade contrasting with the dark roofs of its rising central and lateral towers. The *Cabildo* and Presbytère framed the cathedral with their balanced neoclassical symmetry of street level porticos, second-floor arched windows, and quaint matching cupolas on the center of their mansard roofs. Running along the streets on both lateral sides of the square, a couple of elegant buildings, painted in strong clay-orange colors, with second- and third-floor wrought-iron balconies, completed the frame. On the square's greens people sat or lay down lazily; others sat on the benches or walked around, while a few artists sketched drawings to sell to tourists. The entire scene probably amounted to a regular day at the square, all too familiar for the local vendors and artists, but for me the moment felt special, charged with a sense of both discovery and familiarity at once and shared with K and Carolyn.

We walked up the levee that was across the street from the square on the side opposite the cathedral to see the Mississippi at its sharpest bend in the city. Its greatness once again struck me, as it had when I first had seen it in Saint Louis and when I'd crossed it at various points in Tennessee, Missouri, and Mississippi while on road trips. From this New Orleans levee, however, the river seemed even greater as it flowed powerfully but smoothly toward its delta and the gulf. A large bridge crossed it nearby, tugboats were navigating it, and retro-looking river cruises, harking back to the age of steam-powered boats but probably fully furbished for comfortable tours, were docked nearby. While I was standing on that New Orleans levee overlooking the river, I recalled once again the joy of reading Twain's stories and the experience of staring at that great American river for the first time a couple years earlier at the Gateway Arch in Saint Louis after a baseball game. All those episodes marked for me different aspects of the richness of experiential possibility in *la Yunai*.

I probably could have stared at the river for hours, but we had the French Quarter to experience, and so on we sauntered. We roamed the streets behind the cathedral. It was as if the Old Quarter wanted to hide its affairs from the church or conduct it behind its back. The narrow streets vibrated with music and glowed amid the colorful townhouses with their wide wooden doors, internal patios, and *porticoed* sidewalks underneath balconies that doubled as gardens and had been wrought by the *techne* of fine iron artisans into a multiplicity of patterns and designs. Some of the town houses had become shops, hotels, cafés, or restaurants, but others remained private homes or apartment buildings. K, Carolyn, and I stopped here and there, in shops, record stores, boutiques.

At one point we became hungry, but our money could buy only *po'boys*, and so this poor boy enjoyed his first shrimp *po'boy* of many fish, oyster, and shrimp *po'boys* to follow over the years. And oh boy, it tasted so good!

Onwards we ambled. We stopped to listen to a street jazz band consisting of brass—trombone and saxophones, perhaps a trumpet—and simple percussion that played for all passers-by, strollers, and walkers in the vicinity. The music delighted me, though even I could tell it was not all that fine-tuned. The musicians were trying to make a buck or two on a weekend afternoon from tourists, but they irradiated happiness while playing their music. I surmised they'd rather busk and enjoy it thoroughly than peddle or wither away in a menial job. I appreciated the sentiment—that pleasant joyfulness—that animated them.

We culminated the afternoon having *café au lait* and *beignets* at the famous Café du Monde. Whether we were saunterers doing a touristy thing or broke students on the road or just broke tourists did not matter. To me it felt just right to sit in the *café's* terrace with Carolyn and K, watching people walk by, perhaps talking about music or books or travel dreams or nothing at all, savoring the coffee and *beignets*, and sensing the richness of the New Orleans ambiance. Of all the fine sensible qualities of the moment, it pleased me most to share it with them.

That is why my next memory is so incongruous that I cannot remember or reconstruct inferentially how it came about. Later that day, outside New Orleans, or perhaps some other day during our trip into the bayou, we were on a ferryboat crossing the Mississippi River. We could feel the force of the current as the ferry struggled to reach the other shore. K was happy and calm and delighted to show us the bayous and swamps and rivers she loved. But Carolyn was grieving—the death of her father must still have felt like an open, bleeding wound in her heart. And instead of being attuned to K's calm delight in order to appease Carolyn or to empathize serenely with her, I brooded in silence as I stared at the thick brush and trees on the riverbank. Why did I brood? Though I wanted to take Carolyn's pain away, or at least assuage it, I had no reason to brood. Perhaps it was a bout of unhelpful and misguided empathy? Perhaps I was thinking that although I was attracted to K she would not be attracted to me? My recent experiences with women at our college had been about their disinterest or outright rejection. I did not understand yet that I did not fit into their predetermined mold of a potential waspy husband, and I had not learned yet the kinds of relationships I would find meaningful or to recognize the women that sought in them a viable alternative to their waspy world in a Southern protestant college. Or perhaps I was just a silly boy who at that moment indulged in his tendencies for pseudo-poetic brooding, letting them prevail over more Solomonic tendencies for Ecclesiastic rejoicing in the simple pleasures of life,[2] such as the company of two beloved friends during a trip into a beautiful land of muddy brown waters, lush green foliage, and sorrowful yet blissful blues.

The road trip ended in that funky mood. We traveled back to Arkansas silently, K speeding with her eyes piercing the road like a race car driver, Carolyn thinking or grieving quietly, and I listening to K's cool music— R.E.M., Toad the Wet Sprocket, or any of the other alternative bands whose lyrics and sound pervaded some of our college experiences. The end of the road trip was not quite an end of the world as we knew it, however. We had been no easy riders on our way to Mardi Gras, searching for freedom from an oppressive culture only to find ourselves and our dreams killed by the road-side next to a levee as the Mississippi flowed to the sea. We didn't need to say, like Wyatt in *Easy Rider*: "You know Billy? We blew it."[3] We'd simply been three friends sharing a bit of K's world and exploring where friendship and river and life could take us. We could still have sung the "Ballad of the Easy Rider" with hope, not sorrow, about the flowing river:

It flows to the sea
Wherever that river goes
That's where I want to be.[4]

Our friendship survived the funk, and other trips together were yet to come.

I even had the chance to experience many such trips with only K. In college she was not seeking a waspy husband but an avenue for learning and for the discovery of literatures, worlds, and peoples. As it turned out over time— after a couple more years of friendship, much perseverance and patience, and slow overcoming of my own timidity with her—she came to like me or perhaps simply to allow our attraction to be and grow and develop into a loving relationship. And so over the following years we often traveled together on the road to her lovely land of bayous.

In Baton Rouge I learned to savor urbanized versions of the Cajun dishes, both simple and elaborate, that we'd also search for in our road trips into the heart of Southern Louisiana. I loved the shrimp-stuffed potatoes at the Chimes, a favorite joint of the local university students. Our favorite restaurant, though, was a humble joint in a wooden house in a small town in the bayous to the west of Baton Rouge and the Mississippi River. Engineers and workers from the nearby refinery where K's father worked as a chemist, and local people from the surrounding small towns, had elected it as their place to go for good reason—the food was delightfully tasty, well-spiced, and cheap. Prior to our visits to the restaurant, I looked forward to the thick, hearty gumbo and the fried medallions of alligator tails; afterwards, I savored them for days.

The mixture of social classes, cultures and ethnicities—mechanics and scientists, managers and workers, Anglos, Cajuns, and Afros— among the patrons at the humble joint also made the experience dearer to me. In Baton Rouge we knew mostly church-going, suburban wasps who'd fully adapted to the Southern Louisiana ways of eating and cooking, but not to the lifestyles of the peoples from the bayou and the delta. K had grown up among wasps, in school or at church, and their families. They were caring, loving people, who received me well, and I did love them as I loved K. But I often had a very strong sense that, though my adaptability allowed me to navigate their world, it was *their* very homogeneous world nonetheless. In Baton Rouge we knew the university students and the professionals and the churchgoers, but not the poor blacks or whites. We ate Cajun food but knew no Cajuns. At that joint in the bayous, however, and at similar places, I could see and listen to and talk to them and many other peoples and feel a bit more at home in the heterogeneity of cultures and backgrounds.

I also came to love K's land and to see it through her eyes and mine, through familiarity and wonder, care and interest, longing and desire. She loved the university's Hilltop Arboretum, a diverse botanical garden on the southern edge of town. The Mississippi was not visible, but it flowed nearby. Though the arboretum was no Thoreauvian wilderness, the canopied trails and open spaces in the quiet garden provided a context for returning to one's senses, not in wildness but in tenderness. And it was in tenderness that I became connected to drylands, wetlands, and people in K's Louisiana.

As our road trips took us deeper into those lands, I also got a sense of the history of its peoples in some of its most splendid and most painful dimensions. From Baton Rouge we could drive along River Road on either bank of the Mississippi in the direction of New Orleans to the various preserved plantations dating back to the antebellum era—to the South of a few rich agricultural aristocracies whose splendid ostentation of wealth rested on the pain and sweat and suffering of the poor and the enslaved. On the northeast bank along Highway 44 lay the Destrehan, Houmas, and San Francisco plantations, among others. So long after the civil war and civil rights movements in the United States, it seemed so ironic to me that a plantation with a lavish mansion sustained by slave labor would be named after a man who'd chosen a life of humility and poverty. Not being Catholic I did not consider Francisco of Assisi a saint, but it seemed pretty obvious that he, a simple man, would have renounced any such opulence, especially as it depended on the suffering of so many men and women.

I remember more vividly, however, the plantations on the southwest bank of the Mississippi along Highway 18. Closest to Baton Rouge sat the majestic Oak Alley, which even I recognized—from some source or another in Costa Rica, perhaps a movie or a picture—as the quintessence of the plantation economy's heritage in Louisiana and the antebellum South. Having already taken my American history course in college, I was ideologically prepared to despise the injustice that the plantation house represented. However, when we arrived on the plantation's main road and I saw the moss-covered boughs of its thick, ancient oaks overarching the alley, I was overtaken by the beauty of the place. The carefully landscaped grounds and the grand old house, elegant and poised in the background captivated my gaze. It was perhaps there that I first became puzzled by a question I could only articulate and explore more fully years later: If the good and the beautiful are really unified, how could a site of such dreadful injustice appear to be so beautiful? And how could I, who knew of the historical injustice even if only through books, be so enraptured by the distinguished elegance of the place? The Greek Revival mansion did seem really to embody an ancient Hellenic ideal according to which beauty, goodness, and truth were intimately related and unified. Its solid Doric columns, aligned in perfect symmetry to support the eaves of the roof, provided an artistic counterpoint to the oaks' imperfect symmetry and natural grace. Behind the columns, the ground level porch and second-floor balconies, which surrounded the house on all four sides, invited one to gather for quiet conversation or rest while contemplating the verdant grounds. This overall architectural frame seemed to enclose private chambers where aesthetic attention to form and detail should flow effortlessly. It certainly was not an ideal or a life to which I aspired—but it did captivate me in its admirableness.

I left Oak Alley with this contradictory sensation of admiring beauty in spite of its material origins in horrifying injustice. The Saint Joseph Plantation, however, located just down the River Road from Oak Alley, provided a fast and effective antidote for the uncomfortable fascination. Its Creole manor was less majestic than Oak Alley's mansion—though far from the humble abode of, say, a carpenter, in spite of its Catholic name—and perhaps for this reason the wooden cabins where the slaves lived and the detached kitchen where some of them worked captured my attention and moved me deeply. The fact that the plantation still grew sugarcane harked back to the agricultural economy of Dixie sustained by slave labor.

This experience of respectful and quiet empathy with people who endured a long history of pain became more intense when we visited Evergreen Plantation. It had its own oak alley and neoclassical mansion with eaves supported by Doric columns, front porch, and balcony to which one could ascend by a grandiose external stairwell. But the slave quarters here, aligned in two facing rows, were even more moving. The wooden shacks, raised from the ground by brick foundations probably to avoid flooding or rotting dampness from the ground, with their simple front porches where slaves may have gathered at night, were now surrounded by trimmed grass, moss-draped oaks, and silence. We could only try to imagine in corresponding silence the lives that were once lived there.

And so it was driving through the landscapes and personscapes of Southern Louisiana with K that I grew to know and love its peoples with their cultures and histories and legacies.

Once we also drove straight north from Baton Rouge into Mississippi, speeding on its winding roads, enjoying the power of a man-made machine whizzing by lush nature and small towns. This for me seemed to be an even deeper exploration of the South, a wider humanscape that I also came to love, even with its historical, socioeconomic, and cultural contrasts and injustices.

Some other road trips we simply dreamed about, though we never realized them on the actual road. One such dream was to journey on the blues highway, the historic Highway 61, departing from New Orleans through Baton Rouge, north into Mississippi and Tennessee to Memphis and its Beale Street blues, then continuing northward to Arkansas and Missouri as far as Saint Louis, perhaps eventually taking a detour away from Highway 61 and the parallel course of the Mississippi River toward Chicago. Then perhaps from Chicago we'd drive back while listening to Muddy Waters sing his "Louisiana Blues":

I'm goin' down in Louisiana
Be, be, behind the sun …
Let's go back to New Orleans, boys.[5]

Imagining going on that trip while listening to blues, especially sweet and sorrowful blues from the South, from the Delta, already provided us with an inwardly grounded and outwardly shared experience of personal and trans-personal experimentation on the road.

EXPLORING EXPERIENTIAL POSSIBILITIES

For, again, this is the point: Road trips, like Thoreauvian saunters, are explorations of experiential possibilities while on the move. As we saunter, our destination gradually emerges; in road-tripping, we explore and experiment with ways of getting to our destination. These ways may be actual or potential; they may be realized or simply imagined. We must go on these trips open to their transformative possibilities. Some of these transformations consist in cultivating and fostering meaningful relationships to lands and peoples. And when the transformative experiences have happened—inwardly, outwardly, or both—we must interpret and elaborate their meaning as we continue on our way, along our inward and outward roads of living experience. Some such trips, for me, took place in my first years in *la Yunai*, and I continue to cherish and interpret them to make sense of my place and history in this land.

NOTES

1. Robert Penn Warren, *All the King's Men* (New York: Harcourt, 2002).

2. "Go, eat your food with gladness, and drink your wine with a joyful heart, for God has already approved what you do. Always be clothed in white, and always anoint your head with oil. Enjoy life with your wife, whom you love, all the days of this meaningless life that God has given you under the sun—all your meaningless days. For this is your lot in life and in your toilsome labor under the sun." Eccles. 9:7–10 (Holy Bible: New International Version).

3. *Easy Rider.* Directed by Dennis Hopper (Los Angeles: Columbia Pictures, 1969), film.

4. Roger McGuinn, "Ballad of the Easy Rider" in *Easy Rider* (Dunhill, 1969), 33 1/3 rpm.

5. McKinley Morganfield, "Louisiana Blues" in *Best of Muddy Waters* (Chess, 1967), 33 1/3 rpm.

Chapter 7

Taking the Road Less Traveled By

My first encounter with American literature did not come through books but through a film I watched with a beloved friend after my high school graduation. During my final year, I was supposed to have been reading Miguel de Cervantes's *Don Quijote* for my graduation exams but had spent all of my time reading novels by Gabriel García Márquez and Mario Vargas Llosa, as they spoke more directly to my Latin American experience. I continued to read them after my exams, as Christmas came and passed and the New Year arrived. Unexpectedly, though, early in January, during that summer before I entered the *Universidad de Costa Rica* as a student, an American film spoke even more directly to my heart.

On a Saturday afternoon I felt a bit lonely, as I had called several of my friends to go to the movies with me, but no one was available. Mauri, my best buddy from school, had a date. An intelligent, good-looking guy with poetic charm and an older sister who coached him on wearing cool, fashionable clothes, he knew how to woo girls. R, my good friend turned girlfriend, had just become my ex-girlfriend. We had studied together for our graduation exams toward November and December, and as we spent every afternoon together after school, we had grown closer. For a couple of months I enjoyed our closeness, but then she ended our relationship and distanced herself from me. On that January afternoon I consoled myself thinking that even if we were still close friends, R probably wouldn't have gone to the movies with me. Most of the time her father wouldn't let her go out with me anyway, even on Saturday afternoons.

Come that fateful Saturday in January, then, I decided to go alone to the matinee at the old Cine Magaly in San José to watch *Dead Poets Society*.[1] I knew nothing of the film except that the title and the poster of several students in uniform carrying a teacher on their shoulders had caught my attention.

About an hour before the show, I walked to the bus stop near my house and caught a bus headed toward downtown San José. I got off at the city's National Park and leisurely strolled back toward the theater, enjoying the sunny afternoon. The gentle breeze swaying the tree branches under an azure sky heralded the end of the year, when the rains cease, the flora is verdant, and the cool winds from the northern winter sweep down to our tropics. The scene provided me a quiet calmness.

At the theater's ticket line, though, I felt conspicuous. It was the first time I had ever gone alone to the movies, and everyone else had come in groups. I felt like the only loner in the crowd. As soon as I bought my ticket, I walked quickly into the theater to find a good, inconspicuous seat high up in the balcony section, without stopping to buy popcorn or a soda.

When the theater darkened and the picture began, the film's photography drew me at once into a new world. *Dead Poet's Society* opened with scenes of students in uniform and teachers in academic robes preparing for the inaugural session of the fall semester in a traditional preparatory school in northeastern United States. I admired the gothic architecture of the buildings—the low vaulted ceilings inside the chapel; the stone façades; the pointed arches in windows, arcades, and cloisters; the rising towers. I had never seen anything similar in person, except perhaps the *Iglesia de San Isidro Labrador* in Coronado, several kilometers up the mountains that rose directly east from my home in Guadalupe. But the Church of San Isidro's gray façade and spiraling towers rose in front of a park in the middle of town, not on a school campus. And I had never seen, as I then saw on the silver screen, verdant lawns sloping down to a serene lake, whose still waters reflected the red, orange, and yellow foliage of autumn, or thousands of geese and ducks covering the sky as they migrated south, ahead of winter. All of these elements together created a campus environment unlike anything I had imagined before.

I felt drawn just as strongly to the students' social and personal dynamics as they sought at once bonds of friendship and their own *manera de ser* (way of being) in the midst of conservative mores and authoritarian institutions. As Neil Perry—the obedient, studious son of an autocratic father—welcomed his new roommate Todd Anderson—the introverted younger brother of a former school valedictorian—I felt sympathy for both. Perhaps Neil's caring tenderness with Todd as he adjusted to the new school and Todd's observant attentiveness with Neil as the latter strove to act in a play both appealed to my own introverted sensibilities. The extroverted, charming Charlie Dalton, so unlike me, struck me as interesting to know and fun to be around, and yet he also seemed caring and loyal in friendship; Meeks and Pitts, as pleasant geeks and good friends; Overstreet, as tender-hearted and sincere, if corny; Cameron, as tolerably annoying. I had no experiential sense of being as constrained by traditional mores and scholastic expectations as those boys were—I had no idea students in prep schools, and their parents, really thought their lives' happiness hinged on going to the Ivy League and belonging to the stuffy country-club forever. And I had no grasp of what it would be like to attend an all-boys dormitory school, as I had lived at home and been around boys and girls in school all my life. However, I could understand their yearning to break out, to experiment, to have fun, to be carefree, and to forge friendships.

Then as John Keating, the new English teacher, taught literature to the boys while standing on top of his desk, strolling in courtyards, and even kicking old-style leather balls in *fútbol* fields, I let myself be immersed in the romantic spirit he brought to the stuffy scholasticism of the school. I heeded Mr. Keating's summons for his students to "seize the day"—*carpe diem*—in his opening lesson while they observed the pictures of students long dead in the school's sports memorial hall. I found it eccentric but daring when he asked the boys to call him "O Captain! My Captain!" as in a poem I had not read by a poet I did not know.[2] I sensed that poetry, friendship, and life could all converge as they did for the boys when they revived the Dead Poets Society, when autumn leaves had already browned and fallen and the woods looked bare. I felt their thrill at sneaking out from their residence hall, running over dry leaves through the forest at night, and gathering at a cave in the woods to read verses, sing rhymes, improvise music, and tell stories.

My heart pulsated with the boys' late night meetings to "live deep and suck out all the marrow of life";[3] jumped with Neil's desire to act; sunk with Mr. Perry forbidding his son to play Puck in a production of Shakespeare's *A Midsummer Night's Dream*; yawped like Walt Whitman's barbarian at Neil's joy in acting anyway; sunk deeper when his father condemned him to attend a military school for his disobedience; cracked with Neil's tragic suicide; shattered as Todd ran toward the frozen lake on campus at dawn and heaved on the snow-blanketed lawn upon learning of Neil's death; pumped indignantly at Mr. Keating's unfair dismissal from the school as scapegoat for the young student's death; and beat faster with Todd's brave, standing salute to Mr. Keating, a caring teacher become Walt Whitman's "O Captain! My Captain!"

When the film ended, I came out of the theater in a romantic daze. Outside the theater, the sun shone intensely, and the light blinded me as I came out of the dark room. The brightness and warmth contrasted with the wintry landscapes and snow photographed toward the end of the film. And yet the boys' friendship, their love of literature, Neil's tragedy, Todd's redemption of Mr. Keating and of himself—it all felt plausible to me, even if I was a high school student from San José, born and educated far from the Dead Poets' cultural and natural world of the Northeast.

As my mind raced through scenes and poems, through quotes and authors, someone called my name from behind and brought me out of my daze. As I turned around, I saw my friend M smiling at me. She was a year younger than me and was one of my good friends at school. She was also R's best friend. In fact, Mauri, R, M, and I had become tightly knit over the previous year, as we studied and traveled together with our high school's team in *Antorcha*, a national academic competition. On the bus rides to and from other schools, M and I often sat together and talked. Sometime around April or May, on our way back from Puriscal, a quiet town in the mountains west of San José, I felt tired and sleepy, and M asked me to rest my head on her shoulder as she placed her hand tenderly on my hair. I did not fall asleep, but I stayed quiet and still so I could feel her soft hand caressing me. At our school's library we often studied together, along with Mauri and R, for the competition. M focused on history and I on mathematics, but we both loved reading literature. Ironically, we both seemed to love it even more than R, who focused on Costa Rican and Latin American literature but aspired to be a businesswoman. Perhaps even more ironically, by the end of the year I had fallen for R's quiet softness rather than M's joyful tenderness.

On the afternoon I saw *Dead Poets Society*, M had come to the theater to see the movie with her mother and her younger brother. Her long black hair fell in gentle curls below her thin shoulders; her shiny brown eyes lit up her fair-skinned, oval-shaped face; and her slim figure emphasized her elegant demeanor. Seeing her and hearing her call out my name lit me up inside. I no longer felt lonely, though I felt embarrassed to be at the theater alone. She asked if I was alone; I lied and said I had arrived late and had not seen my friends. She knew I was lying but said nothing. Instead she asked if I wanted to go home with them and have some coffee, and I accepted with delight.

As we walked together to their home in Zapote, we talked about the film and tried to remember the quoted verses and the names of the authors. She had been struck by the words of Mr. Keating in a courtyard, when he was encouraging the boys to find their own stride while walking. We tried to recollect verses whose sense we captured but whose English cadence and rhythm we could not retain:

Two roads diverged in a wood, and I,
I took the one less traveled by,
And that has made all the difference.[4]

While watching the movie, we did not catch that Mr. Keating was quoting Robert Frost's "The Road not Taken." Yet we grasped the significance of the poem for us. I had come to the end of my high school education; M only had one more year left; and we both wondered what path we would take, where we would go, what we would do, how we would live. I had no inkling, not even the smallest suspicion, that less than one year later I would not be studying at the *Universidad de Costa Rica* but would be a student on scholar-ship in Arkansas instead. And I had even less of an inkling of the tragedy that was to come for her, for us. How could we suspect it?

At that moment, after watching the film, I felt most struck by the words from *Walden* that Mr. Keating had cited in his dedication for the first meeting of the boys' society. I had never heard of Henry David Thoreau or the title of any of his works, but I made sure to memorize his last name. I also seized upon the sense of his prose from *Walden*'s "Where I Lived, and What I Lived For," even though my English was too poor to appreciate fully the poetry in his words. In the passage quoted by Mr. Keating, Thoreau writes:

> I went to the woods because I wished to live deliberately, to front only the essential facts of life, and see if I could not learn what it had to teach, and not, when I came to die, discover that I had not lived. I did not wish to live what was not life, living is so dear … . I wanted to live deep and suck out all the marrow of life, to live so sturdily and Spartan-like as to put to rout all that was not life.[5]

As I tried to reconstruct this poetic prose with M, I couldn't quite explain what it meant to me, but I sensed she grasped *how it felt to me*. I wanted the simple life, grounded on bedrock reality, for which *Walden* served as a beacon, the experimental life of individual self-discovery and spontaneous self-expression that Mr. Keating had encouraged in his students. I couldn't articulate this Thoreauvian vision, but my family had nurtured its spirit in me. My mother had filled my heart with love and trust in the world; my father had put me on the road to life; my younger sisters had admired me, foster-ing my confidence; my adventurous uncles had led the way to forests, rivers, mountains, and underwater coves in the sea. Though I couldn't explain my passion, M empathized with it and smiled lovingly at me, as we drank coffee at her home's kitchen table and spoke of the Dead Poets' attempt at living deep and sucking out the marrow of life. Her attentive gaze and soothing company brought me pleasant joy and serenity, steadier than what I had felt that afternoon, at the quiet National Park before the film, as I sensed the cool-ing breeze and warming sunshine on my skin.

The joy of our conversation fluttered inside me over the next few months, as I looked in vain for a Spanish edition of Thoreau's *Walden*—it seemed there was no recent edition, and no used bookstore had an old copy. Mean-while, my summer vacation had ended, and I had started to study at the *Uni-versidad de Costa Rica*. I continued to read García Márquez, Vargas Llosa, Carlos Fuentes, and other *boom* writers from Latin America even as I took my first-year university courses, and I stopped looking for a copy of *Walden*.

One day, I saw a newspaper advertisement for a scholarship program to study in Arkansas. I had a hunch that this could be the chance for an adventure and decided to apply. I called M to tell her about it. She felt thrilled at the prospect of the scholarship and encouraged me, but I wasn't sure I would go even if I got it. I didn't feel tied to my life in San José or at the university. Since running into each other at the *Dead Poets* screening, however, M and I had become closer. I had seen her several times, and I loved calling her to hear her warm voice and easy laughter as we talked. I had begun to feel a growing, deepening love for her. I missed her daily presence in my life, as I had enjoyed it the previous year. But she had started her last year of high school, and I mused that in just one year she would be at the university campus also.

Then, one morning in the middle of that first semester, my friend Mauri called me at home. We used to talk a lot on the phone, so I thought nothing of the early morning call. But this time his voice sounded grave, as if he needed to tell me something difficult and was measuring his words. "What's wrong?" I asked. "*Mae, a M la mataron,*" he said. M had been murdered. My throat contracted, my heart accelerated its beating, and my solar plexus hurt as if it had been stabbed. I couldn't speak. The pain muted me. I couldn't ask anything. I could only agree to meet him at our high school, where our friends would gather for support. When I hung up the phone, I cried. My whole body shook for a few minutes. My mother grasped what had happened and embraced me. She calmed me down so I could react. Then I got ready as fast as I could, left home without having breakfast, and hurried to our former school. I still didn't know what had happened, and I had to restrain the pain so as not to cry on the way. The sun, rising fast on a bright lit sky, announced a hot day, but I felt cold.

When I arrived at our school, I looked for R. Since graduation, we had grown far apart. I had seen her on the university campus a few times, but our conversations had felt impersonal and distant. At that moment, however, I embraced her with all my strength. When I felt the quiet softness in her slender body, my own body relaxed, releasing its tension, and I cried again. We cried desperately, but we cried together, not alone. My body heaved. For the first time in my life, I felt grief so deep and violent that it could not be spoken, only released through the body. When we finally stopped crying, R explained that M and her older brother had been assassinated the night before by her mother's ex-boyfriend. But the details mattered very little to me. M was dead. She had traveled beautifully along her road thus far, and then her life had ended. We would never share again a sunny Saturday afternoon, talking about a film or dreaming about our future.

Over the next several months, I grieved her loss. I walked about campus and the city, and they seemed utterly empty. I discovered a poem from Peruvian César Vallejo that expressed—in verses that I thought M would

love and that, even today, move me in my native Spanish—the violent blow
I had felt:

Hay golpes en la vida, tan fuertes … ¡Yo no sé!
Golpes como del odio de Dios; como si ante ellos,
la resaca de todo lo sufrido
se empozara en el alma … ¡Yo no sé!
Son pocos; pero son … Abren zanjas oscuras
en el rostro más fiero y en el lomo más fuerte.
Serán tal vez los potros de bárbaros atilas;
o los heraldos negros que nos manda la Muerte.
Son las caídas hondas de los Cristos del alma,
de alguna fe adorable que el Destino blasfema.
Esos golpes sangrientos son las crepitaciones
de algún pan que en la puerta del horno se nos quema.
Y el hombre … Pobre … ¡pobre! Vuelve los ojos, como
cuando por sobre el hombro nos llama una palmada;
vuelve los ojos locos, y todo lo vivido
se empoza, como un charco de culpa, en la mirada.
Hay golpes en la vida, tan fuertes … ¡Yo no sé![6]

What had been the strong blow from life that felt like divine hatred to the young
poet? What had been the tragedy that made him feel as if all he had suffered had
become, all at once, like stagnant water drowning his soul? That had cut dark
crevices in his face, in his back, in his heart? That felt like barbaric warriors gal-
loping on wild horses over his chest? That shook his faith so that only the darkness in his gaze could express the depth of his loss? I didn't know, but I felt as if
I understood. I had loved M more intensely than I had realized. Her death had cut
inside me the first of the dark inner crevices that Vallejo had written about, but I
could not speak of it. Only my eyes reflected my pain sometimes, but I turned my
gaze away from people, to the mountains on the horizon or upwards to the sky.

My brief rapprochement with R passed and faded away. I knew she must
have been grieving also, but the chasm grew ever deeper and wider between
us. We loved each other, but perhaps we needed time apart to grieve sepa-
rately. Our hearts would need a long time to heal. I hardly ever saw Mauri at
the university, as he spent most of his time with his girlfriend. Though I made
several acquaintances among my classmates, I did not connect with anyone
on campus. I lost focus in my university courses. I was failing most of them
except calculus. But I continued to read literature—Florentino Ariza's story
of happiness, loss, unrequited love, and persevering hope with Fermina Daza
in García Márquez's *Love in the Time of Cholera* captured me.[7]

As I grieved and felt ever more lost, I was called to an interview in English
for the Arkansas scholarship program, but I did not give it much importance

and did not practice speaking the language in preparation for it. When the program director interviewed me in San José, I did not express myself fluently at all. The flow of my ideas felt broken and disrupted. I made up words, such as "*deportive*" for "sporting." When I left the meeting, I thought I would not get the scholarship to go abroad. A few weeks later, however, after I had failed one more economics exam at the university for lack of studying, a letter arrived in the mail from Arkansas offering me a full scholarship. Initially I read it with a curious indifference. I did not feel excited. I hesitated about what I should do. The more traditional path would have been to pursue a five-year *licenciatura* at the *Universidad de Costa Rica*, make connections and secure employment, and then go abroad with leave for graduate education.

As I sought advice, I felt more intensely M's absence. I wanted to talk to her about my options, about choices, about the road to be taken. In silence without her, I realized I needed to go. One day I told my sister Anto that I had no friends left, really, as we had all disbanded after high school, and without M the campus and the city felt like voids. "There's no one for me here. I am going," I told her. Of course, I had my family. But my parents had educated me according to Kahlil Gibran's philosophy in *The Prophet*—as if I were an arrow, they were the bow, and Life were the archer that shoots the arrow with the bow.[8] They set me free to choose my way but encouraged me to experiment with a different path. Even as grief pushed me to leave, some of the sense of adventure that M had grasped in me came back to the fore. I remembered her loving gaze and her smile as we shared dreams. The words from *Walden* that we had shared and the poem by Frost that she had loved nurtured this sense of life as a road to be traveled, as an experimental walk in the woods. When I left San José for Arkansas, a few days before I turned eighteen, I took my memory of M, the grief and the joy of it, along with me.

NOTES

1. See *Dead Poets Society*. Directed by Peter Weir. (USA: Touchstone Pictures, 1989), film.

2. Walt Whitman, "O Captain! My Captain!," in *Leaves of Grass* (New York: Norton, 1973), 337–338.

3. Henry David Thoreau, *Walden and Resistance to Civil Government*, 2nd ed., ed. William Rossi (New York: W. W. Norton & Company, 1992), 61.

4. Robert Frost, "The Road Not Taken." For a printed version see *The Norton Anthology of American Literature,* 3rd ed., vol. 2 (New York: W.W. Norton and Company, 1989), 1099.

5. Thoreau, *Walden*, 61.

6. César Vallejo, "Los heraldos negros." For an English translation, see *The Black Heralds*, trans. Richard Schaaf and Kathleen Ross (Pittsburg, PA: Latin American Literary Review Press, 1990), 17.

7. Gabriel García Márquez, *Love in the Time of Cholera* (New York: Vintage, 2007).

8. The Prophet says to a woman holding a babe against her bosom and to all parents: "You are the bows from which your children as living arrows are sent forth. / The Archer sees the mark upon the path of the infinite, and He bends you with His might that his arrows may go swift and far. / Let your bending in the archer's hands be for gladness; / For even as He loves the arrow that flies, so He loves also the bow that is stable." Kahlil Gibran, "The Prophet," in *The Collected Works* (New York: Everyman's Library, 2007), 107.

Chapter 8

Tico and *Okie* Migrants in American Literature

I fell in love with American literature while reading under the shade of oak trees in the South. Though I was a mathematics student at our college, I preferred to read the books that K recommended. Any chance I got—fall, spring, or summer—I'd free myself from solving problems or proving theorems, take a book with me, and read in the verdant main lawn, reclining on a grooved trunk or lying on the cool ground under boughs. K had a favorite tree on the lawn, like Paul D at the Sweet Home plantation in Toni Morrison's *Beloved*, and I'd often read by it in hopes she'd come. The more I read, the more we talked, the more we shared that passion, the deeper my love grew not only for the literature we both loved, but for her, her land, and her people—even as we were just friends and I was too timid to tell her what I felt.

Carolyn, my friend from Walla Walla, introduced us during our sophomore year. She and K were roommates in a women's residence hall on campus. For some reason, though Carolyn and I were close friends since the first week of our freshman year, I had never seen her with K. A lot of the time I had been clueless as to what was happening around me anyways. During that first year, I had made a great effort to become fluent in listening to, speaking, reading, and writing English. For a long time, I could just listen to conversations without being able to speak—by the time I processed what was being discussed and thought of what to say, the conversation had moved on. I could only have one-on-one conversations with very patient interlocutors. I had also spent my freshman year strenuously trying to read and writing laboriously. In my American history class, I couldn't understand a thing Professor Haynie, a native Arkansan, ever said. I found his twang soothing but incomprehensible. I only passed the class because I read the whole textbook word by word with a dictionary in hand, and a girl in my class allowed me to sit next to her and read her notes as she took them while listening to Dr. Haynie's lecture. I could understand what she wrote but not understand what he said. Then she let me copy her notes so I could study. She acted as my guardian angel, if I ever had one as a classmate.

Even with difficulties, I had managed to pass a couple of English composition classes to improve my basic writing skills, and I had read, slowly and without full understanding, a few American short stories. My favorite ones had been Mark Twain's—I'd read parts of his *Life on the Mississippi* and some short tales in my first English class during my first Southern summer. Later, during a trip to watch my first baseball game in Saint Louis, I'd remembered Twain's descriptions as I stood in front of the mighty river for the first time. One of his tales, about a steamboat pilot navigating a treacherous passage in the midst of a snowstorm, began thus: "A number of years ago, a Saint Louis and New Orleans packet … was on her way up the river, and at about ten o'clock at night, the sky, which had been clear, suddenly became overcast, and snow commenced falling soon afterwards."[1] I was just learning about incoming storms, over the river or in life, as I witnessed a tranquil scene in the midst of summer. In retrospect I surmise that Samuel Clemens must have learned, from his own piloting experiences, a thing or two about navigating life in the midst of storms and outwitting its tricky passages. As I stood watching the river flow, I could imagine the former life of the river and its people—the large steamboats, the gaudy packets, the captains, the pilots, the stevedores, the merchants, the loafers, the kids running to meet the ships while dreaming of piloting one day, just like young Samuel Clemens. As I stood there watching the darkening sky and imagining a former time, I knew that reading Twain had enriched my experience.

Just so, as I struggled to learn but persisted with the English language over the next few months and years, reading American literature nurtured my living experience in *la Yunai* and helped me engage the land and its peoples. During my freshman year in Arkansas, I bridged my previous experiences reading Costa Rican literature with my new vital and literary explorations in *la Yunai*, especially in order to understand issues of social class and migration in the United States. The college seemed disengaged from the social reality around it. Being on campus, I felt especially distant from the lives that poor migrants must have been living elsewhere in *la Yunai*. Reading literature helped me fill that experiential gap. In particular, by reading John Steinbeck's *Grapes of Wrath* in light of Carlos Luis Fallas's novel *Mamita Yunai*, I sensed that migrant workers, whether in Costa Rica or the United States and regardless of ethnicity or nationality, shared experiences with which I could empathize as an observant foreign student, an engaged sojourner, if not yet an immigrant.

MAMITA YUNAI: STRUGGLE AND SOLIDARITY
IN THE *BANANALES CARIBEÑOS*

Carlos Luis Fallas (*Ca-Lu-Fa*) is one of our most beloved writers in Costa Rica. A working-class man born in Alajuela in 1909, he was the eldest son of a peasant woman who had six other children with his stepfather, a shoemaker. By his own account, *Calufa* received seven years of public education before he had to quit his studies and work as an apprentice in a railroad shop.[2] At age sixteen he moved to the Limón province in the Caribbean region of Costa Rica, where he worked first as a stevedore in the main port and then in the *bananales*, or banana plantations, of the United Fruit Company as a farmhand, mason, dynamite blaster, and tractor operator. At twenty-two he returned to Alajuela, in the Central Valley, where he learned the shoemaking craft, and he earned his living from practicing this craft for many years.[3] He also became a leading figure in the movement for workers' rights in the first half of the twentieth century in Costa Rica and helped to organize several important strikes, for which he was imprisoned. One of them, organized in 1934 against the powerful United Fruit Company— then known as "*Mamita Yunai*"—enlisted 15,000 workers. It was met with violence against the workers by the local police at the service of the company's interests. *Calufa* was once again incarcerated but went on hunger strike before being released. Eventually he was elected to a position in Alajuela's local government (1942) and then to a seat in Costa Rica's legislature (1944).[4]

Calufa also wrote fiction that portrayed the lives and experiences of laborers in gold mines and banana plantations, and of peasants and poor people in our country's rural and urban settings, with tenderness, humor, solidarity, and love of neighbor. I read his novel *Mamita Yunai*, first published in 1941, during my first year of secondary education in Costa Rica. It moved my heart to feel compassion and indignation for the struggles of landless peasants and migrant workers in the Caribbean feuds of the *Yunaited Frut Cómpani* during the first decades of the twentieth century.

Though my father had taken me on many road trips around Costa Rica by then, I had only been to the Caribbean coast twice. On one of those occasions, my family had gone camping to Cahuita National Park. We had spent a week right on the beach, sleeping in a single large tent pitched under the shade of wide-leaved *almendros* and low-hanging boughs of large trees. The lush, verdant rainforest met the turquoise waters of the Caribbean Sea on a beach of bone-white sand. Entire troops of white-faced capuchin monkeys in search of food passed through, and even hung out, on the trees near us. Our neighbors had been a couple from New Zealand who had come on their honeymoon. We all had timed our visit so we could see, at sundown behind us in the west, the full moon rising, huge and round and bright, over the darkening waters in front of us to the east. I had been most often to the Pacific coast, and I had seen many sunsets over the expansive ocean—the sky burning in reds, oranges, and yellows, before cooling into greens, light blues, and deeper blues as I raised my sight over the horizon to the celestial dome above me. I had never seen, however, the full moon rising over the waters of the sea to the east and becoming the queen of the warm Caribbean nights. That image remained my most vivid memory of *nuestro Caribe*, and the virgin rainforest and limpid sea waters at Cahuita the main sources of my concept of the region as a natural paradise. I had, however, no experience and very little inkling of the socioeconomic history of the region.

Reading *Mamita Yunai* as a student from the urban lower middle class during my first year of high school, then, opened my eyes to a harsh social reality I had not known. The narrator of the novel, Sibajita, a former worker in the plantations of the United Fruit Company, travels through the Caribbean lowlands to the remote mountains of Talamanca. His mission is to act as an overseer for the *Bloque de Obreros y Campesinos* (the Workers and Peasant's Party) at a remote voting poll during a presidential election. At the poll, most of the voters will be indigenous *Bribris* and *Cabécares* whose lives and struggles are perennially ignored by the government except at election time, when their votes are exchanged for petty favors. The election is rigged in favor of the party in government. Sibajita's mission is to minimize fraud at that remote poll so perhaps his own party, which has support among some of the stevedores at the port and the farmhands at the *bananales*, can have some candidates elected into congress for the Limón province. As he narrates his vicissitudes to achieve his mission, he describes the rough conditions of dispossession and exploitation among the indigenous *Bribris* and *Cabécares* who live in the Talamanca Mountains, the *Mekatelyu*—or creole English-speaking afro-descendants from the lowlands, and the *mestizo* migrant workers from the rest of Costa Rica and Central America who come to work at the *Yunaited Frut Cómpani*'s banana plantations in the Costa Rica of the late 1930s.

As I read, I learned of a great migration of Costa Rican *afrocaribeños* from Limón across the border to Panama. They crossed rivers, swamps, and mountains on foot in order to seek better economic conditions at the Panama Canal. They had no other options; *Mamita Yunai* had decided to abandon several plantations in their region, since overproduction of the fruit had led to excessive supply and falling prices in the foreign markets.[5] Many of their ancestors had come from Caribbean islands to work in the construction of railroads or to settle in fishing villages, but now they had to migrate to work at the Canal.

Then, as Sibajita makes his way up the mountains, sometimes on foot and more often on rivers, upstream, hitching a ride aboard *cayucos* or canoes rowed by silent indigenous men, I began to imagine the rough Talamanca wilderness in which the native peoples toiled. As Sibajita tells it, with the arrival of the United Fruit Company the "*indios*" had been dispossessed of their remaining ancestral lowlands in the Talamanca Valley, where the flat terrain and humid climate favored the growth of banana trees. They had been constrained thus to the isolated Talamanca Mountains, that even *Mamita Yunai* could not penetrate. Circumscribed to rougher terrains and harsher environments, they barely survived by growing corn and plantains, so indigenous men had no option but to descend to the lowlands and work as farmhands and peons at *Mamita Yunai*'s plantations. There they suffered from malaria, dysentery, and alcoholism until they could no longer work. For Sibajita, the brave Talamanca peoples, who had not been fully "civilized"— conquered and dominated—by the Spaniards during the period of coloniza- tion, had been defeated instead during the republican period by the new "civilizing" wave of capitalism and liberalism embodied by the company and Costa Rica's servile government.[6] During a sleepless night in the mountains, he cries:

> Y el plácido valle de Talamanca se estremeció al paso de la jauría azuzada por los yanquis … Querían tierra y hombres-bestias que la trabajaran. Y ya los pobres indios no pudieron contener el avance de la "nueva civilización"… Entró la locomotora y sacó millones y millones de frutas para los gringos. Y mientras en la capital de la República los criollos imbéciles o pillos aplaudían la obra "civilizadora" de la United, en Talamanca corría el guaro y el sudor y la sangre también.[7]

As I heard Sibajita's cry in the dark, for the first time my heart felt the pain of the long-suffering *Bribris* and *Cabécares* in Talamanca—a few hundred kilo- meters, but so many worlds, away from my San José. I heard Sibajita's lam- entations as a plea for compassion with the indigenous people of my country more than as an ideological denunciation. Today I could say that Sibajita's socialism is a humanist cry for solidarity rather than an orthodox political doctrine. In this sense, Carlos Luis Fallas's *Mamita Yunai* is in line with the Marxist humanism of many Latin American authors—present, for instance, in the essays of José Carlos Mariátegui or the poetry of Pablo Neruda.[8] At the time of my first reading in high school, I could not articulate the matter in this way, but I could empathize with the humanist pain Sibajita felt at witnessing the misery and marginalization of the native peoples of Talamanca.

For me at that age, the most moving story in *Mamita Yunai* was not just one of humanist solidarity but of close personal friendship among three young men: Sibajita, Herminio, and Calero. In the narrative, as Sibajita finds his way out of the mountains of Talamanca after the fraudulent election, he runs into Herminio, a long-lost friend. They embrace each other like loving brothers and begin to reminisce about their lives together, years earlier, in the company's feud. Along with Calero, they had worked together for years at the fruit company's plantations as farmhands and dynamite blasters. Sibajita arrived in Limón from Alajuela, in the Central Valley, when he was around nineteen years old; Herminio and Calero from Esparza, in the Pacific low-lands, also at a similar age. Their goal was to work hard at the plantations, earn and save money, and then fulfill their youthful dreams. Sibajita and Herminio wanted to travel the world. For Sibajita, this aspiration found its source in the novels of Jules Verne and Emilio Salgari.[9] At the point of reading this, I began to empathize most strongly with Sibajita. He spoke of travel and exploration born from literary discoveries. The road trips around Costa Rica with my father had already planted wanderlust in me. My father had also bought me some novels by Jules Verne which I enjoyed, but I preferred Emilio Salgari's stories, and he bought me as many of his novels as he could find in San José's bookstores. My favorites, like *The Pirates of Malaysia* or *The Tigers of Mompracem*, had the audacious pirate Sandokan as their protagonist, living his adventures in faraway lands bathed by the Indian Ocean. How exciting it was, then, to find that Sibajita also dreamed of seeing the world that Salgari's novels described! I empathized with his desire to see also South America, Egypt, or India. For a schoolboy from San José, those lands seemed as distant, but reachable in daydreams, as for a teenaged man working in the *bananales*.[10]

However, Sibajita, Calero, and Herminio's economic reality in the feud turned these dreams into impossible fantasies. The tragic turn in the story of friendship and solidarity comes when Sibajita, Herminio, and Calero, feeling trapped and exploited, take a chance at earning better wages and working overtime to leave *Mamita Yunai* once and for all. After torrential rains, a landslide blocks a rail line in the plantations. Since Sibajita and Herminio are skilled dynamite blasters, the company's main engineer, the Italian Bertolazzi, agrees to pay them a higher wage and overtime to clear the landslide, blasting its massive rocks and giant trees. They fool the engineer into thinking that Calero, an unskilled but strong and dexterous farmhand, is also a skilled blaster, and the three of them set to work overtime for weeks. When they expect to receive their wages and leave, however, their foreman takes their money from the Italian engineer but does not pay them. He runs away to Limón with the dynamite-blasters' wages. When Calero threatens Bertolazzi, the police agents—who are always at the company's service—pummel and imprison Calero and later expel all three friends from the plantations. They have to flee further into the jungle and search for work in the *volteas*, overseen by a mean *gringo* foreman, felling trees and cutting away the forest to clear the way for agricultural expansion. They do not earn enough money, eat poorly, and become terribly sick from drinking dirty water.[11]

Just as they are deciding to leave any way they can, a tree falls on Calero, crushing him to death. Sibajita and Herminio cry. They want to take him out of the jungle for burial, but their foreman convinces them that it is pointless. They bury his body right in the clearing, knowing his body will rot and fertilize the land to grow bananas for *Mamita Yunai*.[12] When the two survivors return to the plantation, Herminio avenges Calero by cutting Bertolazzi open with his *machete*. His destination is prison in San Lucas, an island in the Gulf of Nicoya, on the Pacific coast.

Many years later, when Herminio's prison sentence ends, he is too ashamed to return to his and Calero's hometown, Esparza, and instead returns to the misery of the *bananales*. After Calero's death and Herminio's imprisonment, Sibajita does manage to flee the company's feud, but his experiences and memories lead him to become a labor activist.[13] When he returns to oversee an electoral poll in Talamanca, he finds Herminio by chance and recalls their story—one of joint suffering, fraternal love, and humanist solidarity.

In many ways, the tragic story of these three friends follows a pattern that Sibajita's narrative explains to be the result of the greed of *yanquis*. Like many other characters, Sibajita identifies *gringos* with this cruel greed when he decries injustice and exploitation at the plantations. For instance, when he describes how the workers spend their wages at the company's *comisariato* to buy poor quality rum at very high prices to flood their pained hearts and minds with alcohol, he rails against blond bankers from Wall Street who reap *Mamita Yunai*'s profits and ironizes about the opportunities these generous bankers endow upon the workers.[14] From the workers' perspective, greed and avarice are the main characteristics of the United Statesians they know through their merciless advancement of the fruit company's financial interests.

Sibajita, however, who is inquisitive and reflective, at the end of the novel does not attribute *Mamita Yunai*'s greed and cruelty to nationality or culture, but to economic class. When their reunion is ending and Sibajita is about to continue his journey away from the mountains of Talamanca to the port of Limón, Herminio, whose life of misfortune had continued upon his return to the *bananales*, wishes he could cut the throat of all *gringos* in one swift swing of his *machete*. But Sibajita tries to appease Herminio's rage by explaining that it is only a few *machos* or blondies who exploit people, while there are millions of workers in the United States who are themselves exploited: "*Así pensaba yo también, Herminio. Pero no son todos: son unos cuantos que viven sangrando a los pueblos. Allá, en el país de los gringos, hay también millones de hombres que sufren como nosotros. ¡Hay que luchar de otro modo para cambiar la vida, hermano!*"[15] The path Sibajita chooses is through building workers' unions and promoting workers' rights through democratic political struggle. This is the path of social and political solidarity.

THE GOSPEL OF LOVE

As I reconsider these issues over two decades later, I recognize that *Calufa* and his fictional counterpart Sibajita would have found a philosophical friend in American philosopher Charles Peirce. In the midst of aggressive United Statesian economic expansion and the accumulation of wealth by a few industrial barons, Peirce denounced the "gospel of greed" in 1893 and advocated to replace it with the "gospel of love."[16] For Peirce, in the nineteenth century the science of political economy had been abused by apologists of self-interested accumulation of wealth to draw a false general conclusion that came to this: "Intelligence in the service of greed ensures the justest prices, the fairest contracts, the most enlightened conduct of all the dealings among men, and leads to the *summum bonum*, food in plenty and perfect comfort. Food for whom? Why, for the greedy master of intelligence."[17] In my way of understanding Peirce, political economy is a theory that upon specific hypotheses draws strict logical inferences. The falsity above consists in drawing from such theoretical reasoning a general principle for guiding people in matters of vital importance, such as affairs that pertain to the human ideals of justice and truth. Matters of vital importance such as justice, fairness, and goodness ought to be guided by sentiment—say, by sympathy that recommends fraternity and solidarity—though advised by reason in order to be effective. Theory and practice, thinking and living, are not disjointed but coordinated; however, in ethical living, theoretical principles ought not to trample the insights and recommendations of natural sentiment. [18] But the false generalization of theories of political economy fostered a doctrine that Peirce labelled the "gospel of greed." Its central philosophical principle was "that greed is the great agent in the elevation of the human race and in the evolution of the universe."[19] This principle was the antithesis of Peirce's agapistic thesis that "growth comes only from love, from—I will not say self-*sacrifice*, but from the ardent impulse to fulfill another's highest impulse."[20] The agapistic principle sustained and fostered the "gospel of love" which claimed "that progress comes from every individual merging his individuality in sympathy with his neighbors."[21] For Peirce, sentiment provided the affective insight into the truth of the gospel of love. Peirce's agapistic ethics relied on sentimentalism, that is, on the "doctrine that great respect should be paid to the natural judgments of the sensible heart."[22] In Spanish, I think this is well-expressed by the dictum that we ought to listen to our *corazonadas*, that is, to the hunches of the heart. In particular, a "strong feeling" in favor of the "gospel of love" and its core philosophical principles indicated to Peirce that such principles bespoke "the normal judgment of the Sensible Heart."[23]

Calufa, I think, would have agreed with Peirce that progress comes from sympathetic solidarity. His characters in *Mamita Yunai*—Sibajita, Herminio, and Calero—personify this kind of agapistic impulse, whereas the contractors and foremen that exploit these workers personify the selfish impulse that sustains the gospel of greed. As for me, as a young reader I felt Sibajita's sympathetic impulse to be ethically admirable and commendable. His path of social solidarity and care of his friends and neighbors recommended itself to my heart.

FROM *LOS BANANALES* TO THE PROMISED LAND: READING *THE GRAPES OF WRATH*

During my first year in *la Yunai*, I discovered a counterpart for Sibajita's democratic path of political struggle and solidarity in John Steinbeck's *The Grapes of Wrath.* After my first semester at college in Arkansas, the director of my scholarship program, David T., asked me how I was doing. Even though David was an economics professor and I had intended to study economics, I said: "I am bored. I don't like the business school. I'd rather read." I must have said something like that in choppy sentences, without announcing that I was already considering a transfer to the mathematics program. Worried, my tall, skinny, dirty-blond-haired, mustached professor, dressed in pants, button-up shirt, and conservative tie as if he were a banker, walked over to the shelves of his office library and picked up a copy of John Steinbeck's *The Grapes of Wrath.* "Here. Read this one. It'll bring economics to life," he said, and handed me the hardback book.

I would have been suspicious of the economics comment, except that I recognized the title. Several years earlier, in my neighborhood in San José, my "secret" girlfriend Carmen had told me that she had just read "*Las uvas de la ira*" at the university. We kept our relationship "secret" because my parents and hers were alarmed about it, since she was already a college student when I was just starting high school. One evening when her parents were not home, we were standing in the doorway of her house, holding hands, and she looked at me with her dark hazelnut eyes when she said, in her sweet, thoughtful voice, that it was the best book she had ever read. She had not mentioned the author's name, but I had seized upon the title: *Las uvas de la ira*, intriguing and suggestive. Five years later, in Arkansas, I had not yet read the novel—Carmen broke up with me for a college boy before I thought to borrow it from her. As soon as David T. handed me a copy in the original English from his personal library, I remembered Carmen's words about it. If she had loved it so deeply, I had to trust her sensitivity and read the novel. From the initial pages, I sensed what she had felt when reading the story of a dispossessed family of farmers from Oklahoma. And what I sensed—sorrow and solidarity—felt significant.

David had been right to say that Steinbeck's novel would bring economics to life. The economic processes that sparked mass migration seemed clear as I read. The dust bowl dries all the corn planted by the tenants or squatters of small farms in Oklahoma. They lose their crops.[24] The owners do not receive their share of the crops and have to borrow from banks. But the soil is exhausted; it is does not yield rich crops anymore. Season after season, the tenants do not produce as much, and the owners become more indebted, until the latter lose control, or even ownership, of their land to the banks. These heartless institutions take effective control of the land, forcing the owners to mechanize large-scale production.[25] Through their arms in the legal system, the banks throw these tenants off the land. These men and women, these families, are angry. They know that legal possession is not coextensive with just ownership, that the land is for those who work, live, and die on it.[26] Against justice, they are pushed out onto Highway 66. The former farming tenants sell all of their possessions at negligible prices out of desperation and buy overpriced clunkers. As I read, I gathered that economists would have liked me to call that rip-off the "opportunity cost." The expelled tenants bear that "cost" so that they can migrate west, to California, to the Promised Land of Peaches and Oranges and Grapes.[27] These economic themes were similar to those of *Mamita Yunai* and other novels of Costa Rican social realism. Even if the economic processes were somewhat different, the consequences of dispossession, exploitation, and suffering were the same.

However, it wasn't the economic dynamics but the suffering, sorrow, hope, passing joy, deep disillusionment, sadness, mourning, renewed strength, struggle, loss, perseverance, and solidarity of the people called "Okies" that truly mattered. I surmised that these experiences—Okie experiences, United Statesian experiences, American and human experiences—must have been what took hold of Carmen's sensitive heart years earlier, just as they took hold of mine while reading in Arkansas, just across the border from Oklahoma.

The story begins with Tom Joad, a convict on parole, returning home to find that his family of farming tenants has been expelled from their land. They are preparing to migrate westward to California, where they have heard there is work at fruit farms. Grampa, Granma, Pa, Ma, and his siblings are all going. Even though Tom cannot leave the state without breaking the terms of his parole, he decides to go with them. Casy, a former pastor known by the Joad family, joins them. And thus a story of migrants' sorrows and joys, pleasures and pains, struggles, defeats and triumphs ensues.

Perhaps because of the overtly religious culture in which I was immersed while reading, I felt quite drawn to Casy's story from the outset. As he walks home across fields and farms, Tom Joad runs into the former preacher as he is taking refuge from the scorching sun in the shade under a tree. As they talk,

Casy explains why he had left his work and disappeared for a long while. Even as he preached, he had been "sinning," laying with women on the grass after preaching at meetings.[28] Tom smiles upon hearing this and confesses he has done the same with girls after religious meetings. But the preacher worries about it to the point of giving up his mission. What seized me, though, was the way the preacher resolves, over time, his self-doubt and anguish. He concludes that there is no sin but just good and bad things people do to each other, and that Christian love means caring for the flesh and blood neighbor standing next to you.[29] This insight leads Casy to humanize his understanding of the Holy Spirit: "Maybe it's all men an' all women we love; maybe that's the Holy Sperit—the human sperit—the whole shebang. Maybe all men got one big soul ever'body's a part of."[30] Casy's faith in this insight leads him to re-conceive his religious mission. It motivates him to go with the Joads and the Okies, to participate in their exodus to the Promised Land.[31] Casy doesn't yet know how, but he resolves to help the folks around him along their earthly road to California, to assist them in their concrete, daily vicissitudes.

Initially I followed the narrative thread of the Joads' struggles as they make their way westward in an old, beat-up truck. Securing food, water, and shelter on the road proves difficult, even hazardous. Soon, tragedy strikes the family. As Grampa lies dying in a tent as they camp and Casy tends to him, Granma demands a prayer, and the preacher begins to enounce the Lord's Prayer from Jesus's Sermon on the Mount. Granma exclaims hallelujahs, glories, and amen just as the prayer goes on praying and her husband dies. Then she walks away with dignity, and as she sits down quietly, all the other family members gather, squatting on the ground, and Pa becomes the head of the family.[32] They could confer together, and later they could grieve together. The law demands that they report the death to the authorities, but burying the corpse would cost forty dollars they cannot spare in order to get to California, and no one in their family has ever been buried a pauper. The solution, Pa says, is to bury him in the land themselves. This would mean breaking the law, but the preacher claims that moral duties are prior and higher.[33] Like Antigone's burying her brother Polyneices against the human decrees of her uncle Creon, king of Thebes, but according to divine justice,[34] and like the Trojan hero Aeneas's burying his father Anchises in a foreign land as he searches for the place to found the new Troy,[35] Pa and his family bury Grampa in the land by the side of the road that leads west to California. The family's men dig a deep grave, and then Pa lays his father down gently into it. In this way, with as much dignity and respect as they could muster and offer, the Joads bury their patriarch.

When I read this, I felt for the Joads. I could not fully empathize with their grief, however, for my own paternal grandfather, Enrique, had not yet died. He died over a year later, in the spring semester of my sophomore year. After

I had read *The Grapes of Wrath*, during the summer between my freshman
and sophomore years, I returned to Costa Rica for a few weeks. During my
stay I went to see my grandfather often during the mornings. I knew not to
look for him at home, though. He was retired already, and every morning,
after breakfast, he left home to spend the day outside. My grandmother,
Dora, always had clean, well-ironed dress pants and *guayabera* shirts ready
for him to wear. Since his fifties, his right leg had been amputated from the
knee down, so he folded his pants' right leg up at the knee and secured it with
safety pins. He was very agile and dexterous at walking with crutches, so he
often hopped onto a bus to go to downtown San José. Those buses were not
outfitted to serve handicapped passengers, but he managed to get in and out
of them with resourceful grace. Many retired men gathered daily to talk at
the square in front of the main post office building, and he often joined them.
Sometimes I looked for him there. Other times, he simply walked to the shopping center near his house to find a bench in the shade where he sat and peo-
ple-watched. We talked about baseball and *fútbol* and the United States. As a
young man he had studied English in Texas and had worked as an accountant
for the US embassy in Costa Rica until his retirement, so he had an affinity
for US sports and culture. When that summer ended and I needed to return to
Arkansas, he asked my father not to let me leave again for the United States.
My father, though, said that I was the one to decide and that he thought I had
to continue along my path. When I said goodbye to my grandfather and gave
him a hug and kiss on the right cheek—I had kissed him since I was little and
had never stopped even as a teenager—my grandfather cried. I had never seen
him cry, and I felt moved. But I left again for my sophomore year.

One Sunday morning in the spring, very early, I got a call in my dorm
room. It was my mother on the phone, and she told me that my grandfather
had died overnight, in his sleep, of a heart attack. I listened to her quietly
and asked her what would happen next. My family would hold a wake in the
evening, and they would bury him on the next day. Burials in Costa Rica happen fast as families tend to stay together and people don't have to travel long
distances for funerals. This meant that, even had I had the money for a last-
minute air ticket, I wouldn't have made it in time for the funeral anyway. But
we didn't have the money. Even international calls were extremely expensive
then, so we spoke briefly. I waited until we hung up, and then I cried. For the
second time in my life, I felt grief at death that shook my body to the core. It
was only the first death in my family after I emigrated, though.

After I calmed down, I got up, showered, and walked over to the school
cafeteria to have breakfast. It was early and hardly anybody was there. I sat
down alone to eat at a table near the windows. As I sat there, I saw K and
Carolyn come into the cafeteria, get breakfast, and sit down, but I did not call
out to them. I wanted to be alone and quiet. I did not go to church that day. I

walked to the edge of campus, near the *fútbol* field, and sat there quietly for a long time, watching the trees sway in the wind and feeling my grieving heart at odds with the joyful blossoming of spring. A few days later, to my surprise, I opened my mailbox on campus to discover a letter from my grandfather. He had mailed it from Costa Rica before he died. He did not write me often, but he had sent me a gift. He had gathered several five, ten, and twenty-five cent coins from Costa Rica that did not circulate anymore, glued them to a square of transparent cellophane paper, and mailed them to me with a note. He missed me. Standing still with his gift in my hand, I wondered if my grandfather had felt that he would die soon when he prepared it. Had he felt death approaching when he had made the gift and mailed it to me? Had it been for that reason that he did not want me to leave? I could never know it for sure, but I guessed that may have been the case.

As I grieved over the next few weeks, eventually I recalled the scene of Grampa's death in *The Grapes of Wrath*. Then I could empathize with the Joads' sorrow with greater understanding. I had *felt* in my flesh and bones now, and thus come to understand, that the death of beloved people is one of the sorrows of migrants and immigrants while they are away from home. But this insight came only over a year after reading the novel.

While still a freshman, as I continued to read the Joads' story after Grampa's death, I began to focus my attention on Ma. When the novel opens with a scene of the agricultural devastation caused by the dust bowl, the emphasis is on the perseverance of men. As they regard the ruined corn, their women look to see whether these hard men will break down. When they realize their men will not give in to despair or hopelessness but will persevere, the women feel relieved: "After a while the faces of the watching men lost their bemused perplexity and became hard and angry and resistant. Then the women knew that they were safe and that there was no break."[36] When Grampa dies, even Ma repeats this kind of *machista* concept as she recites to a concerned friend an expression her own father often used: "Anybody can break down. It takes a man not to."[37] I am loathe to admit that at that age I found this idea of male fortitude appealing, so much so that I underlined Ma's words and wrote them down in my little notebook of quotations from my readings. It seemed cool to me to be a stoic man who would not break.

As the Joads' westward migration continues, however, Ma emerges as a central figure with an admirable steadfastness and fortitude all her own, deeper and firmer than any man's. At a turning point, she defies Pa's authority to make decisions regarding the future of the family. When the vicissitudes of travel seem to demand that the Joad family separate, Pa, in consultation with his brother and son, decides that Tom and Casy stay behind to repair a car while the rest of the family members continue onwards. Standing still and determined, holding a jack handle in her hand to defend herself in case

Pa tries to overpower her, she disobeys Pa's orders, refusing to go. Pa tries to enforce his authority and demand that she fulfill her proper duties as wife and mother. But Ma was determined, as the family witnessed her rebellion. With firm resolve, she overthrows the patriarchy for the sake of family unity.[38]

Ma's most heroic feat for the family, however, comes at the Mojave Desert. Granma is very sick while traveling on the truck's bed, and Ma tends to her, lying by her side. As the Joads make their final push by traveling across the desert nonstop at night, Ma remains silent. She knows that that they cannot stop or they might not make it across—the truck might break down and her young children, Ruthie and Winfield, and her pregnant daughter, Rose of Sharon, might not make it one more day in the harsh sun. So she stays still and quiet by Granma's side as they continue their exodus across the desert. Finally, they reach the town of Mojave, and they leave the desert behind as they start ascending the mountains at dawn. They drive through Tehachapi as the sun comes up behind them, so they can see the Promised Land of vineyards and fruit farms below them.[39] Ma crawls down from the truck's bed to see it too. She looks haggard and exhausted. Pa asks her whether Granma is bad. Only then Ma reveals that Granma is dead.[40] Like Moses, Granma had died after a long, trying exodus just prior to reaching the Promised Land. Ma had known it and had remained silent and still by the corpse all night so that the family would not break down and they could reach the land of their hope. As her son Tom comes to place his hand on her shoulder to console her, Ma says, "Don't touch me … I'll hold up if you don' touch me. That'd get me."[41] She embodies, at that moment, the very fortitude that her father had enshrined as a male virtue. "Anybody can break down. It takes a woman not to"—this is the reversal that she personifies.

That sort of fortitude now reminds me, as I write this, of my grandmother Dora. During the summer after her husband, my grandfather Enrique, died, I returned to Costa Rica again. Though I could no longer find my grandfather in his usual hangouts, I often visited my grandmother at her house in the afternoons, as I had done while growing up. She offered me tea and biscuits. It was a bit unusual, as Costa Ricans drink coffee in the midafternoon, not tea. But she always offered me tea on a well-set table, as she had learned from her family. She set bright-colored individual tablecloths on her Formica-topped kitchen table, not on the large, wooden dining room table. She placed her white teacups and small plates for biscuits on the bright cloths, and we drank tea together. For several weeks I visited her, and we talked about the lives of my sisters and father and mother and uncles and aunts and cousins and great aunts and great uncles and even second and third cousins, and about my studies and my life in the United States. But she embodied a silent fortitude of her own, and I could not bring myself to ask directly about *abuelito* Enrique's death, about how she was feeling, about her *duelo* or grieving process. One afternoon, however, right before I returned to Arkansas for my junior year, I finally asked her how she felt as I sat next to her at the kitchen table: "*¿Cómo se siente? ¿Le hace falta abuelito?*" She put her left arm on the table, bent it up at the elbow, lowered her head, and placed her face in her left hand. She did not respond. But when I touched her arm, she began to cry. She shook gently as she sobbed. She did not say a word, and I knew just to stay there, touching her shoulder quietly as she cried. She embodied her own kind of silent fortitude even in her crying. She soon recomposed herself and got up to take the tea set to the kitchen sink and clean the table. I got up quietly and helped her. We never spoke about her *duelo* again during the years that she lived as a widow.

In *The Grapes of Wrath*, Ma finally grieves when the Joads have arrived at a government camp for migrants where they have been welcomed and have found temporary respite from their troubles. She does not cry. She allows herself to voice her grieving, to share it with her husband.[42] But she continues to strive to hold the family together, even as things soon begin to fall apart for the Joads and their hopes drown in sorrow.

In the dry terms of economics, the problem is that the masses of migrants provide an excessive supply of labor in a context where there are no effective workers' rights.[43] To make matters worse, when wages are low already, latifundium-owning banks force smaller farmers in California to keep wages even lower.[44] The result is human tragedy: instead of the Promised Land, at the end of their exodus, the Okies arrive in a feudal land of servitude. In California, they find not only exploitation and misery but also hatred, repression, and violence against them.

They found what migrants often find, whatever their origin and wherever they arrive. For as I read *The Grapes of Wrath*, my gradual realization that the Joads, and all the *farming* people, had become *migrants* struck me most forcefully. At the onset of the exodus, the narrator heralds the theme: "The cars of the migrant people crawled out of the side roads onto the great cross-country highway, and they took the migrant way to the West."[45] All too soon they discover that rich landowners and poor store clerks hate them.[46] Reading *Mamita Yunai* and similar novels in Costa Rica had attuned me to the stories of migrant agricultural workers in Central America. I was also aware of the stories of Latino migrants in the United States.[47] But it came as a surprise to me to read the story of other migrants within the United States—*Okie* migrants within their own country. Thus, all of the people on exodus, represented by the Joad family, became for me the central character.

The lucid descriptions of economic *life* in large fruit and vegetable farms in California may well have been descriptions of banana latifundiums owned by the United Fruit Company in Costa Rica's Caribbean region.[48] By reference to *Mamita Yunai*, then, I seized quickly upon the pain of troubled lives as the ejected Okie farmers become migrants. They keep their senses tied to the land—they treasure its smells, its textures, its sound as it breaks and is sowed, its taste in the savory crops, and the sight of growing plant life on a well-tilled field—and so they understand the sensual, organic impoverishment that results from agricultural industrialization.[49] Yet, "the questing people were migrants now."[50] They became dispossessed migrants fleeing westward from Kansas, Oklahoma, Arkansas, Texas, New Mexico, and Nevada, seeking dignified work, food, and shelter, a quiet and humble home, only to become feudal serfs in California.[51] Their migration may well have been a description of poor *costarricenses*, *nicaragüenses*, and *hondureños* scurrying for work in the *bananales* of *Mamita Yunai*. Just as Okies in *los Yunaited Esteits*, they migrated because they were hungry and desperate. This cross-national, cross-cultural, inter-American, human commonality of experience must have been what Sibajita expresses when he explains to Herminio that there are millions of workers in the United States who are themselves exploited.[52] There must be some way, some path, without hatred, without rancor, to transform these lives, life itself, from pain to well-being.

For this reason, one appeal for justice that anonymous Okies voice in *The Grapes of Wrath* struck me as misled and divisive: "We ain't foreign. Seven generations back Americans, and beyond that Irish, Scotch, English, German. One of our folks in the Revolution, an' they was lots of our folks in the Civil War—both sides, Americans."[53] Okies, I thought, did not deserve justice in California because they were United Statesians, not even because they were Americans. They deserved justice, compassion, and love because they were human. The narrator describes how foreign workers had been brought as serfs to California earlier, before the Okies' exodus, when the agroindustry brought Mexican and East Asian farmhands to work for low wages. Farm owners said: "They don't need much. They wouldn't know what to do with good wages. Why, look how they live. Why, look what they eat. And if they get funny—deport them."[54] Chinese, Japanese, Mexicans, Filipinos, and Okies in California; *ticos, nicas, catrachos, cuzcatlecos, panas, cubanos, jamaicanos*, and *chinos* in Limón—they all deserve justice, care, and love because they are all human beings, capable of feeling pleasures and pains, joys and sorrows, happiness and sadness, and capable of loving and caring for others and for themselves.

In the end, however, just as Sibajita chooses the path of social and political solidarity in *Mamita Yunai*, so also in *The Grapes of Wrath* Casy, Tom, his sister Rose of Sharon, and all the Joads choose the path of empathy, solidarity, and loving cooperation. Casy heralds this theme in his prayer of thanksgiving for breakfast on the day the Joads go on their westward journey. For him, holiness is found in the togetherness of mankind.[55] Through a poetic plea, the narrator depicts cooperation as the solution to the social problem of dispossession.[56] Gradually, as people who plant and harvest the land but cannot enjoy its fruit share their sorrow and hunger, they unite in a common defense of justice.[57] The farming migrants' united defense of social justice in response to exploitation and greed, I came to understand, gave meaning to the novel's central metaphor, *las uvas de la ira*: "[I]n the eyes of the hungry there is a growing wrath. In the souls of the people the grapes of wrath are filling and growing heavy, growing heavy for the vintage."[58]

I found these themes of empathetic solidarity and communion played out most movingly in the denouement of the Joads' story. Upon seeing the struggles of the migrant workers in California, Casy reconceives his religious mission in order to organize the people and form labor unions. But he gets in trouble with law enforcement and with anti-union vigilantes, and so does Tom, who has to go into hiding.[59] The Joad family is thrown into greater confusion and grief.[60]

As Tom spends time in hiding, a man living like a woodchuck in the brush and thickets near a culvert by a fallow field, he recalls all his conversations with Casy, including the preacher's main insight when he abandoned his mission and fled to the wilderness to reflect.[61] As Tom tells it to his Ma, Casy went to the wilderness to find his soul but instead discovered that it was only part of a whole universal soul, and thus that people are good in society, not alone.[62] Tom further recounts a summons for companionship, cooperation, and mutual support that Casy once cited from the book of *Ecclesiastes*: "Two are better than one, because they have a good reward for their labor. For if they fall, the one will lift up his fellow, but woe to him that is alone when he falleth, for he hath not another to help him up."[63]

As a result of his personal reflections in his own wilderness, Tom decides to take up Casy's mission. He must leave the family; he cannot burden or endanger them any longer. But he can find purpose in working for the people, for the migrants, for the dispossessed and suffering and exploited. Ma is troubled as they sit in Tom's cave of vines. She might never hear from him again; the family might never know whether he is alive or dead. Tom responds with Casy's spiritual insight that an individual person only has a part of a universal soul.[64] Prompted by Ma, he concludes: "Then I'll be aroun' in the dark. I'll be ever'where—wherever you look. Wherever they's a fight so hungry people can eat, I'll be there."[65] Tom realizes that he has taken up Casy's voice, ideas, and mission. I thought he could also give those ideas his own meaning in his own purposeful life. In my interpretation, in my own web of associations, at this moment Tom also became Sibajita.

Once Ma leaves Tom behind, her heart torn and ragged, she returns to the family as flooding rains begin to fall. They fall for days, and the stream near the Joads' camp begins to creep up the bank. As the men struggle to build a dike to protect their few belongings, Rose of Sharon—Ma and Pa's pregnant daughter, Tom's sister, who had been abandoned by her husband upon their arrival in California—goes into labor. The flooding rains keep falling. The dike breaks. Rose of Sharon's baby is stillborn.[66] As the waters rise, Pa's brother, Uncle John, is asked to bury the baby. He takes the little corpse out in a box, but instead of burying the baby he releases the box to float downstream.[67] Like a dead baby Moses without Pharaoh's daughter awaiting to rescue him from the Nile's waters, Rose of Sharon's baby floats down the stream, bearing witness to the cruelty of the Joads' dispossession and misery in front of the landowners, vigilantes, and clerks.

Rose of Sharon emerges, in the final scene, as the surprising heroine. The Joads flee the rising waters and the continuing deluge to a barn on top of a hill. There they find a frightened boy whose father is dying of starvation. He had given all his food and drink to the boy until it ran out and had not saved nourishment for himself. Having lost her baby, Rose of Sharon looks with pity at the starving man and lies down next to him, in order to provide him the nourishment that she could not give to her stillborn child. In an act of tenderness and loving care, she gives him the gift of life.[68]

This final act of fortitude and loving solidarity stunned me. Rose of Sharon had been afraid for her baby's well-being during the entire exodus and travails in California. It seemed as if she could foresee her tragedy. And yet, in the hour of her greatest suffering, she offered the most significant act of loving care in *The Grapes of Wrath.*

After I finished reading, I thought about it for days. This was unlike any of the novels in Costa Rican social realism that I had read. The greatest act of solidarity comes from a female character, a seemingly weak one. Perhaps this had been what had impressed and moved Carmen so deeply about *Las uvas de la ira.* Here was a story about dispossessed farmers, about exploited migrant workers in large latifundia—a familiar theme for us. And yet, the characters with the most admirable fortitude to go along with loving tenderness were women—Ma and her daughter, Rose of Sharon. I had discovered something new in American literature—something I would have liked to talk about with Carmen, to share with M, whom I missed, and to discuss with K, when she arrived in my life.

NOTES

1. Mark Twain, "Ghost Life on the Mississippi," in *Early Tales and Sketches: 1851–1864,* eds. G.M. Branch and R.H. Hirst, vol. 1 (Berkeley: University of California Press, 1979), 147.

2. Carlos Luis Fallas, *Mamita Yunai,* 2nd ed. (San José: Editorial Costa Rica, 1986), 13.

3. Ibid.
4. Ibid., 13–14.
5. Ibid., 25.
6. Ibid., 69–70.
7. Ibid., 70.
8. See José Carlos Mariátegui, *Seven Interpretive Essays on Peruvian Reality*, trans. Majory Urquidi (Austin: University of Texas Press, 1988), and Pablo Neruda, *Canto General*, 3rd rev. ed., trans. Jack Schmitt (Berkeley: University of California Press, 2011).
9. *Fallas, Mamita Yunai*, 123.
10. Ibid., 124.
11. Ibid., 162–168.
12. Ibid., 168–169.
13. Ibid., 177–179.
14. Ibid., 132.
15. Ibid., 180.
16. See C. S. Peirce, "Evolutionary Love," in *The Essential Peirce: Selected Philosophical Writings*, eds. N. Houser and C. Kloesel, vol. 1 (Bloomington: Indiana University Press, 1992), 352–371.
17. Ibid., 354.
18. See C. S. Peirce, "Philosophy and the Conduct of Life," in *The Essential Peirce: Selected Philosophical Writings*, ed. Peirce Edition Project, vol. 2 (Bloomington: Indiana University Press, 1998), 27–41. For my interpretation in relation to a long line of debate regarding the relation between logic and ethics, theory and practice, and reason and sentiment in Peirce's thought, see Daniel G. Campos, "The Role of Diagrammatic Reasoning in Ethical Deliberation," *Transactions of the Charles S. Peirce Society* 51, no. 3 (2015): 338–357.
19. Peirce, "Evolutionary Love," 354.
20. Ibid.
21. Ibid., 357.
22. Ibid., 356.
23. Ibid., 357.
24. John Steinbeck, *The Grapes of Wrath* (New York: Viking, 1986), 6–7.
25. Ibid., 40–41.
26. Ibid., 43.
27. Ibid., 111–115.
28. Ibid., 28.
29. Ibid., 30.
30. Ibid., 31.
31. Ibid., 67.
32. Ibid., 176–177.
33. Ibid., 179.
34. See Sophocles, *Antigone, Oedipus the King* and *Electra*, trans. H.D.F. Kitto (Oxford: Oxford University Press, 2008).
35. See Virgil, *The Aeneid*, trans. David West (New York: Penguin Books, 1991).

36. Steinbeck, *Grapes of Wrath*, 6.

37. Ibid., 181.

38. Ibid., 217–219.

39. Ibid., 292.

40. Ibid., 293.

41. Ibid., 294.

42. Ibid., 414.

43. Ibid., 244–245.

44. Ibid., 380.

45. Ibid., 249.

46. Ibid., 264–266.

47. See, for instance, Cesar Chavez, *An Organizer's Tale: Speeches*, ed. Ilan Stavans (New York: Penguin Classics, 1988), and Francisco Jiménez, *The Circuit: Stories from the Life of a Migrant Child* (Albuquerque: University of New Mexico Press, 1997).

48. Steinbeck, *Grapes of Wrath*, 299.

49. Ibid., 362–363.

50. Ibid., 362.

51. Ibid., 300.

52. Fallas, *Mamita Yunai*, 180.

53. Steinbeck, *Grapes of Wrath*, 299.

54. Ibid., 298.

55. Ibid., 105.

56. Ibid., 194.

57. Ibid., 448–449.

58. Ibid., 449.

59. Ibid., 495.

60. Ibid., 503.

61. This is another representation of Casy as Christ-figure, in this case through an allusion to Jesus in the wilderness. See Luke 4:1–13 (Holy Bible: New International Version).

62. Steinbeck, *Grapes of Wrath*, 535.

63. Eccles. 4:9–10 (NIV).

64. Steinbeck, *Grapes of Wrath*, 537.

65. Ibid.

66. Ibid., 567.

67. Ibid., 571–572.

68. Ibid., 580–581.

Chapter 9

Sacramental Awakenings in the South

In the spring of my sophomore year of college, two years after M's death, I started to read *Walden*. I had guarded in my heart its basic themes of simplicity, spontaneity, liberty, self-expression, and experimentalism— heralded by Mr. Keating in *Dead Poets Society*[1]—even as I had kept reading mostly along the political and social lines of the Latin American literature that I knew, even as I had approached Anglo-American literature from that direction by reading Steinbeck. I had found a copy of *Walden* on the library shelves soon after my arrival on campus, but I quickly realized that my English did not match up to Thoreau's poetic prose yet. However, having read *The Grapes of Wrath* and other American novels by then, I sensed with the arrival of spring—in the budding tree branches, the blooming plants, the blossoming shrubs, and my cherishing of M's friendship—that I needed to read Thoreau.

Reflecting on *Dead Poets Society*, I had a clearer sense of why it had struck me so forcefully. Though M and I couldn't articulate it when we commented on the movie, its philosophical novelty for two young students in Costa Rica with a shared romantic streak lay in the themes of personal awakening, experiment, and self-development. Our readings through the public education system had fostered sensitivity to social injustice and critical awareness of oppressive political contexts or conservative cultural mores, especially in agrarian societies. But Keating and the Dead Poets had emphasized the exploration and cultivation of the genuine self—of finding one's own voice and perspective within society, just or unjust; of remaining attentive to the possibilities of directing one's own life along alternative paths; and of preserving the freedom and spontaneity to walk along these alternative paths. I thought that by turning to *Walden* as a sophomore I could get a sharper understanding of the issues M and I couldn't quite express two years earlier. So I finally checked out a yellow-paged paperback copy of Thoreau's account of his *Life in the Woods* from the library, and I began to read it under the protection of my beloved oaks on the main lawn.

The first paragraph puzzled me and then drew me into *Walden* by its contrast between *living* in the woods and *sojourning* in civilization: "When I wrote the following pages, or rather the bulk of them, I lived alone, in the woods, a mile from any neighbor, in a house which I had built myself, on the shore of Walden Pond, in Concord, Massachusetts, and earned my living by the labor of my hands only. I lived there two years and two months. At present I am a sojourner in civilized life again."[2] I had to stop reading at once, get back to the library, find a dictionary, and look up the verb "sojourn." When I understood its meaning, I learned it by heart and used it in most of my attempts at writing poems later in college. Prone to romantic excess, I conceived of myself as a sojourner in *la Yunai*, just as Thoreau took himself to be sojourning in civilization when he published *Walden* after returning from the pond.

For someone who was simply staying temporarily in civilization, however, Thoreau sure had a message to deliver. Having availed myself of a dictionary and settled in to read in one of the library's couches in front of the bay windows that overlooked the lily pool and main lawn, I heard his cry loud and clear:

> The mass of men lead lives of quiet desperation. What is called resignation is confirmed desperation. From the desperate city you go into the desperate country, and have to console yourself with the bravery of minks and muskrats. A stereotyped but unconscious despair is concealed even under what are called the games and amusements of mankind. There is no play in them, for this comes after work. But it is a characteristic of wisdom not to do desperate things.[3]

Mr. Keating, I remembered, had cited the first sentence to the boys as he enticed them to find their own voices, their own paths, in life. By the time I was a sophomore, I thought I could see some of my peers personifying the danger that Thoreau and Keating warned the boys about: "I see young men, my townsmen, whose misfortune it is to have inherited farms, houses, barns, cattle, and farming tools; for these are more easily acquired than got rid of. ... Why should they begin digging their graves as soon as they are born?"[4] I was nineteen years old when I read this, about a decade younger than Thoreau when he went to the woods, and I thought he was pointing at a real peril from a clearer perspective than mine. As I read his warning I must have paused to think about my acquaintances. Perhaps I thought of Jimmy H., a former roommate—a spoiled suburban brat who was so concerned with his Gap clothes and his car and already worried about how much money he was going to make when he graduated. He seemed well on his way to digging his own grave so he could lie in it alongside many other living dead, until actual death came to summon him. For my part, I had the self-righteous sense that I was *not* digging my own grave. At least I had figured out as a freshman that pursuing an economics degree in the business school would suffocate my soul, and I had fled to save my mind and heart through mathematics and literature. I did not aspire to wearing a suit and tie every day except Saturday, as the stiffs who sat next to me in marketing class.

Despite my haughtiness, however, I had no experiential inkling of what those lives of quiet desperation felt like to the people who lived them. Thoreau seemed like an older brother warning me of a danger I could not quite grasp yet. I had no idea what it might feel like to lie awake at night thinking that you are not living the life you wanted to live. I could not imagine my chest aching and my breath becoming dense and weary from being trapped in a path I did not want to follow, carrying on my shoulders responsibilities I could not bear. I knew I wanted no part in desperation, but I had no sense of the sentiment that settles in your heart and mind and darkens your perspective. At the same time, my very naïve youthfulness perhaps allowed me to focus on the last sentence in Thoreau's famous warning—not the sentence decrying the despair of the masses but the one offering hope to his readers: "It is a mark of wisdom not to do desperate things." Where could I find this wisdom? How could I pursue it?

Deliberateness, I guessed, was the opposite of desperation. The dictum "It is a mark of wisdom to do deliberate things" suggested itself to me as the positive Thoreauvian characterization of wisdom. Had I been reflective and prescient enough as I read, I would have noticed that Keating and the Dead Poets had already suggested this emphasis on deliberateness when they cited Thoreau at the opening of every meeting: "I went to the woods because I wished to live deliberately, to front only the essential facts of life, and see if I could not learn what it had to teach, and not, when I came to die, discover that I had not lived."[5] But I would only come to read those verses, and recall their affective impact some days later.

Thoreau, at any rate, emphasized deliberateness in the passage immediately following his characterization of wisdom: "When we consider what … is the chief end of man, and what are the true necessaries and means of life, it appears as if men had deliberately chosen the common mode of living because they preferred it to any other. Yet they honestly think there is no choice left."[6] People, Thoreau claimed, choose their way of life even as they believe they have had no choice in the matter whatsoever. They choose without consciously and earnestly deliberating within themselves. Yet, he continued, "alert and healthy natures remember that the sun rose clear. It is never too late to give up our prejudices."[7] I had to stop at this point to understand the image and its implications. The sun rises bright and clear to bring a new day in which we can choose a different way of life. The sun sets, and night falls upon our anguish and desperation. But the sun also rises.

Every dawn, then, I could wake and say with Thoreau: "Here is life, an experiment to a great extent untried by me,"[8] one that no one can prescribe for me but that I must discover for myself. I surmised I should subscribe to his experimentalism if I wanted to discover something new and original in human possibility: "Man's capacities have never been measured; nor are we to judge of what he can do by any precedents, so little has been tried."[9] Yes, so little has been tried! As a young Central American venturing into life as a student and sojourner in a foreign land, I wanted to yawp these poetic sentences aloud. In concluding his initial exhortation, Thoreau exclaimed:

> How vigilant we are! determined not to live by faith if we can avoid it; all the day long on the alert, at night we unwillingly say our prayers and commit ourselves to uncertainties. So thoroughly and sincerely are we compelled to live, reverencing our life, and denying the possibility of change. This is the only way, we say; but there are as many ways as there can be drawn radii from one centre.[10]

A beautiful mathematical metaphor revealed to me that there are infinitely many possible ways to live, and any one of them is available to us if we remain alert.

It took me a full day at the library to read and comprehend the first few pages of "Economy." When I had done so, I felt as if I wanted to talk to M or write her a letter and mail it, telling her how I was finally reading *Walden* even as I found myself sojourning in the South. But I could not write to her. Yet I also wanted to talk to K, to tell her how I "dug" what Thoreau had to say about experimenting with infinite possibilities in life. I was too shy to call her, but on the next chance I got I looked for her in the school cafeteria to tell her I had started reading. She told me that Dr. Long, one of the professors at our English department, had written his dissertation on Thoreau's use of the Bible, especially the New Testament, in *Walden*. When I returned to my dorm room, I re-read one of the passages I had pondered on my first reading day: "But men labor under a mistake. The better part of the man is soon plowed into the soil for compost. By a seeming fate, commonly called necessity, they are employed, as it says in an old book, laying up treasures which moth and rust will corrupt and thieves break through and steal."[11] I could then recognize Thoreau's allusion to the Sermon on the Mount. I did not know the exact passage and had to look for it in the gospel of Matthew (6:19), but I grasped the origin of Thoreau's recommendation. I had not taken any courses yet with Professor Long, but K loved his survey course on American Literature, and his influence on her clued me into looking for the spirit of Jesus's gentle sermon in Thoreau's sermons to his contemporaries.

I could not have interpreted the nature of the sway that *Walden* held over me for the next few weeks of laborious but rewarding reading. Thoreau's *Life in the Woods* cast a spell on me, and every hour I could spare I acquiesced to its draw. Today, E. B. White's interpretation of the work clarifies my own experience:

> I think it is of some advantage to encounter the book at a period in one's life when the normal anxieties and enthusiasms and rebellions of youth closely resemble those of Thoreau in that spring of 1845 when he borrowed an axe, went out to the woods, and began to whack down some trees for timber. Received at such a juncture, the book is like an invitation to life's dance assuring the troubled recipient that no matter what befalls him in the way of success or failure he will always be welcome at the party—that the music is played for him, too, if he will but listen and move his feet. In effect, that is what the book is—an invitation, unengraved.[12]

I felt eager to accept the invitation, at least to read *Walden* and see if I could make a go at the life to which it summoned me.

Following my unreserved acceptance of the reading invitation, it took me numerous days to plod through the introductory chapter on "Economy." Yet I marveled at how prudential Thoreau's writing could be. I had come to read *Walden* in search of the poetry that had enchanted M and me in San José, but in addition to poetry I also found practical wisdom. If I wanted to live an experimental life, I needed to heed some basic philosophical principles on life's "economy." I had already left our college's business school, where studying economics did not mean learning to interpret the just ends deliberately chosen by a society in order then to plan effective strategies for achieving those just social ends. For my professors and peers, economics did not consist in the art of fostering the well-being of whole persons in just social contexts. For them, the alleged science of neoclassical economics rather sought to devise theoretical systems in which utility-maximizing individuals could pursue their own self-interest and unperturbed businesses could maximize profits by supposedly satisfying those needs. Partly for these reasons, I had fled in disgust. So my heart and mind provided already fertile ground for Thoreau's "Economy" before I even started reading. From the ground where I stood looking at the world around me, I did not need to be moved or swayed but rather enlightened.

In the introductory chapter to *Walden*, Thoreau expounded the central principle of economy of life that guided his experiment at the pond and his life afterward. The principle is: "the cost of a thing is the amount of what I will call life which is required to be exchanged for it, immediately or in the long run."[13] Thinking in terms of the vital cost of pursuing and acquiring things clarified for me the problem with the consumerism that the "Jimmy

Hs" on campus had already embraced before even turning twenty years old. There is an economic trade-off between the aims we pursue and the life we must invest to pursue them. So Thoreau recommended that once I had secured the necessaries of life, I do not pursue the superfluities but actually just live:

> When he has obtained those things which are necessary to life, there is another alternative than to obtain the superfluities; and that is, to adventure on life now, his vacation from humbler toil having commenced. The soil, it appears, is suited to the seed, for it has sent its radicle downward, and it may now send its shoot upward also with confidence. Why has man rooted himself thus firmly in the earth, but that he may rise in the same proportion into the heavens above? — for the nobler plants are valued for the fruit they bear at last in the air and light, far from the ground.[14]

Nowadays, the metaphor of human beings as trees that become deep-rooted in order to rise to higher and higher altitudes reminds me of a forty-meter tall *espavel* or wild cashew tree (*Anacardium excelsum*) that rises above the canopy of the surrounding tropical forest in Carara National Park in the Pacific lowlands of Costa Rica. The trunk's diameter at its base may be about two meters long. Thick and sturdy, the *espavel* digs deep and wide roots so that it may grow tall. Its upper branches, way above the forest's understory, support and sustain rich ecosystems of epiphyte plants—such as bromeliads with twisting leaves that trap water and orchids with webbed roots that swell as they capture moisture—myriad insects, and birds—such as toucans and scarlet macaws. Strong vines and lianas descend all the way from the *espavel*'s canopy to the forest's ground. I love to climb as far up those vines as my strength and agility will allow, so that I can regard the surrounding undergrowth from above. When I walk by this tree, I remember that Thoreau encouraged anyone who would listen, including himself, to aim at living the life of a towering *espavel*.

Thoreau's metaphor also reminds me of the lyrics from the song "Flowers" by Tennessean folk musician Casey Black:

I hold my petals out to the air of possibility,
And I shoot my roots down just as deep as the earth will let me.
I think the point is to grow tall and always stay green
And bow when the colors of fall come.[15]

Sometimes I hear him play in New York City, and when he drawls these lyrics I wonder if he has read *Walden* and think it very likely. At any rate, the *espavel* rising above the surrounding canopy at Carara, Black singing "Flowers" at his gigs, and I walking in the tropical forest agree with Thoreau when he writes, "In the long run men hit only what they aim at. Therefore, though they should fail immediately, they had better aim at something high."[16]

As I interpret it today and instinctively grasped it during my sophomoric reading, Thoreau's principle of economy of life is philosophical. In fact, he presented the whole experiment at Walden Pond as a philosophical experiment to simplify life, to live only according to the most fundamental principles: "To be a philosopher is not merely to have subtle thoughts, nor even to found a school, but so to love wisdom as to live according to its dictates, a life of simplicity, independence, magnanimity, and trust. It is to solve some of the problems of life, not only theoretically, but practically."[17] Though I could not articulate it then, I sensed that a conception of the "good life" undergirded Thoreau's vital economics. His understanding of philosophy linked theory to practice, thought to living, as I would discover many years later in Socratic and Hellenistic conceptions of philosophy.

As a college student, I also sensed what was going awry with an entire system that promoted marketability for the business world as the chief end of education: "Even the *poor* student studies and is taught only *political* economy, while that economy of living which is synonymous with philosophy is not even sincerely professed in our colleges."[18] Thoreau's philosophical economy of living would criticize rather than promote the vital cost of pursuing material comfort as one's main goal. Again and again, as I reflected upon "Economy," I returned to the dictum that the things that underwrite such comfort "are more easily acquired than got rid of."[19] Perhaps it was all too easy to agree with this, for I was a poor student who could not buy much—a poor relative to most of the "waspy Jimmys" with whom I interacted. And perhaps I was sliding a bit into the consumerism inherent to the United Statesian dream, because I had arrived in *la Yunai* with half a duffle bag of clothes, but by my sophomore year I had at least a full suitcase and a bunch of crafts from Costa Rica on display in my half of a dorm room. Yet, I think I heartily accepted and tried to live according to the motto—"the cost of a thing is the amount of what I will call life which is required to be exchanged for it, immediately or in the long run."[20] I wanted life, not things. I wanted to be free to amble, to ramble, to saunter, to experiment. As the Spanish saying goes, *después nadie te quita lo bailado.* After you have accepted life's invitation, nobody can take away from you your having danced at the party.

In this vein, I appreciated Thoreau's insistence that life experiments must be individual and self-expressive. Thoreau was not making prescriptions but suggestions, recommendations on how to live. Today I may say that his ethics are not normative but suggestive:

> I would not have any one adopt my mode of living on any account; for, beside that before he has fairly learned it I may have found out another for myself, I

desire that there may be as many different persons in the world as possible; but I would have each one be very careful to find out and pursue *his own way*, and not his father's or his mother's or his neighbor's instead. The youth may build or plant or sail, only let him not be hindered from doing that which he tells me he would like to do. It is by a mathematical point only that we are wise, as the sailor or the fugitive slave keeps the polestar in his eye; but that is sufficient guidance for all our life. We may not arrive at our port within a calculable period, but we would preserve the true course.[21]

At the same time, I grasped that even though Thoreau recommended individual experimentation and self-expression, he did not advocate isolation or aloofness from others; rather, we must cooperate: "If a man has faith, he will coöperate with equal faith everywhere; if he has not faith, he will continue to live like the rest of the world, whatever company he is joined to. To coöperate in the highest as well as the lowest sense, means *to get our living together*."[22] This ethos seemed akin to the one recommended in *The Grapes of Wrath*. The possibility of cultivating this cooperative spirit founded upon faith alongside a strong individual experimentalism allured me. It also posed a difficult question for me. How could I achieve a balance between the cooperative and experimentalist strains in my inward life?

Nowadays, I find that E. B. White illuminates this issue when he writes that Walden "is the report of a man torn by two powerful and opposing drives— the desire to enjoy the world ... and the urge to set the world straight."[23] Since before my college years in Arkansas, I had interpreted the tension between these two impulses in my own life as the tension between the call of the author of Ecclesiastes to enjoy the simple joys of life and the burning desire for justice of the prophet Jeremiah. In the Hebrew book of wisdom, the Preacher advises: "Go then, eat your bread in happiness and drink your wine with a cheerful heart; for God has already approved your works. Let your clothes be white all the time, and let not oil be lacking on your head. Enjoy life with the woman whom you love all the days of your fleeting life which He has given to you under the sun; for this is your reward in life and in your toil in which you have labored under the sun."[24] I desired to heed these summons to enjoy food, drink, and intimate love in the face of the ceaseless toils of human life. If I could simplify life in this way, I could find joy akin to felicity. However, I could not accept the Preacher's underlying despair at the vanity of life. As many young idealists, perhaps, I sensed that a life of work for justice, solidarity, and cooperation could not add up to a vain life, even if individual hopes could often appear to be defeated. In the face of persecution and derision for his vain cries for justice, the prophet Jeremiah felt deceived by God and overcome by his foes. And yet he did not give up on his task. His desire for justice, personified in his God, felt like a fire burning in his bones:

But if I say, "I will not remember Him
Or speak anymore in His name,"
Then in my heart it becomes like a burning fire
Shut up in my bones;
And I am weary of holding it in,
And I cannot endure it.[25]

Thoreau's attempt at addressing both his drive for enjoyment and his drive for justice spoke directly to my own struggle to learn to enjoy simplicity while finding a way to live a life of service and solidarity—that is, to get my living together with my neighbors. However, many years still lay ahead before I found a way to strike this balance in teaching philosophy to students in a public college.

During my own college years, I felt the tension without finding release. Even as I felt the need for equilibrium between my yearning to be cooperative and my zest for experimentalist sauntering, I had come to read *Walden* because of the latter tendency—that is, because of my inner drive toward experimenting and cherishing a life of spontaneity. This had been the strain in American literature—heralded by yawping verses from Whitman, Frost, and Thoreau—that had enchanted M and me two years earlier. Thus, I delighted in sensing that the life of simplicity that Thoreau advocated was not one of toil or asceticism, but rather of freedom and vital celebration: "I am convinced, both by faith and experience, that to maintain one's self on this earth is not a hardship but a pastime, if we will live simply and wisely; as the pursuits of the simpler nations are still the sports of the more artificial. It is not necessary that a man should earn his living by the sweat of his brow, unless he sweats easier than I do."[26] I wanted to live simply and wisely, and I thought that Thoreau's philosophical principles for an economy of life could provide a guide toward living that way.

All of my considerations regarding Thoreau's "Economy" were enmeshed for me with the lifestyles that surrounded me on campus and in town. They are reflected, perhaps, in a failed but revealing poem that I wrote as a senior a couple of years after reading *Walden*. I entitled it "The English Language, Thoreau, and the Word 'Shampoo.'" The opening stanza reads:

Weird, spooky sounds,
smooth English words
baffled my mind while I,
the foreigner, the sojourner,
the non-Yankee, non-redneck *amigo*,
sat in an Atlanta bus station.

I was trying to be playful with English sounds and cultural stereotypes, but at that time I really took myself to be sojourning in *la Yunai*, just as Thoreau

took himself to be sojourning in civilization when he published *Walden* after
returning from the pond. The poem continues as a dialogue:

Nope sir, I told the old man next to me,
I didn't come for the Milk Duds,
Nor to search in the Union
For Uncle Sam's promised land.
Why then, stranger,
Why did you come?
I came to hear,
To see in wild ecstasy
The sexy lips of American women
When they simply say "shampoo."
I came to learn the language
That haunted my dreams
Since I heard Ophelia's soft speech
In San José's English theater.
To listen, to learn, to think
with a different mind, I came.
And, after discovering
The red leaves in autumn
And the taste of Dr. Pepper,
While trying to understand
This society's endless rush
To make money and live on pizza,
While asking who I was
In these United States of America,
I found Thoreau's soothing voice
In an old, yellow-paged *Walden* paperback.
Writing beautiful English words he taught me to
Front only the essential facts of life.
And in the end that's why I came, sir,
To read Thoreau in English,
To enjoy living every second, and,
When our "fragmented modern world" wearies me,
To admire the beauty of American women's sexy lips
As they simply say "shampoo."

I tried to capture in one poem all at once: My love of the English language,
my attraction for K and the way she spoke, my desire to enjoy life with the
woman whom I loved in the face of the frivolity of materialist lifestyles,
my adverse reaction to United Statesian consumerism, and my affinity for
Thoreuvian simplicity. If the poem has any value, it is as a reflection of
my perspective as a Central American student who wanted to find a path to

felicity in the midst of the many conflicting ends and values that surrounded me in *la Yunai*. I was in the country that gave the world Milk Duds, Dr. Pepper, pizza delivery, and the United Statesian dream, but that also nurtured the philosophical poet who wrote *Walden*. And Thoreau's *Life in the Woods* served as my lantern in the midst of much obscurity.

SACRAMENTS AND AWAKENING TO LIFE'S POSSIBILITIES IN THOREAU'S *WALDEN*

Still, my reading of "Economy" as reflected in my poem did not dig deep enough into the philosophical ground undergirding Thoreau's stance. I focused too much on the anti-consumerist aspects of Thoreau's principle of economic simplicity. Perhaps I had not sufficiently grasped that such economic aspects of simplicity were but a sacrament—that is, "an outward and visible sign of an inward and spiritual grace."[27] In fact, *Walden* is gravid with sacraments in need of inward and spiritual interpretation. The experiment at Walden Pond is itself a sacrament.

Thoreau begins the second chapter, "Where I Lived and What I Lived For," with an imaginative experiment—he surveys farms and land, and he imagines how it would be to live there. He claims, "At a certain season of our life we are accustomed to consider every spot as the possible site of a house."[28] When I read this at twenty years of age, that season of my life had not yet come. I could not imagine owning anything to be anchored anywhere. But I grasped that for Thoreau the imaginative experience was the real joy; he did not wish to own anything: "My imagination carried me so far that I even had the refusal of several farms—the refusal was all I wanted—but I never got my fingers burned by actual possession."[29] Indeed, I embraced Thoreau's recommendation to his "fellows" that they preserve their freedom to enjoy life without possessing things for as long as possible, so that they can plant a better seed and reap a more plentiful harvest later.[30] In this case I gathered that material freedom from the responsibilities of owning a farm was related to the spiritual freedom to live one's own life. But I did not conceive of this relationship yet as a sacrament—the material freedom from planting and harvesting a farm *signified* the spiritual freedom to cultivate one's inner life in order to harvest a better crop.

Thoreau's main experiment, however, consisted in living at Walden Pond. He announces his purpose to live life with utmost pleasure within sight of his neighbors, who are asleep to the possibilities of life and in need of awakening: "I do not propose to write an ode to dejection, but to brag as lustily as chanticleer in the morning, standing on his roost, if only to wake my neighbors up."[31] I sensed the tension in this purpose, since Thoreau's life experiment at Walden was as much individual as social; he wanted his experiment to be pondered by his very neighbors at Concord.

More importantly for me, however, the image of the rooster summoning people to seize the day heralded the central metaphor that ensued: awakening. Thoreau urged that I must awaken to the living possibilities that each morning brings with it. He offered the image of a cleansing bath in the pond at dawn as a religious ritual, one that I now also see as a sacrament—a ceremonial cleansing of the body to signify an inward cleansing: "Every morning was a cheerful invitation to make my life of equal simplicity, and I may say innocence, with Nature herself … . I got up early and bathed in the pond; that was a religious exercise, and one of the best things which I did."[32] As I read this and subsequent passages, like a young E. B. White I also heard an invitation that I could not refuse. I wanted with all my youthful might to accept it:

> The morning, which is the most memorable season of the day, is the awakening hour. Then there is least somnolence in us; and for an hour, at least, some part of us awakes which slumbers all the rest of the day and night. Little is to be expected of that day, if it can be called a day, to which we are not awakened by our Genius, but by the mechanical nudgings of some servitor … to a higher life than we fell asleep from; and thus the darkness bear its fruit, and prove itself to be good, no less than the light.[33]

I did see the irony of my enthusiasm, since I was a night owl and did not like to wake up early. Most of the time, I needed an alarm clock to help me along. But I felt released from insincerity when Thoreau allowed that, to a nocturnal being like me, the metaphorical "morning" could mean the night hours in which my thought kept pace but with the light of distant stars—the hours in which I felt most alert to life and the possibilities of self-cultivation: "To him whose elastic and vigorous thought keeps pace with the sun, the day is a perpetual morning. It matters not what the clocks say or the attitudes and labors of men. Morning is when I am awake and there is a dawn in me. Moral reform is the effort to throw off sleep."[34]

Thoreau's exhortations demanded careful reading, pondering, reflecting, and re-reading, so that it took me several afternoons and evenings to get through the first few pages of "What I Lived For." My blossoming romanticism intensified this response, leading me to imbibe passages inviting me to a poetic life: "The millions are awake enough for physical labor; but only one in a million is awake enough for effective intellectual exertion, only one in a hundred millions to a poetic or divine life. To be awake is to be alive. I have never yet met a man who was quite awake. How could I have looked him in the face?"[35] By this poetic life, Thoreau means one that creates an inner world capable of affecting the very quality of daily endeavor and sentiment in the outer one:

> We must learn to reawaken and keep ourselves awake, not by mechanical aids, but by an infinite expectation of the dawn, which does not forsake us in our soundest sleep. I know of no more encouraging fact than the unquestionable ability of man to elevate his life by a conscious endeavor. It is something to be able to paint a particular picture, or to carve a statue, and so to make a few objects beautiful; but it is far more glorious to carve and paint the very atmosphere and medium through which we look, which morally we can do. To affect the quality of the day, that is the highest of arts.[36]

I read this passage time and again, imagining how I might cultivate such a high ethical art. Looking back upon those days, it is sometimes strange and marvelous to recollect how the poetic sermons of a nineteenth-century Transcendentalist from New England could move so much a *muchacho* from Central America. Our cultural worlds and even our personal ways of being seemed so different as to be disjointed, and yet I sensed continuity of sentiment and aspiration between us. It felt as if I had an older brother, Enrique, who fostered my well-being and with whom solidarity and fraternity prevailed, in spite of his apparent chanticleer's cockiness. Unlike him, I did not feel any inclination to wake up my neighbors; like him, I felt eager to wake myself up and "elevate my life" so as to affect the quality of my days. *Carpe diem*, I recalled.

Indeed, I recalled the *Dead Poets Society* when I finally came to read the passage that drew me irresistibly, and for the rest of my life, to American literature on a Saturday afternoon in my hometown of San José. The metaphor of awakening in the morning to life's possibilities sets up the passage from *Walden* that inspired the boys of the Dead Poets Society, M, and me:

> I went to the woods because I wished to live deliberately, to front only the essential facts of life, and see if I could not learn what it had to teach, and not, when I came to die, discover that I had not lived. I did not wish to live what was not life, living is so dear; nor did I wish to practise resignation, unless it was quite necessary. I wanted to live deep and suck out all the marrow of life, to live so sturdily and Spartan-like as to put to rout all that was not life, to cut a broad swath and shave close, to drive life into a corner, and reduce it to its lowest terms, and, if it proved to be mean, why then to get the whole and genuine meanness of it, and publish its meanness to the world; or if it were sublime, to know it by experience, and be able to give a true account of it in my next excursion.[37]

After more than two years of searching, yearning, and quietly grieving M, I came to read the sentences whose meaning I had tried to interpret with my beloved friend. I could now read them with a better, albeit struggling, grasp of Thoreau's English and in the context of both the literary work and the culture that yielded it. The South, I surmised, was not New England, and yet there must be some cultural continuity to illuminate my reading. The mid-nineteenth-century consumerism of United Statesian culture seemed only to have become worse. However the American resistance to pursuing superfluities, the rebellious, countercultural undercurrent to focus on the necessaries, and the individual impulse for deliberate experimentation remained present for anyone who observed carefully. Life along the cultural and spiritual borders of United Statesian society—say, reading for self-cultivation a yellow-paged *Walden* paperback in the library of a liberal arts college in a small southern town, where the mass of citizens gathered at Walmart—that American border life, I sensed, still provided alternatives.

Reflecting upon the passage, I recalled that resignation was another name for the quiet desperation Thoreau's spirit resisted. Deliberateness, a conscious cultivation of spontaneous and simple living, served as his antidote. I decided to keep this contrast between deliberateness and desperation always in view. Wisdom consisted in perceiving the contrast and choosing a deliberate life. As my poem reveals, the heart of the matter for me lay in the conscious effort "to front only the essential facts of life." Thoreau wanted to face reality, a reality that would provide the bedrock truth upon which to found his life and answer the question "What should I live for?" This sounded like a wise call to me.

From this point onward, in fact, Thoreau developed two interrelated themes, namely, simplicity and reality. Today I would put the matter as follows: I must simplify my outward life as a *sacrament* of inward simplification, so that I may burrow into reality and discover that it is itself simple and principled. At that time, I seized upon a powerful sentence that I endeavored to turn into a guiding maxim for inward and outward simplification: "Simplicity, simplicity, simplicity! I say, let your affairs be as two or three, and not a hundred or a thousand. … Simplify, simplify."[38] To let my affairs be few and essential; then to enjoy food and drink and friendship and life with the woman whom I loved—striving for these ends seemed worthy of a good life.

Once again, I had to pause and re-read and think for days before I could go on with reading. What could it mean to "simplify, simplify" for a Central American student in the South? I pondered how I could focus on the essentials. Intellectually, I had already decided to focus on mathematics and literature. This now struck me as sound. Having tried economics, business, and other ways of keeping busy without reflecting much seemed by then like mistakes for me. I was years away from identifying philosophy as my field to till, but in the serenity of mathematical reasoning and the insight into human nature resulting from reading literature, I found the principled intellectual simplicity Thoreau described: "If you are acquainted with the principle, what do you care for a myriad instances and applications? To a philosopher all *news*, as it is called, is gossip."[39] Materially, I thought the simplification process came naturally for me, since I never did strive to acquire the comforts, gadgets, *chunches* (things "useful" for inessential purposes), and *tiliches* (useless junk) on offer at the local Walmart and in Little Rock's malls. I did not perceive, however, my own accumulation of books and compact disks and even artisan crafts that I had brought with me from Costa Rica after my freshman year. In my own way, I had started to accumulate stuff.

Socially, I surmised that I should cultivate a few meaningful friendships rather than many superficial acquaintances. For an introvert like me this happened naturally, anyways, as Carolyn, K, Adrian, Tim, and Luis—my sauntering, road-tripping, reading, music listening, and *fútbol* playing friends—were the people with whom I felt some connection stronger than circumstance. However, as a sophomore, I still felt a strong impulse for becoming acquainted with many people, fitting into various groups—social clubs, *fútbol* teams, devotional groups, and even churches—and trying many different kinds of relationships. Personally, I did guard my spaces and times for solitude—for being with myself while walking about campus or town or while reading in the library or under trees in the lawn. I read *Walden* during spring, and at lucid moments it inspired me to come to my senses. I spent hours just feeling the warmth of the new season on my skin, listening to the melody of singing red robins, and regarding colorful cardinals flying among oak branches or hiding in shrubs—enchanting patches of redness highlighted against a background of green foliage.

As I continued my self-examination, I seized upon another maxim: "Let us spend one day as deliberately as Nature .... Let us rise early and fast, or break fast, gently and without perturbation; let company come and let company go, let the bells ring and the children cry — determined to make a day of it."[40] On the whole I found that I knew how to spend a day with myself, walking or reading or sensing, as deliberately as Nature. But my yearning for companionship also seemed so strong as to not allow me to "let company come and let company go" spontaneously. On a given day I might be able to do it. But could one live that way every day? I felt far from attaining this degree of freedom expressive of inward simplicity. I could not just let M come into and go from my life. I lamented her absence, even if silently. And now I could not just let K come into my life without becoming an important part of it. On this point, I did not know whether I was misunderstanding Thoreau or whether I understood him but disagreed.

As I neared the end of "What I Lived For," I became more enthralled by Thoreau's exhortations until wanting to yawp them, even coming to the point of declaiming them aloud to myself under a sheltering oak tree:

Let us settle ourselves, and work and wedge our feet downward through the mud and slush of opinion, and prejudice, and tradition, and delusion, and appearance, that alluvion which covers the globe, through Paris and London, through New York and Boston and Concord, through Church and State, through poetry and philosophy and religion, till we come to a hard bottom and rocks in place, which we can call *reality*, and say, This is, and no mistake; and then begin, having a *point d'appui*, below freshet and frost and fire, a place where you might found a wall or a state, or set a lamp-post safely. ... If you stand right fronting and face to face to a fact, you will see the sun glimmer on both its surfaces, as if it were a cimeter, and feel its sweet edge dividing you through the heart and marrow, and so you will happily conclude your mortal career. Be it life or death, we crave only reality. If we are really dying, let us hear the rattle in our throats and feel cold in the extremities; if we are alive, let us go about our business.[41]

I had not traveled yet as a student to the cities of the North and the capitals of Europe, and I did not imagine I would make a living as a public university teacher in New York over a decade later. But I lived in a kind of southern Concord, where a conservative college took the place of lyceum, and church-condoned dogmas played a prominent role in the lives of busy citizens, and the buzz and gossip of the village's market resounded at Walmart. So I thought I grasped what Thoreau meant by needing to burrow beneath opinion, prejudice, tradition, delusion, and appearance until striking bedrock reality. I felt alive and ready to go about simple living. I desired to found my vital matters upon a solid point of support, one that could be discovered in inward simplicity and manifested in outward economy.

While I delved deeper into *Walden*, I consciously searched for ways to cultivate inward simplicity in studying mathematics for clarity of thought and serenity of mind, continuing to read at leisure for mirth and perspicacity, cherishing my friendships with K, Carolyn, Luis, Adrian, and Tim, and enjoying the sensuality of spring. Thoreau was to me what the classical writers were to Thoreau in "Reading"—wiser interlocutors with whom conversation led to insight into the essentials of life. In "Sounds" I found a beautifully expressed counterpart to my cavorting with *Primavera* and frolicking around oak trees and along the rail line on the edge of campus during furtive nocturnal walks:

There were times when I could not afford to sacrifice the bloom of the present moment to any work, whether of the head or hands. I love a broad margin to my life. Sometimes, in a summer morning, having taken my accustomed bath, I sat in my sunny doorway from sunrise till noon, rapt in a revery, amidst the pines and hickories and sumachs, in undisturbed solitude and stillness, while the birds sang around or flitted noiseless through the house, until by the sun falling in at my west window, or the noise of some traveller's wagon on the distant highway, I was reminded of the lapse of time. I grew in those seasons like corn in the night, and they were far better than any work of the hands would have been. They were not time subtracted from my life, but so much over and above my usual allowance. I realized what the Orientals mean by contemplation and the forsaking of works... . This was sheer idleness to my fellow-townsmen, no doubt; but if the birds and flowers had tried me by their standard, I should not have been found wanting. A man must find his occasions in himself, it is true. The natural day is very calm, and will hardly reprove his indolence.[42]

I grew in those cavorts, frolics, and reveries like the corn in the fields of Mesoamerican peoples. As Thoreau appealed to the standard of birds and flowers—say, of the cardinals and bluebonnets of southern spring—I recalled Jesus's words in the Sermon on the Mount:

For this reason I say to you, do not be worried about your life, *as to* what you will eat or what you will drink; nor for your body, *as to* what you will put on. Is not life more than food, and the body more than clothing? Look at the birds of the air, that they do not sow, nor reap nor gather into barns, and *yet* your heavenly Father feeds them. Are you not worth much more than they? And who of you by being worried can add a *single* hour to his life? And why are you worried about clothing? Observe how the lilies of the field grow; they do not toil nor do they spin, yet I say to you that not even Solomon in all his glory clothed himself like one of these.[43]

In such passages, I interpreted Thoreauvian experimental simplicity to be one way to actually live the advice of the Preacher from *Ecclesiastes* and of the teacher from the Sermon on the Mount. K's words about Dr. Long's dissertation had clued me into this. Nowadays, I think Thoreau's experiment at Walden was, at least in part, a sacrament of his inward attempt at living the good life according to his understanding of the Sermon and other writings sacred to him. I find this to be reflected in the parable of "The Bean-Field." Thoreau described his field as "half-cultivated" or somewhere between a "wild" and a "cultivated" or "civilized" field.[44] But his agricultural husbandry was sacramental. What he really wanted to plant were not beans but spiritual or moral seeds, namely, "sincerity, truth, simplicity, faith, innocence"—seeds we all should plant and cultivate in ourselves and in a "new generation of men."[45] Similarly, in "Baker Farm" Thoreau reflects upon the significance of an indolent day spent fishing by citing *Ecclesiastes*: "Remember thy Creator in the days of thy youth. Rise free from care before the dawn, and seek adventures. Let the noon find thee by other lakes, and the night overtake thee everywhere at home. There are no larger fields than these, no worthier games than may here be played. Grow wild according to thy nature."[46]

The parable of cultivating the bean field and the figure of the sauntering fisherman who finds himself "everywhere at home" reveal earnest aspirations. Even in college, I thought Thoreau to be sincere in trying to make his living coherent with his thinking and writing. Occasionally I found his denunciations of his neighbors to be merciless and his exhortations to become scalding tirades. I found him to be too ascetic with his body and incapable of expressing love and intimacy through touch. After celebrating hearing, seeing, touching, tasting, and smelling in so many ways in his detailed observations, in "Higher Laws" he became dualistic and argued for a purity of spirit by a severe ascetic negation of sensuality.[47] This had been already heralded in his rejection of bodily intimacy during earnest dialogue with visitors.[48] Here I parted ways with Thoreau. At the outset of "Higher Laws," he had written: "I found in myself, and still find, an instinct toward a higher, or, as it is named, spiritual life, as do most men, and another toward a primitive rank and savage one, and I reverence them both. I love the wild no less than the good."[49] But then he turned ascetic. I wanted to shake Henry back into his senses. I wanted to retort: "Give me spiritual and sensual intimacy; I reverence them both and love the sensual no less than the spiritual."

And yet my older brother Henry—who is sometimes accused of pride or insincerity and who even today often frustrates me—had made a clear fallibilist statement for his position:

> If I seem to boast more than is becoming, my excuse is that I brag for humanity rather than for myself; and my shortcomings and inconsistencies do not affect the truth of my statement. Notwithstanding much cant and hypocrisy—chaff which I find it difficult to separate from my wheat, but for which I am as sorry as any man—I will breathe freely and stretch myself in this respect, it is such a relief to both the moral and physical system; and I am resolved that I will not through humility become the devil's attorney. I will endeavor to speak a good word for the truth.[50]

He struck me as self-aware and frank. He may not have known all of his inconsistencies and blind-spots, but he knew he had them. Frankness, especially, seemed like a quality I did not have and my culture of origin did not encourage. Thoreau said directly what he thought to be true.

There also were moments when Thoreau became more sympathetic toward his neighbors. I saw him as a caring person then. In "Former Inhabitants; and Winter Visitors," Thoreau wrote of weathering snowstorms when, for "human society, [he] would conjure up the former occupants of these woods."[51] These passages revealed Thoreau's sympathy for humanity, as he expressed his sensibility for the suffering of the poor and downtrodden. He tells their stories with loving tenderness, for instance, the story of "Cato Ingraham ... . Some say that he was a Guinea Negro. There are a few who remember his little patch among the walnuts, which he let grow up till he should be old and need them; but a younger and whiter speculator got them at last."[52] He told of Zilpha, who spun linen for the "townsfolk" and whose house English soldiers set on fire during the war of 1812: "She led a hard life, and somewhat inhumane."[53] He remembered seeing Breed's hut burn in a blaze caused by mischievous boys. The night after the fire, Thoreau went out on a walk, heard moaning, and found the only survivor of the family staring at the smoldering cinders and muttering to himself. Thoreau recorded that the man "was soothed by the sympathy which my mere presence implied" and showed him an iron hook from "the well-sweep which his father had cut and mounted."[54] This hook was "all that he could now cling to," and Thoreau wrote that he "felt it, and still remark it almost daily in my walks, for by it hangs the history of a family."[55] The passage about Breed's hut put Thoreau in a softer light, as he felt sympathy, and the despairing man felt comforted. Thoreau then honored the memory of the history of the family. I surmised, then, that when Thoreau wrote that the mass of men lead lives of "quiet desperation," he was not condemning them but rather expressing his own sympathetic care for their well-being, even if sometimes his tone was contemptuous.

I weathered the winter chapters, as I did not have the experiential sense of living through and learning to enjoy a long northern winter or the intellectual background to understand Thoreau's naturalist and transcendentalist aims in those sections. When "Spring" arrived, however, I noticed how a hopeful Thoreau found in his neighbors the possibility for spiritual renaissance. For him, awakening and renewal in Nature heralded the possibilities of awakening to our ethical lives. In the most moving passage, he wrote:

> A single gentle rain makes the grass many shades greener. So our prospects brighten on the influx of better thoughts. We should be blessed if we lived in the present always, and took advantage of every accident that befell us, like the grass which confesses the influence of the slightest dew that falls on it; and did not spend our time in atoning for the neglect of past opportunities, which we call doing our duty. We loiter in winter while it is already spring.[56]

For me, this passage again harked back to the Sermon on the Mount: "But if God so clothes the grass of the field, which is *alive* today and tomorrow is thrown into the furnace, *will He* not much more *clothe* you? You of little faith!"[57] Have faith that the gentle rains will come, Thoreau added.

This faithful message was immediately followed by the possibility of regarding our neighbors with grace, as they are themselves awakened to a new day:

> In a pleasant spring morning all men's sins are forgiven. Such a day is a truce to vice. While such a sun holds out to burn, the vilest sinner may return. Through

our own recovered innocence we discern the innocence of our neighbors. ... [T]he sun shines bright and warm this first spring morning, recreating the world, and you meet him at some serene work, and see how his exhausted and debauched veins expand with still joy and bless the new day, feel the spring influence with the innocence of infancy, and all his faults are forgotten.[58]

Thus, Thoreau's own words soothed my misgivings about his unsympathetic and self-righteous excesses.[59]

When I came to Thoreau's "Conclusion," then, I felt attuned to Thoreau's own renewed faith in humanity and alternative possibilities for living. He issued a renewed call to remain free and spontaneous, awake to the possibilities of life, especially our inward life. However, he also sensed, after two years at Walden, that he had other experiments to conduct, other ways to attend to vital matters. In tentative terms, as if offering a guess, he explained that he left the woods to preserve his spontaneity in pursuing other paths of life:

> I left the woods for as good a reason as I went there. Perhaps it seemed to me that I had several more lives to live, and could not spare any more time for that one. It is remarkable how easily and insensibly we fall into a particular route, and make a beaten track for ourselves. I had not lived there a week before my feet wore a path from my door to the pond-side. ... The surface of the earth is soft and impressible by the feet of men; and so with the paths which the mind travels. How worn and dusty, then, must be the highways of the world, how deep the ruts of tradition and conformity![60]

I read these sentences carefully, and then I became very still and quiet. K had warned me to look for the reasons why Thoreau left the woods—the counterpart to the passage that inspired the boys of the Dead Poets to go into the woods. Thoreau left because he had several other lives to live. And immediately after that he spoke of non-conformity in terms of avoiding the wearing and following of beaten tracks. I then recalled M's reaction to Robert Frost's "The Road Not Taken," how she'd been moved by it to wonder what life paths we'd choose as I entered the university and she started her final year of high school. Thoreau had expressed here a similar sentiment, though the poetry was different. Thoreau could live his other lives; Frost could follow roads not taken; I could saunter, road-trip, experiment. In contrast, M's life had been ended all too soon—she would not live other ones, choose new roads, blaze new paths, saunter, road-trip, or experiment. I hoped, however, that I could take her along my saunters and road-trips and share with her my experiments, carrying her in my heart while I conversed with Henry for encouragement.

By his own reflection Thoreau again exhorted me to experiment and simplify:

> I learned this, at least, by my experiment: that if one advances confidently in the direction of his dreams, and endeavors to live the life which he has imagined, he will meet with a success unexpected in common hours. ... In proportion as he simplifies his life, the laws of the universe will appear less complex, and solitude will not be solitude, nor poverty poverty, nor weakness weakness. If you have built castles in the air, your work need not be lost; that is where they should be. Now put the foundations under them.[61]

This is the final passage I recall from my college reading. I discussed it with K toward the end of my sophomore year. Literature seemed to be drawing us closer and closer. Spring had fully arrived and began to give way to summer. Thoreau continued writing to end *Walden* with the summons to remain awake so the new day could dawn and the morning sun could rise.[62] But I think my heart and mind held on to these sentences: I wanted to get on with simple living and put the foundations under the lives I could imagine. Some of these I would live in *la Yunai*, Henry's and K's homeland.

NOTES

1. See *Dead Poets Society*. Directed by Peter Weir (USA: Touchstone Pictures, 1989), film.
2. Henry David Thoreau, *Walden and Resistance to Civil Government*, 2nd ed., ed. William Rossi (New York: W. W. Norton & Company, 1992), 1.
3. Ibid., 7.
4. Ibid., 2.
5. Ibid., 61.
6. Ibid., 5.
7. Ibid.
8. Ibid.
9. Ibid., 6.
10. Ibid., 7.
11. Ibid., 3.
12. E. B. White, "Walden—1954," in Henry David Thoreau, *Walden and Resistance to Civil Government*, 2nd ed., ed. William Rossi (New York: W. W. Norton & Company, 1992), 360.
13. Thoreau, *Walden*, 21.
14. Ibid., 10.
15. Casey Black, "Flowers" in *Lay You in the Loam* (Catbeach Music, 2013), compact disc.
16. Thoreau, *Walden*, 18.

17. Ibid., 9.
18. Ibid., 35.
19. Ibid., 3.
20. Ibid., 21.
21. Ibid., 48.
22. Ibid., 48–49.
23. White, "Walden—1954," 363.
24. Eccles. 9:7–9 (New American Standard Bible).
25. Jer. 20:9 (NASB).
26. Thoreau, *Walden*, 48.
27. Ibid., 47.
28. Ibid., 55.
29. Ibid.
30. Ibid., 57.
31. Ibid.
32. Ibid., 60.
33. Ibid.
34. Ibid., 61.
35. Ibid.
36. Ibid.
37. Ibid.
38. Ibid., 63.
39. Ibid., 64.
40. Ibid., 66.
41. Ibid.
42. Ibid., 75–76.
43. Matt. 6:25–29 (NASB).
44. Thoreau, *Walden*, 106.
45. Ibid., 110.
46. Ibid., 139. The first sentence is from Eccles. 12:1 (NASB).
47. Ibid., 146–149.
48. Ibid., 95.
49. Ibid., 140–141.
50. Ibid., 33–34.
51. Ibid., 171.
52. Ibid., 171.
53. Ibid.
54. Ibid., 174.
55. Ibid.
56. Ibid., 209.
57. Matt. 6:30 (NASB)
58. Thoreau, *Walden*, 209–210.
59. The explanation for Thoreau's evolving sympathy toward his neighbors may be found in the way he composed *Walden* throughout a decade of work. See Robert Sattelmeyer, "The Remaking of Walden," in Henry David Thoreau, *Walden and*

Resistance to Civil Government, 2nd ed., ed. William Rossi (New York: W. W. Norton & Company, 1992), 428–444. Sattelmeyer identifies two main stages of Thoreau's work to compose *Walden*, the first 1847–1849 and the second 1852-1854. By 1849, two years after leaving the pond, Thoreau thought his work was nearly finished, but as his friendships, domestic relations, literary fortunes, and sense of his own literary métier changed, the manuscript underwent thorough transformation (429). Sattelmeyer's central thesis is that the evolution of *Walden* is an expression of the evolution of Thoreau's life over nearly a decade of "spiritual and intellectual growth" (431), from the time he went to the pond to the time he published the book. In particular, in the first stage Thoreau focused on his criticism of American culture and society, offering his own experimental life at Walden as a counterpoint, while in the second stage Thoreau's focus turned to introspective self-examination and to an investigation of the relationship of perfect correspondence between human beings and Nature. For Sattelmeyer, "Thoreau became increasingly concerned with his own awakening and less obsessed with waking up his neighbors" (438). During this second stage, he composed the chapters from "The Ponds" to "Conclusion." These are more "introspective, meditative, and descriptive and [contain] relatively few passages of sustained satire" (433). Even when he returns to the themes of "Economy," Thoreau's "criticism is muted by sympathy," for example in his account of the Irish farmer John Field and his family in "Baker Farm" (433).

60. Thoreau, Walden, 215–216.

61. Ibid., 216.

62. The final sentence reads, "Only that day dawns to which we are awake. There is more day to dawn. The sun is but a morning star." Ibid., 223.

Chapter 10

Philosophies of the Heart
in American Literature

Anthony lived across the hallway from my dorm room during my junior year. An African-American guy from a small town somewhere in the South—I can't recall now if he was from Arkansas, Louisiana, Mississippi, Alabama, or Tennessee, he had come to our college on a scholarship to play football. Of average height but thick-bodied, strong-legged, and muscular from his neck to his calves, he played as a starting offensive lineman on the varsity team. He preferred to live in a single room in our dorm, near the library, rather than room with teammates in the distant residence hall near the football field. According to him, most of the players on the team were rowdy. They lived across the road from the field so they wouldn't have to walk far going to and coming back from practice. Anthony, though, was a dedicated business-major and needed the quietness of our hall to study.

Our single rooms were tiny: a bed, a desk, a drawer, and a sink took up most of the space. My window looked out onto the softball field behind the library. Across the field, there rose the main auditorium. In order to feel less constrained in my room, I often left my door open while reading or studying at my desk. So I often saw Anthony coming or going, and we chatted a bit every day, about football and *fútbol*—we understood little of each other's sport but wanted to learn—or school or life in general.

One time he said, "Hey, man, I always see you reading. What are you reading?" I said that I enjoyed reading American literature, mainly fiction but also poetry. A very practical guy, he spent most of his time studying business—management, marketing, accounting—and only read what humanities courses required. But to my surprise he said, "What do you recommend that I read?" I was not sure. But at the time I had been reading William Faulkner intensely, in part because the fictional world of Mississippi's Yoknapatawpha County revealed to me the origins of Gabriel García Márquez's *Macondo* in the

141

Colombian Caribbean, in part to understand the South, in part simply for the pleasure of reading great literature. So I said, "How about Faulkner? Have your read him?" He hadn't. I would have thought Faulkner to be required reading in high school, if not college, especially in the South. Anthony immediately borrowed my paperback copy of *The Portable Faulkner*. I had bought it at the college's bookstore, courtesy of my scholarship fund, and felt happy to lend it to my friend.

Around that time, two short stories had opened my eyes to the history of race relations in the South. I had been dumbfounded at discovering, through reading "Red Leaves,"[1] that some Native American tribes in the South had enslaved Africans during the nineteenth century, in emulation of the European influence that assailed them. The results of such emulation had been disastrous. At a revealing juncture in the story, various Native American characters discuss the problem. They are pursuing a runaway African slave who does not want to be sacrificed and interred with the tribe's recently dead chief, and they wonder whether all that work to keep slaves is worth it. The first explains that the slaves are too valuable, but it is troublesome to find things for them to do. Nonetheless he adds, "We must do as the white men do." Asked by a second to explain what that means, he elaborates: "Raise more Negroes by clearing more land to make corn to feed them, then sell them. We will clear the land and plant it with food and raise Negroes and sell them to the white men for money." A third one wonders, "But what will we do with this money?" They think silently for a while until the first one concludes, "We will see."[2] The absurdity of emulating European economic dynamics becomes evident. I wondered, if Anthony were to read this story, what he would think about the dynamics of "doing business."

I mostly wondered, though, what he would think if he read "That Evening Sun."[3] The story is set in Jefferson, Mississippi, after the Civil War, as the culture of the Old South is falling to pieces. The economic and political dynamics are changing gradually, even as traditional social hierarchies and race segregation endure. Nancy, a black servant who washes clothes and occasionally cooks for the Compson family, is afraid that her husband, Jesus, will kill her for prostituting herself to a white man, Mr. Stovall. A cashier in the bank and a deacon at the Baptist church, the man has not paid her the last three times. When she denounces Mr. Stovall publicly by yelling in the street, he knocks her down and kicks her teeth out. She is arrested for the disturbance, and when she attempts to commit suicide in jail, the jailer beats and whips her. Afterward, back in her cabin, Nancy is terrified, sensing that her husband has returned to murder her for the offense. The Compson children witness Nancy's fearful comings and goings to and from her cabin.

In the midst of this, the narrator's portrayal of Jason, the youngest Compson, suggested to me how white kids learned to differentiate between themselves and "niggers." Five years old, Jason is constantly asking who is a "nigger" and whether he is one. When Nancy is telling Dilsey, the Compson's main cook, that she thinks Jesus has returned to kill her, Jason's interventions surprised me:

"How do you know he's back?" Dilsey said. "You ain't seen him."
"Jesus is a nigger," Jason said.
"I can feel him," Nancy said. "I can feel him laying yonder in the ditch."
"Tonight?" Dilsey said. "Is he there tonight?"
"Dilsey's a nigger too," Jason said.
"You try to eat something," Dilsey said.
"I don't want nothing," Nancy said.
"I ain't a nigger," Jason said.[4]

The conversation continues until the most revealing moment:

"I ain't a nigger," Jason said. "Are you a nigger, Nancy?"
"I hellborn, child," Nancy said.[5]

Jason has heard the term "nigger" and seems to know that it is derogatory, but he does not know how to apply it. He doesn't know yet that it is race that makes a person a "nigger." He witnesses the violent and impoverished world of Nancy and Dilsey—a world that Nancy may literally call hell, but to him that's just the way the world is. In that world, Nancy is convinced she will be murdered, and, at the end of the story, she no longer resists death. It doesn't matter whether she gets killed or not; the threat of violence has deranged her already. The Compson children witness it, as Jason is trying to figure out who the "niggers" are.

I wondered if this is how it happened—how Southern white kids came to internalize racist concepts.[6] Faulkner's story reminded me of another one by Flannery O'Connor. In "The Artificial Nigger," a grandfather and his grandson from rural Georgia visit "the city"—Atlanta.[7] The grandfather, Mr. Head, wants to teach his ten-year-old grandson, Nelson, a moral lesson—namely, that the city is dangerous and full of "niggers." There have not been any in their county since the white residents chased the last one off twelve years earlier, and so he says to Nelson: "You ain't never seen a nigger."[8] Nelson, who knows he had been born in Atlanta, wants to appear more knowledgeable than his grandfather. A little know-it-all, he retorts: "How you know I never saw a nigger when I lived there before? ... I probably saw a lot of niggers."[9] Then comes a quick exchange that was as revealing to me as the one in Faulkner's story:

"If you seen one you didn't know what he was," Mr. Head said, completely exasperated. "A six-month-old child don't know a nigger from anybody else."
"I reckon I'll know a nigger if I see one," the boy said.[10]

However, in the train to Atlanta later that day, Nelson sees a "huge coffee-colored man … coming slowly forward" through the car in which he sits with his grandfather.[11] The man is elegant and dignified, wearing a light suit, a yellow satin tie with a ruby pin in it, and a sapphire ring on the hand that holds the cane with which he walks deliberately. When the man has passed, Mr. Head asks his grandson what he saw. Nelson responds that he saw a man, a fat man, an old man.[12] Then, in a petty moment of triumph, Mr. Head tells him, "That was a nigger."[13] Nelson, however, complains: "You said they were black. … You never said they were tan. How do you expect me to know anything when you don't tell me right?"[14]

And, sadly, Nelson seemed to me to be right—to learn the concept he must be instructed properly; he must be taught how to be a racist if he was to become one. On the train, he saw a dignified, large, old man. Nelson only saw the man as a "nigger" when his grandfather told him to do so, even if Nelson had already internalized that he must despise the old man for being one. Indeed, from O'Connor's story I gathered that generations of white people had needed a shared hatred of blacks to keep whites together. In the story, after a frightful experience getting lost in the city, Mr. Head and Nelson are reconciled and united by their mutual bewilderment at the sight of "a plaster figure of a Negro sitting bent over on a low yellow brick fence that curved around a wide lawn" in a white suburban neighborhood.[15] The grotesque figure which holds "a piece of brown watermelon" mesmerizes them until Mr. Head exclaims, "An artificial nigger!"[16] The boy wonders why there should be such a miserable-looking plaster figure on that brick fence. The grandfather, after pondering the question and wanting to regain the child's respect for his wisdom, responds, "They ain't got enough real ones here. They got to have an artificial one."[17] Even when there are no black people around, as in that suburban neighborhood, whites must construct blacks as different and threatening to reinforce the notion of white superiority.

I wondered what Anthony would have to say to all of this. A couple of months later, when he returned my copy of *The Portable Faulkner* to me, he said that he had enjoyed reading from it, that it was good writing. But before I could ask anything about specific stories or his interpretations, he asked me why I had started to read Faulkner. I said that I wanted to understand why white and black students never sat together in the cafeteria, why the black athletes hung out by themselves and the white kids didn't seem to reach out to them either. He stood there silently, as if pondering what to tell me. Then he said, "I see. Yeah, man, that's messed up. This place is messed up, isn't it?" Then he turned around and, after thanking me for the book, went back to his room without elaborating. I wondered what he meant by tagging the question "isn't it?" to his words. Maybe he thought that we shared our not being white and both understood the same things. Or maybe he thought that even if I didn't know why, I would figure it out, perhaps by reading Faulkner or perhaps by continuing to observe the experiences around me. Maybe he didn't want to dwell on it. Or maybe he didn't want to say what he thought or knew. I, at any rate, kept wondering about other parts of his question: Which place? Our subtly segregated campus? Or the South? Or the United States? And how is it messed up for Anthony? For others?

I only knew partially the experience of Luis, my Afro-Costa Rican friend. His Southern girlfriend's "waspy" family had resisted their relationship until she ended it under pressure. But I did not know the details and could only surmise them. By that time, however, reading literature had become one of my main sources of insight into the nuances of Southern society and of imagination regarding mores and social practices in other regions of *la Yunai*. So I figured I would keep reading and observing the experiences around me to understand.

FREEDOM, LOVE, AND THE HEART IN
TONI MORRISON′S *BELOVED*

On a sunny afternoon during the fall semester of our senior year, K came to find me at the main lawn on campus. I noticed the spring in her step as she walked toward me. Her green eyes shone in the bright light, and she flashed her endearing smile. From a short distance, even before she reached me, she exclaimed, "Toni Morrison was awarded the Nobel Prize in literature!" She'd just heard the news at the English department. Her smile became laughter, and she clapped excitedly. She felt sheer joy. Yet she expressed worry that conservative traditionalists in the department—the guardians of the cannon, even in American literature—might claim that Morrison won because she was a black woman, as if her literary merits were reducible to and explained away by politically correct charity from the awarding committee. It had been many years since another American, Saul Bellow, had won the Nobel Prize, and even the non-traditionalists expected John Updike or Philip Roth to win sometime, but not Morrison. K had urged me many times to read Morrison: "Perhaps *The Bluest Eye* or *Sula*," she'd advised me. But I hadn't read any of her books yet. So when K told me about the award, her joy, and her worry, I had nothing to say and couldn't hold forth on what I thought. As usual, though, I trusted her perspicacious sense of literary beauty and artful writing. At once I thought the time had come to read Morrison's work, but now K encouraged me to begin with the masterpiece: "Read *Beloved*." So *Beloved* I sought and found in the library's shelves before anyone else could get to it, and I proceeded to read it on the library's comfortable armchairs in front of the large bay windows that faced the lily pool. Once I started reading, I could not stop for several days.

The opening scene in a house haunted by dreadful sorrow, confusing and frightful as it was, brought my thoughts back to the first time I had crossed the Mason-Dixon Line from Kentucky into Ohio, specifically into Cincinnati, during a missionary road trip. As soon as my group approached the Ohio River and crossed it into the northern city, even an uninformed Central American could see the sudden presence of African Americans driving around, whereas to the south, for miles and miles and miles, there had been none. I surmised that they lived and toiled in Cincinnati neighborhoods on the northern banks of the Ohio River. The experience of having seen those Cincinnati roads and neighborhoods personally drew me, all the more powerfully, into the story of the suffering black family living in the spiteful house at 124 Bluestone Road, on the outskirts of the city. The story of Baby Suggs, Sethe, Denver, Howard, Buglar, Paul D, and a baby's ghost full of venom could be the ancestral story of any of the families I'd seen during my brief passage through the city.[18]

As the stories of these characters began to unfold, I began to have, for the first time in four years as a student in *la Yunai*, a clear sense, a vivid apprehension, of just how terrible the daily and life-long suffering of slaves had been. I had read about slavery as a political, social, and economic event in my American History class with Professor Haynie. I had not grasped, however, how painful the human toil had been. Some of that pain had been written, as if through an ideogram, in the scars on the backs of slaves such as Sethe. A former slave on a Kentucky plantation, Sethe had been raped and flogged by her white owners just before she escaped to Ohio. She had been nursed and kept from dying by a white girl, Amy Denver, a former indentured servant who was wandering the Kentucky woods on her way to Boston. Amy had found Sethe wounded, exhausted, and pregnant. As the good Samaritan in the Christian Gospels, she had cured the wounds on Sethe´s back, which she described as drawing a chokecherry tree. And she had delivered Sethe's baby—later named Denver in thankfulness—on an abandoned boat on the banks of the Ohio River. With the help of Stamp Paid, Ella, and others—former slaves who now lived in Cincinnati and helped fugitive slaves to escape to freedom—Sethe had arrived at Baby Suggs's house at 124 Bluestone Road.

There, reunited with her mother-in-law and her other children—Howard, Buglar, and a nameless girl—Sethe had enjoyed twenty-eight days of freedom in the midst of a loving community. During that time, she had heard Baby Suggs preach of the redeeming, healing power of love and the human heart. As the narrator tells it, after the physical and moral hardships of slavery Baby Suggs thought that she "had nothing left to make a living with but her heart—which she put to work at once."[19] Baby Suggs opened her "great big heart" to the black community of Cincinnati in the Clearing—an open space deep in the woods outside the city—and preached about grace through self-love. The power of her message moved me as I read her sermon; it spoke directly to my heart, as I'd begun to search for secular ways to understand the principles of love and grace—to rescue them from other-worldly heaven and bring them back down to earth, where people do suffer and toil; to liberate them from the formalities and strictures of the churchgoing world around me and make them living principles.

Baby Suggs's message of possible redemption for those who had undergone hurtful injustice in this world made sense to me. To imagine grace and attain it, the downtrodden former slaves needed to love themselves.[20] So it was up to them to love their own flesh, just as it depended on them to love their own hands to touch and caress each other, their own feet to walk and dance, their own mouths to eat and speak, their backs, their arms, their unnoosed and straight necks. And finally, it was up to the suffering and the downtrodden to love their own life-preserving guts, their life-giving organs, and their own love-nourishing hearts: "More than your life-holding womb and your life-giving private parts, hear me now, love your heart."[21]

When I finished reading Baby Suggs's Sermon in the Clearing, I could only return to it again and again and again. Each time, it shook me. To love one's own life-sustaining heart—to care for it, to trust it, to nurse it, to guard it, to heal it, to nourish it—so that one could let its love flow from self to neighbors: This seemed to be the kernel of the ethical principle "to love your neighbor as yourself,"[22] though at the time I could not articulate the theme in those terms. All I could do was read Baby Suggs's message over and over and over and imagine what it meant to the people who listened and, when Baby Suggs had finished speaking the Word, sang in harmony to give her music as she danced. When her heart could speak no more words, it still beat to make her dance.[23]

For a while, I could not read beyond this passage. I had read it at my desk in my single, small dorm room. I had walked to the window, to look out at the green softball field and blue sky outside. Then I had returned to my desk to read again and walked again to the window. I was on the opposite side of campus from K, but I felt like walking to find her just to talk about that sermon. In connection with this passage in *Beloved*, I recalled the final scene of James Baldwin's short story "Sonny's Blues"—the story that had moved K and me so deeply when we had read it in our American Short Story class. Sonny, a black boy from Harlem, had survived being orphaned as a teenager, the threat and violence of his neighborhood's streets, his heroin addiction, and imprisonment. He had survived mostly by gathering strength and consolation from playing blues and jazz at the piano. In the story, he does not preach lovingly like Baby Suggs in *Beloved*, but he does play his piano wholeheartedly so that others will listen and will be freed from their pain through listening. "Belief in God is an inclination to listen"[24]—I thought about this opening verse for Robert Lowell's poem "No Hearing," as I read once again the final scene in "Sonny's Blues." Sonny's brother, the story's narrator, listens to Sonny struggle at the piano during his first gig in a Greenwich Village venue after being freed from prison. But then he listens to Sonny play "Am I Blue" and senses that, as Sonny played, he "began to make it his. It was very beautiful because it wasn't hurried and it was no longer a lament. I seemed to hear with what burning he had made it his, with what burning we had yet to make it ours, how we could cease lamenting. Freedom lurked around us and I understood, at last, that he could help us to be free if we would listen, that he would never be free until we did."[25] By way of his own struggles, Sonny had gone through what his parents and black ancestors had gone through—long migrations, violent deaths, small joys, tragic deaths, cherished hopes, constant striving. He was playing it back with the blues, making their pain one with his and making others listen, so that their freedom, their liberty to listen and respond wholeheartedly, could be real and meaningful. Sonny played his piano and Baby Suggs preached and danced to the beat of her heart so that their listeners could be free to live and love. As I thought of this, I wanted to say this to K, to share it with her. I knew she would listen to me.

When eventually I did continue reading *Beloved* beyond Baby Suggs's sermon at the Clearing, I felt crushed. Perhaps I had expected what would come next, since the narrator had already heralded Baby Suggs's sad death, and I wanted to hold on to Baby Suggs's gospel of saving grace in the flesh. But immediately after hearing her sermon as if it were spoken not only for the long-suffering black people of Cincinnati but for all the downtrodden in America, I learned that, in the end, "Baby Suggs, holy, believed she had lied. There was no grace—imaginary or real—and no sunlit dance in a Clearing could change that. Her faith, her love, her imagination, and her great big old heart began to collapse twenty-eight days after her daughter-in-law arrived."[26] Her faith in the possibility of earthly grace in the flesh broke down when, upon the arrival at her house of four slave-catching white men, Sethe had attempted to murder all her children and succeeded in slitting with a handsaw the throat of her daughter—later named Beloved on a tombstone bought in exchange for sex with the engraver.

As I read, the story's themes of love, grace, and freedom grew ever more intertwined and dire for me. At a crucial juncture later in the narrative, Stamp Paid's belated understanding of Baby Suggs's prostration reveals the central moral issue of the novel: "Now, too late, he understood her. The heart that pumped out love, the mouth that spoke the Word, didn't count. They came in her yard anyway and she could not approve or condemn Sethe's rough choice. One or the other might have saved her, but beaten up by the claims of both,

she went to bed. The white folks had tired her out at last."[27] Baby Suggs's ethical ambivalence, not being able to condone or condemn Sethe's infanticide
in the face of the cruelties of slavery, destroyed the loving life she had left to
live. After Beloved's death, Baby Suggs confined herself to bed, where she
wanted only to regard bright colors, to observe colorful pieces of cloth, since
white people seemed to be the endless source of evil in her world. Human evil
had destroyed the possibility of human grace and loving redemption.

This crushed my heart, just at it had crushed K's. When we talked about
it, we could feel the despair of a woman who had lost her last hope at restoring joy through loving grace after a lifetime of sorrow. I wanted to believe
in Baby Suggs's gospel of saving grace in the flesh, but her story threatened
to destroy the possibility of such grace. That possibility seemed too fragile to
withstand the destructive power of cold-hearted human cruelty. I had to read
through the pain of Sethe's whole story for faith in that gospel of grace in the
flesh to be reaffirmed.

In spite of her pain, Sethe perseveres in her life. She struggles to go on living in isolation from her community, in a violent house haunted by Beloved's
ghost, but she continues to care for Denver and for herself. When Paul D, a
former slave and her friend from Sweet Home, arrives at her house eighteen
years after she had fled and they had been separated, she opens herself up
to the possibility of restoring her life through love—through *eros*, but also
more than *eros*: through a caring, nursing, restoring love. She tries a new life
with him, one in which they can help each other heal and thrive, even though
she knows it is dangerous to love too much because—as so many characters
claim from experience in *Beloved*—loving most often leads to loss and pain.
But Sethe does try because freedom is meaningless if it does not mean freedom to love. This struck me, and still strikes me, as the heart of the matter
in *Beloved*.

When Paul D asks Sethe whether it is true that she killed her own daughter, love motivates Sethe to try to explain it to him. With moving words she
explains to him that, upon her escape from Sweet Home in Kentucky and her
arrival at the house in Cincinnati, she felt free to love for the first time in her
life. She had made independent decisions during their escape, experiencing
freedom for the first time, and she had succeeded. More importantly, she
felt that she could protect, care for, and love her children as her own, not a
someone else's property:

> Look like I loved em more after I got here. Or maybe I couldn't love em proper
> in Kentucky because they wasn't mine to love. But when I got here, when I
> jumped down off that wagon—there wasn't nobody in the world I couldn't love
> if I wanted to. You know what I mean?[28]

In an equally moving passage, the narrator explains why Paul D under-
stands what Sethe means. He had been imprisoned in Georgia for murdering
his cruel new owner after being sold away from Sweet Home, only to suffer
more vexing humiliations. While in prison, Paul D had learned to love only
small things, like a tiny star or a blade of grass, because these could not be
taken away from him:

> Anything bigger wouldn't do. A woman, a child, a brother—a big love like that
> would split you open in Alfred, Georgia. He knew exactly what [Sethe] meant:
> to get to a place where you could love anything you chose—not to need permis-
> sion for desire—well now, that was freedom.[29]

Freedom to love is the greatest, truest freedom—the freedom that Sethe could
not give up to go back to slavery, the freedom she could not bear for her
children to live without.

As a student living and learning in *la Yunai*, where quotidian political and
cultural discourse seemed to make so much of the ideal of liberty, where a
Yankee state even had as its motto "To live free or die," I found this account
of freedom to be deeply significant. Freedom is most meaningful when it is
freedom to love, to care, to heal, to nurse, to teach, to encourage, to offer solidarity, to support and help each other. This is not freedom *from* strange others
but freedom *to* cultivate relations with neighbors. Years later, as a student of
philosophy, I could articulate this freedom to love as the most meaningful
form of positive, rather than negative, freedom. In the philosophical terms of
Charles Peirce, I could articulate it as agapistic freedom: freedom to cherish
unconditionally the object of our agapistic love—our beloved persons—and
to nurture them so that they can grow and thrive.[30]

Upon that first reading of *Beloved* in Arkansas and discussing it with K, I
also found it significant that for this freedom to love to be effective—to lead
to actual loving care—its source must be a "great big heart"—big like Baby
Suggs's heart had been until its pain became unbearable; great like Sethe's
heart remained in spite of the unbearable pain; big like Paul D's heart which,
after years sealed shut like a rusted tin box buried in his chest, had burst open
again in order to love and care for Sethe even through their struggles. Years
later, as a student in Pennsylvania, I learned to articulate this theme in terms
of Peirce's view that the ethical judgments of the "sensible heart"—an organ
of affective perception and insight—deserve our deepest respect as moral
guides.[31] Even later, as a teacher in Brooklyn discussing the novel with my
students, I learned to express this alternatively in terms of William James's
view that the best ethical whole for a community can be ascertained only by
listening to the voices of all persons who are part of the community and make
claims on each other. As we listen to these claims, the "only force of appeal

to *us*" that moves us to respond is our heart.[32] When a person appeals to our attention and care, we find guidance and encouragement in "our own human hearts, as they happen to beat responsive and not irresponsive to the claim."[33] The heart, a sensible organ of ethical perception, is the living source that nurtures and makes effective our freedom to love.

Moreover, with my students I have learned that the hope to understand Sethe or to accept her devastating act of infanticide and continue to cherish her even without complete understanding lives in our empathetic hearts. We need what philosopher Evgenia Cherkasova calls a *philosophia cordis* or philosophy of the heart. As she argues, across different civilizations the heart is the vital center of a person's body and at the same time the core of a person's emotional, spiritual, and moral life.[34] In a *philosophia cordis*, the heart mediates between body and mind or spirit, feeling and thinking, nature and consciousness. It is the primal organic bond that holds these opposites together. Moreover, a *philosophia cordis* "does not preclude clarity of thought, but it does require attunement to life's ambiguity and innuendo."[35] It is not through the logical evaluation of arguments but through the sensible, wholehearted understanding of human stories and their contexts that we can have ethical insight. In a *philosophia cordis*, the "ethical ideal of wholeness, or wholeheartedness, requires a shift from the arguments of the discriminating intellect to creative engagement with the fullness of lived experience."[36]

Cherkasova draws such a philosophy from Dostoevsky's novels which, according to her, present a "genuine *philosophia cordis*, sensitive to the harmonies and discords of life; a philosophy which willingly appreciates, listens, and responds to the primal 'songs of the heart.'"[37] She argues that Dostoevsky's work "acknowledges the primary role of the heart in moral conduct, expresses skepticism concerning the moral worth of speculative reason, and passionately searches for harmonious communion of human hearts flourishing in love."[38] For Dostoevsky, "the heart is a unifying motif that joins the palpable, sometimes acutely physical, rhythms of life and its spiritual melody. ... His philosophy of the heart is an artistic perspective that expresses, through an intricate psycho-biological imagery, a genuine concern with the tragic disintegration of human nature, and a quest for harmonious, loving communion of humanity, nature, and deity."[39]

Furthermore, this philosophy, focused on the heart as the organic and sentimental center of a person's moral life, brings along with it an ethic of love—an ethic that focuses on the duty of vital, active love and the duty of genuine trust.[40] According to this ethic, "a warm and vital commandment to love is at the core of all human responsibility ... [a]s ethical creatures human beings are under the obligation to love."[41] But love is not merely a matter of sentiment; it demands hard work, the active engagement with those who are beloved.[42] Moreover, love is a matter of choice—chosen not through rational deliberation, sticking to the facts, weighing the consequences, or making a formal categorical decision to love. Choosing love is choosing to learn the language of the heart, to be receptive to its expressions.[43] Cherkasova lucidly sums up this ethic of love from a Dostoevskian perspective:

> In Dostoevsky's moral universe, our duty is first the duty of taking care of our hearts; this implies learning to take our inner life and that of other people seriously, to love others and trust them, to listen to the summons of the living life, and develop a sense of belonging in the world. These obligations are unconditional, they do not depend on a person's situation and they do not guarantee any gratification. We must only remember that evil dwells and flourishes where the heart's life-giving sources are contaminated, where its essential bonds to the hearts of other human beings are ignored, and where love is forgotten.[44]

I draw Cherkasova's *philosophia cordis* and ethics of love into my discussions with my students regarding *Beloved*, especially when we discuss Sethe's act of infanticide. The heart is the sensible organ in Paul D's inner life that Sethe hoped to appeal to in her explanation. Either his empathetic heart could understand her—or perhaps lovingly accept her without understanding—or it could not. Empathy for Sethe and for her story is the only avenue Paul D could have to continue to love and care for her effectively. Sethe knows there are no justifying arguments or rational explanations that could ever secure his understanding and his continued loving care.[45]

Initially, Paul D cannot accept her choice. He condemns Sethe's care for her children's well-being—care even to the point of killing them, as they would be safer dead than brutalized as slaves. He condemns it as misguided love: "Your love is too thick."[46] But she stands her ground: "Love is or it ain't. Thin love ain't love at all."[47] She could not allow schoolteacher, the slaveowner, to take away her and her children's freedom to love. Conflicted, his own sorrows resurfacing, Paul D leaves her. However, it is ultimately Sethe's cherishing love, the way she gathers the broken pieces of Paul D's own life, that brings him back to her, to care for her and nurse her back to health, to offer effective companionship, and to cultivate the hope of shared happiness. He recalls the words of his friend Sixo, another slave at Sweet Home. Sixo had explained why, anytime he could, he walked furtively thirty miles in the dark just to visit the woman he loved: "She is a friend of my mind. She gather me, man. The pieces I am, she gather them and give them back to me in all the right order."[48] Freedom for Sixo, Paul D, and Sethe is meaningful when it means freedom to experience this gathering love—mediating, cherishing, nurturing, giving love born of their great big hearts.

This sort of insight, all broken in pieces and poorly articulated, I could share with K. She helped me gather its parts, put them in order, so that I could make sense of the experiences of people I had encountered and met in Arkansas, in Kentucky, in Ohio, in my struggle to live among and love my neighbors in *la Yunai*. K helped me interpret Morrison's *Beloved*, and *Beloved* helped me understand some of the history of sorrow and restored joy, of loss and renewed hope born of big great hearts, among downtrodden people in America.

NOTES

1. William Faulkner, "Red Leaves," in *The Portable Faulkner*, rev. exp. ed., ed. Malcolm Cowley (New York: Penguin, 1977), 57–84.
2. Ibid., 63.
3. William Faulkner, "That Evening Sun," in *The Portable Faulkner*, rev. exp. ed., ed. Malcolm Cowley (New York: Penguin, 1977), 391–410.
4. Ibid., 399.
5. Ibid.
6. For a clear account, from the perspective of Charles Peirce's philosophy, of how racist ideas are internalized as nonconscious habits that guide action, see Lara Trout, *The Politics of Survival: Peirce, Affectivity, and Social Criticism* (New York: Fordham University Press, 2010).
7. Flannery O'Connor, "The Artificial Nigger," in *A Good Man is Hard to Find and Other Stories* (New York: Harcourt, Brace, Jovanovich, 1992), 98–126.
8. Ibid., 102.
9. Ibid.
10. Ibid.
11. Ibid., 106.
12. Ibid., 106–107.
13. Ibid., 107.
14. Ibid.
15. Ibid., 124.
16. Ibid.
17. Ibid., 125.
18. Toni Morrison, *Beloved* (New York: Vintage, 2004).
19. Ibid., 102.
20. Ibid.
21. Ibid., 104.
22. Mark 12:31 (Holy Bible: New International Version).
23. Morrison, *Beloved*, 104.
24. Robert Lowell, "No Hearing 3" in *Collected Poems*, eds. Frank Bidart and David Gewanter (New York: Farrar, Straus and Giroux, 2003), 638.
25. James Baldwin, "Sonny's Blues," in *Going to Meet the Man: Stories* (New York: Vintage, 1995), 140.
26. Morrison, *Beloved*, 105.

27. Ibid., 212.

28. Ibid., 190–191.

29. Ibid., 191.

30. For Peirce's "agapism"—the doctrine that love, or "sympathy," is really effective in the world—see Charles S. Peirce, "Evolutionary Love," in *The Essential Peirce: Selected Philosophical Writings*, eds. N. Houser and C. Kloesel, vol. 1 (Bloomington: Indiana University Press, 1992), 352–371. For this interpretation of *agape* as unconditional love that cherishes and nurtures the well-being of the beloved persons so they can grow and thrive, see Douglas Anderson and Michael Ventimiglia, "Learning and Teaching: Gambling, Love, and Growth," in Douglas R. Anderson, *Philosophy Americana: Making Philosophy at Home in American Culture* (New York: Fordham University Press, 2006), 170–173.

31. Peirce, "Evolutionary Love," 356.

32. William James, "The Moral Philosopher and the Moral Life," in *Pragmatism and Other Writings*, ed. Giles Gun (New York: Penguin, 2000), 250.

33. Ibid.

34. Evgenia Cherkasova, *Dostoevsky and Kant: Dialogues on Ethics* (New York: Rodopi, 2009), 9.

35. Ibid., 11.

36. Ibid.

37. Ibid.

38. Ibid.

39. Ibid., 15

40. Ibid.

41. Ibid., 20.

42. Ibid., 19.

43. Ibid., 21.

44. Ibid.

45. Morrison, *Beloved*, 192.

46. Ibid., 194.

47. Ibid., 195.

48. Ibid., 321.

Chapter 11

Playing *Fútbol* in *la Yunai*

The trash-talking *gringo* received a pass in midfield, his back turned toward our goal. I stepped up to mark him. I pressed my forearm against his back so he could not turn, and with my right foot I reached around him to dispute the ball. Then I clipped his left knee with mine, leaning my weight on him, and he fell to the ground. He jumped up, screaming at the young referee: "That bitch clipped my knee." The referee called the foul, but he gave no yellow card to either one of us. So I knew: "Let this guy talk trash; I'll get him later."

Since kickoff his entire team, upon hearing us talk to each other in Spanish in the field, had taken to speaking among themselves in mock Spanish, imitating the sound of our language. They spoke like Speedy González, saying "*ándale, ándale, arriba, arriba*" like the mouse from that stupid cartoon and laughed as a group. I had asked him directly, "What's your problem?" But he did not respond. He just looked away, as if seeking for a pal to tell him what to do. Yet, on the smooth, well-lit green field under the clear, starry sky, *el gringuito* kept disparaging us all game long. As the match progressed and we outplayed and outscored his team, he grew more frustrated. We had been efficient that night on defense. As the end of the game neared, I knew payback time was coming.

On that cool evening, in one of the Central Pennsylvania valleys between the beautiful Allegheny and Appalachian Mountains, we had been playing an intramural *fútbol* match. It was spring officially, but at night we could still feel the bite of winter chilling our bodies. Perhaps the chill was a bit harsher for those of us who did not grow up in wintry climates—especially for *el peruano* Martín and me, a *josefino* from Costa Rica. But even César, Ariel, Fer, Gerardo, and *Meque*—the Argentines—and *el yorugua* Manuel, the Uruguayan, had to bundle up. Doug and Bryan, *los estadounidenses*, perhaps were a bit more comfortable.

Doug hadn't been comfortable, however, with the taunting by the frat boys on our opposing team. His sensible heart burned with the most fury upon hearing his compatriots say things that shamed him. He told a couple of "little punks" to "shut up," but he was the goalkeeper and did not have a chance for physical contact, as we would not let the opposing team near our goal.

For the rest of us, this was not the first time hearing such stupidity. We had experienced it before. It was common for college students in such teams to seek ways to berate or deride us during games. Most of them were cowards. They never confronted or addressed us directly. They just made derogatory jokes or provoking comments among themselves so that we could overhear them: "Why don't they just go home?" "In America we speak English."

Most of the time, we simply tried to outplay our opponents and silence them with skill and goals. As the Spanish saying goes, "*goles son amores*," meaning in this case that trash-talk is worthless and it is only goals that count. But this time I could not exercise so much self-control.

Eventually the *gringuito* chased a long, wild pass to the left corner of the field. As I ran to mark him, he was turned away from me, facing the sideline. I saw my chance. I launched my body feet first through the air, with my left-foot I swept the ball away from in front of him, and with my right one I intentionally swept his right leg clear off the ground. He fell hard and once again cursed. I knew it had hurt. I stood up and walked away silently, pretending nothing had happened but ready for a red card expelling me from the game. The referee did call the foul but issued only a yellow card as warning. It mattered very little—the game was over.

It should have been a moment of triumph. We won. For all his talk, mister frat boy had accomplished nothing, and he would be remembering me for a few days as he iced his ankle to alleviate the pain. However, after the match ended, I watched my opposing player limp away from the field. As my heart gradually stopped racing and my blood ceased boiling, regret overcame me. I should have just outplayed him without the deliberate violent foul. His ankle would hurt, bruise, and swell, but my chest felt tight, and my heart weighed like a brick. This foul had been worthy of a hooliganish rogue, not a *futbolista* playing with grace among mates and rivals in *la Yunai*.

How had I lost my footballer-self—the one educated by *don* Israel Santana and *Feo* Rojas, coaches in my beloved *Club Deportivo Saprissa*, in the Costa Rica of my youth? How could I find that finer, more graceful self again?

PLAYING WITH THE KICKERS IN ARKANSAS

Over the years playing *fútbol* in *la Yunai*, I found my temper had become more explosive and my fuse shorter while confronting disrespectful, often blatantly racist or xenophobic opponents. My impatience had begun to emerge very gradually during my years as a college student in Arkansas, but it had grown in intensity subsequently to become, perhaps, a kind of intemperance.

When I arrived in Arkansas, there was a club team, the Kickers, at my college that played in the state's interuniversity tournament every year. Most of the players were foreigners. In fact, a majority were Central Americans who had come to study through the same academic scholarship I had. Others were from the Caribbean and Africa. A few were highly skilled. Bornwell, a tall, strong, fast midfielder who displayed great vision of the entire field had played in the Olympic qualifying team for Zambia. Luis, an elegant midfielder who played with graceful control of the ball and dribbled with ease and flair, had played briefly in a professional first-division team in Costa Rica before leaving the sport to study. I did not play quite at their level, but I was a good left-back who could double as a fast left-winger and, occasionally, play creatively in midfield. There were a couple of *chapines*—our goalkeeper Noel from Guatemala City and Víctor from Chichicastenango, another talented midfielder—and *catrachos*—such as *el gordo* Francisco from Tegucigalpa— who also played nicely. Others were less skilled but enthusiastic. Together, we constituted a good club for our level, with a sense for playing well and seeking offensive flair, though with a tendency to be porous on defense. We were, that is, a fairly typical Central American team. Most importantly, we all liked to play club *fútbol* for fun.

My first experiences playing in Arkansas had been in fact very pleasant and memorable. I had arrived on a hot summer and spent many late afternoons playing, and sweating profusely, at the college's field on the south end of campus. To reach it, one had to walk beyond the farthest parking lot and cross a bridge over a small creek. But it was a beautiful field—level, green, and surrounded by trees on both sides. In that far edge of campus we could share a common experience from our upbringing, whether in El Salvador, Zambia, Belize, Jamaica, or anywhere: playing *fútbol* every summer day with friends. We constructed bonds of friendship and relived experiences that brought us home.

I particularly cherished the friendship I cultivated with Luis, my fellow *tico*, on the field. There are some friendships that are forged mainly on a sporting field, and they have a special, distinctive character. They are friendships based on common goals and a mutual understanding that is often tacit and unspoken. I first met him in the hallway of our college dorm as I was moving in. Alonso, another *tico*, introduced us. Luis smiled, shook my hand, and quickly asked me if I played *fútbol*. I answered "¡sí!" enthusiastically, explaining that in Costa Rica I had played in the minor divisions of a professional club, my beloved *Club Deportivo Saprissa*, besides playing for my elementary- and high-school teams. That's when I learned that he'd played for the *Club Sport Cartaginés* in Costa Rica's first-division. Luis claimed that he could tell I played football by my stride. I thought there must be something to it, since I'd also recognized something in him distinctive of a *futbolista*, perhaps the deliberate, measured spring in his bow-legged gait. Be that as it may, I did recognize quickly that we could be friends. And on that college field in Arkansas, I learned to admire his elegance, gracefulness, agility, and creativity with the ball. He would dominate the midfield with his skill, dribbling, passing, and vision. Only Bornwell could challenge him for control of midfield by playing a very different style of *fútbol*—fast, strong, direct. When I was on the opposing side of a friendly match, I tried to mark Luis effectively and persistently. I managed to challenge him, to force him to raise his skill significantly. But I knew he had an edge over me in skill which I could only try to overcome with my tenacity. Occasionally, we would go together to the field simply to pass the ball, run together, and even try to dribble and mark each other playing a one-on-one game. Those one-on-ones were intense, well-disputed, and the catalyst of unspoken, tacit understanding regarding not only how each other played but also each other's affective dispositions.

During that summer there were many friendships to be fostered and a lot of fun to be had *en la cancha*, even if sometimes the friendly matches got heated. I, who was eighteen years old and had little self-awareness on the field, in fact completely lost my temper one afternoon over what I perceived to be poor play by my teammates. I was yelling and demanding better passing, more cohesive movements. Playing forward, I thought I was moving well into open spaces, but the right pass wasn't coming from midfield. Víctor, the talented *chapín*, kept hogging the darn ball. When yet another pass did not come to me as he dribbled in midfield, I yelled at him in exasperation: "*¡Pasámela, güevón!*" He was a senior student, more mature and even married, and lost his patience with me. He just wanted to have fun, not win a meaningless match. "*Callate, me tenés harto,*" he screamed to shut me up, and we got into an argument. But after the game was over, we quickly forgot it. I thought of him as a kind, level-headed person, and I knew I had been the hot-head. And so the summer passed.

When the fall semester came, it was time for the interuniversity club tournament in Arkansas. Club teams from any university could sign up; in fact, there could be several clubs per college, though that was rare. The tournament was organized as a round-robin with home and away games between each pair of clubs. A victory counted for two points, a draw for one. The club with the most points at the end of the round-robin won the championship. In the two years prior to my arrival, a rivalry had been established between our club, made up mainly of *centroamericanos*, and the club team at the University of Arkansas at Little Rock, whose line-up was almost exclusively composed of Arab students. The teams had disputed the championship both years, and each team had taken one title. The upcoming season, then, offered the chance to establish which club was the better one. Of course, this was all a matter of youthful pride, because neither club really had any support from the universities. "Soccer" was still of little interest to colleges in Arkansas, and those of us who played did it out of love and paid for our own uniforms, rides, referees, and so on. For foreign students with little or no income, this was not easy—it was a labor of love; or rather, it was play out of love.

So we started playing. One Saturday we'd host a team; the next, we'd travel to play away. We'd borrow some cars, squeeze in and pack them full of our stuff, and ride. For the first game of the season, the academic director of our scholarship program helped us to borrow an old station wagon, probably from the 1970s, that was property of the university. We started driving away to Arkadelphia, but the wagon was so overloaded on the back with us and our stuff that on the highway it began to veer and slide, from right to left, from left to right, and back. Foolishly, we kept driving for a few minutes, until we realized that eventually we'd have an accident if we kept going. We drove back to campus, now worried we'd have to forfeit. But we solved the problem. One of us begged a roommate to borrow an additional car in order to distribute people and weight, and we went on the road again. We arrived safely and just in time, full of expectation and hoping to beat the club at Ouachita Baptist.

Bornwell, however, had withdrawn from the team. I'd heard that the year when our club had won the title against the Arabs from UALR, Bornwell and Luis had played together in midfield, combining dribbling with passing, attacking with tough marking, while César, another Costa Rican who'd just graduated and left, had been an effective forward. During his college years, in fact, César, who was tall, wiry, and strong, had displayed such a powerful left-footed shot, that the coach of the American football team had tried to recruit him to be the kicker of punts and field-goals. César refused because he would've had to forfeit his academic scholarship, and he had chosen to play fine association football (soccer) instead. But now he was gone also. And so our season did not begin well.

In the first half, we were surprised by a goal from Ouachita Baptist on an error by our defense. One of their midfielders kicked a long, wild ball forward, but David, our tall, strong, but slow Jamaican central defender, did not control it properly. A speedy forward stole the ball from him and outran him to score on Noel in our goal. I was playing left-winger and was frustrated by the mistake on the back but sought to play near Luis on midfield to see if we could muster something offensively together. We tried all game long, failing, until near the end of the game, he dribbled two defensive midfielders and advanced toward the area. I was running ahead of him to his left, along the gap in between their central defender and right-back. As the central defender stepped up to mark him, Luis was able to slip the ball past him, leaving me face to face with the goalkeeper, a tall, blond, thick-set guy. He charged toward the ball, but I barely beat him to it, lifting it gently over him and into the net. I was a bit stunned that I'd been able to get the ball past him. So I did not react. It was as if the play had developed in slow motion, and so my reaction was also delayed. The yelps of my teammates, who ran toward me, finally spurred me into joy. David embraced me, lifted me up, and flashing a wide smile on his thickly bearded face, said, "Thank you!" I seized upon this detail because no one had ever *thanked* me for a goal. But I think he'd felt responsible for the early mistake and now felt relief. We could go home with a 1–1 tie in an away game—an acceptable way to begin the season, the hope of improving left intact.

We did not improve much that season, however. In spite of Luis's leadership, we kept playing mediocre games, mostly tying and occasionally winning, but not convincingly. I scored a few more goals as winger but did not really influence the overall performance of the team as much as I would have liked—or rather, as I dreamed I would, since I still had the imagination of a boy who wants to win the big game for his team. We did not win the big game either. We lost to the Arabs at UALR, who clearly outplayed us, and we finished in third place for the season.

Our joy, then, consisted not in winning, but in traveling and simply *playing* together. Our Saturday trips to small towns such as Conway, Arkadelphia, Clarksville, or Siloam Springs provided a chance to see, beyond other colleges and campuses, the state and its people, especially at diners and roadside family restaurants when we could afford a stop. We also had the chance to get to know one another on the road and off the field. *El gordo* Francisco and Ricardo *el pana* were the comedians; Noel, quiet and intellectual; Luis, good-humored but socially aware, a defiant Afro-Latino in the South; all of us, young, friendly, and adventurous. Then the season ended. The cool air of late fall turned chilly, and since even an Arkansas winter was too cold for us then, we would not play again, even informal *mejengas*, until springtime. Then came summer school and the late afternoon games in the heat and humidity. By the time summer ended, we were ready for a new season. Luis, Ricardo, and Noel would be seniors, I a sophomore. The promising *Catracho*—tall, lean, strong—had arrived to play defensive midfield. We thought we had a chance to win again. We wanted to play.

That season, however, everything changed. "Soccer" was becoming more popular among United Statesians. Their national team had qualified to the FIFA World Cup in 1990. Students who'd played in high school were looking increasingly for chances to continue playing. And so a group of *gringo* kids from our college had decided to found their own club team to play in the tournament. They called it Rogues. And, as time would show, what a bunch of damn rogues they were.

Hard as I try to remember, I do not know how or why exactly the segregation started. When I arrived, the university's club had been around a long time, and it had such an unimaginative English name, Kickers. It was made up almost entirely of foreign students, but this seemed to be because only foreigners were interested in playing association football. So I do not know why it was that the *gringos* started their own club. Did we exclude them? Was our team a clique? Did they feel uneasy among foreigners? Or were they simply not interested in mixing with us? I am not sure, though I am confident that if we excluded them it was unintentional—perhaps the bond of friendship through shared experiences as foreigners created a clique that could seem impenetrable to others. At the same time, most of those guys had grown up in the suburban or rural South. They were white, protestant, and affluent by US standards but superrich and privileged by worldwide ones. However, they probably had not had much contact with foreigners while growing up. They may have been unaccustomed to interacting with people from other cultures. Maybe these conjectures explain why everything happened. Or maybe I am grasping for reasons to understand passions.

On my second season our team was again a disappointment. We won some games, tied others, lost a couple. *El Catracho* and Luis made a fine defensive-offensive pair in midfield; I improved in my second year as winger, though sometimes I joined the pair in midfield; Noel remained a reliable keeper; Ricardo *el pana* displayed sporadic flashes of creative ingenuity as forward; and that was about it. Our defense was a disaster again. On one of our first games, we allowed two goals within the first ten minutes. Frustrated, I dropped all the way back to play full-back and asked the full-back to move to center so we could play with three central defenders. I thought it was a fine idea to avoid further damage and regroup at half-time. But this year we had a coach, a kind Arkansas man with experience coaching high school, and he pulled me out. I had actually kicked a couple of fine shots at goal early in the game and was outraged at him: "*They* make the mistakes, and you pull *me* out!" I yelled. I thought I was so important and smart and righteous. Not only was I a fine winger; I was a strategic genius. But he calmly explained that since I no longer was pushing up offensively and had stayed back, he simply thought I was injured. He was standing on the opposite sideline and could not tell why I had dropped back. He disarmed my stupid outrage with his calmness and humbled me. He was right. He was our coach. I had no reason to accuse him after unilaterally changing our tactics within the field without consulting him or suggesting it. At the end of the game, I apologized to him and shook his hand. Our team lost the game, but we recovered our form to tie or win others.

The first time we played the Rogues that season, in fact, we won decisively. I want to say that we trashed them 4–0, but I am not sure I remember correctly. It may just be the passions informing memory, as they often do. I do know we outplayed them and won fairly. Luis had a particularly fine game, once again dominating midfield with elegance and gracefulness and scoring a couple of goals. But on our second match of the season against the Rogues, I came face to face, for the first time in such explicit ways, with a nasty aspect of living as a foreigner in *la Yunai*. Enmity between our clubs had grown after the first match. The Rogues had been frustrated for losing, and we had taken pleasure in beating them on the field. Up to that point, though, I thought it was merely a sporting rivalry—intense, competitive, passionate, but in the end respectful, not hateful, of the rivals and their dignity. But I was wrong.

It was the custom in that tournament that the home team would hire the referees from the overseeing federation. This time the Rogues were the home team and hired the referees. The game started. From the beginning, it was hotly disputed, aggressive, physically rough, more heart than brains. We could not get our passing game going; they were pressing us hard and counter-attacking fast. One thing I've always found about *gringo* players is that they run tirelessly, like track-and-field athletes, all game long. They are persistent, energetic, and committed to the match, so they force you to play until the last minute to beat them. But I also thought the referee was being quite permissive with their rough style of marking. Some of our players were getting frustrated. Then they scored. *¡Qué madre!* They were overwhelming us in midfield, so I dropped back from left wing and into midfield to try some give-and-gos with Luis, filter passes in between defenders to Ricardo up-front, and help *el Catracho* with marking. The coach let us try this, and it worked. We tied the game.

But this time the Rogues were relentless and playing better than ever before. And they were not all rogue-ness. They had two Brians who were exceptional. One—dark-haired, short, thick-set, and strong-legged, like Diego Maradona minus the curls—played right-fullback. I knew his style well because I confronted him several times as left-winger. He always marked me fairly though tenaciously. He also had a neat passing game, good vision of possibilities for play in the field ahead of him, and he could run up the line fast in counterattack. When I dropped back and into the middle from the wing, he found an open corridor to advance along the right sideline. The other one, Brian P.—curled dirty-blond hair, taller, his proportional build approaching the Greek athletic ideal—was a talented midfielder who could both mark defensively and explode offensively with dribbling and passing. No doubt he had been a standout player in his high school in Birmingham, Alabama. I knew them both a bit from playing informal games on campus, and I respected them on and off the field. We had never conversed, but

I always greeted and acknowledged them when I saw them around. This afternoon in particular they were playing fine football for their team. The Alabaman scored. *¡Qué sal!* They were beating us again.

The first half ended. During half-time, we tried to regroup. But some of my friends were growing in frustration at their roughness and the referee's complacency. He'd even overlooked a foul in the penalty area. Ricardo and Luis, in particular, had been fouled hard by their central defender. We knew he was dirty. That was his game—no style, no elegance, no marking fairly, no passing to start building his team's play; only speed, strength, roughness. His approach to every play was to tackle the rival and kick the fucking ball away. When refs are permissive, though, this can work. And it was working. We were losing our cool. And so we wasted the half-time, I thought, complaining about the situation rather than thinking about how to win. Then again, I was not the one getting hammered. Luis was already limping.

The second half started. Play was broken often by fouls and balls kicked out of bounds. Luis got hammered again. No call. His limp grew worse, but he stayed on the field. On the sideline, the Rogues' substitutes had started their taunting: "Go back home! Get back to Mexico! No more *Menudo*! This is America!" They were surrounded by their friends and girlfriends, who laughed and celebrated their provocations. They looked at us with furious eyes and spiteful grins. I was at once bewildered, amused, and enraged— bewildered because I had never experienced a sporting rivalry which had become so adversarial that players *themselves* became hooligans; amused because I could not believe they all were so stupid as not to know that Central America is not Mexico and that *Menudo* was a boy band from Puerto Rico that no self-respecting *centroamericano* would ever listen to; enraged because I understood at once who they were when their social masks came off.

Yet we all kept playing hard and well. After several minutes and much sweating, we scored. Luis got a pass near the half-moon outside the penalty area and shot hard and low just inside the post to the keeper's right-hand side: 2–2. We were ecstatic. I ran along the sideline, in front of the Rogue subs, to celebrate the goal with our friends. We quickly talked to each other on the field. Now we were even and could play a bit more calmly, move the ball around the field and let them chase it. They could not run forever.

Then disaster happened. Only a couple of minutes later, they advanced, a forward chased the ball in the penalty area, our defender came to mark him, and, it seemed to me, their forward dived. So it seemed to all of us. But the referee called a penalty kick. Then half of my teammates lost their temper completely. They charged the referee, surrounding him to challenge the call. The referee was impassive and would not call back the penalty, of course. I was frustrated but thought that even if they scored we could draw even again. Many of my *Kickers*, though, started to say we should leave the field in protest. Luis and *el Catracho* were especially adamant. Luis, in particular, felt the injustice burning inside him. I thought we should stay and play the match, even if it was unfair. Noel, in the goal, was always calm and conciliatory and tried to be the diplomat among us. Our team imploded. Half of my teammates walked away, leaving the field. Then, in frustration, I exploded and yelled at my friends: "*No se vayan, cobardes.*" I called them cowards. Luis tolerated me and just walked away. But *el Catracho* felt offended. He came back and swung a fist at me. I was stunned. Others grabbed him and carried him away. Our fans and friends had walked onto the field to calm us down. Tania, a Sino-Guatemalan friend, was crying. I felt sad for her, regret for what I'd just yelled, anger at the redneck Rogues. I stayed on the field with Noel. But the game was over. We'd lost by forfeit.

The Rogues ran to celebrate with their sub players and friends. Then they all, even the Brians, started chanting more loudly: "Go back home! Damn Mexico! No more *Menudo*!" I observed them from a distance, adding moments of detached disbelief to those of anger and bewilderment. They derided us under the bright lit sky on the soft, grassy field. Their venomous chants seemed so out of place on a quiet, windless Arkansas afternoon meant for play. Their aggressive, spiteful, arrogant, and unapologetic chants stung all of us. "Such loving Christians they are," I thought with irony. Only Lenny, a tall redhead with a gentle heart, a perennial sub, tried to discourage his teammates.

I do not remember what happened next. In the last moment I can recall, I stood on the field, watching Tania cry, my Kickers leaving angry and indignant, and the Rogues disgracing themselves in that far edge of campus where they felt immune from moral accountability. They were not at an early morning chapel service, an evening devotional, or Sunday morning church service, where they could be seen and judged. They were at a far-off *fútbol* field where the only witnesses, besides their friends who said nothing to stop them, were the foreigners they despised.

I must have returned to my dorm to shower, must have had dinner at the cafeteria, must have gone walking or to a movie on campus, and a Sunday I cannot remember must have come and gone. I must have gone to church. All the Rogues must have gone to church also to worship their Lord, wearing suits and ties, with their girlfriends in long, flowery dresses.

Then during the Monday morning chapel service, which all the students were required to attend, the daily campus announcements were given. To my surprise, the student who made them reported the result of the weekend club "soccer" game, congratulating the Rogues. But results had never before been reported; this was the first time such an announcement was made during chapel. Those guys also controlled the media! Well, just the campus gossip, I guess. They must have known the students in charge of announcements, or they went to the president's office, where requests for announcements could be made. I did not feel stung, though. Neither did my friends. I just thought they were such petty, small-minded pieces of shit. We moved on. It was, after all, Monday, and our studies would now continue anyway.

The experience left a profound mark, however. Luis was limping for days because of the violent fouls he received. Even weeks later he told me, "*yo creo que ese mae me jodió.*" That hack, the Rogue central defender, had injured him seriously, and his foot would not heal. But what could Luis do? Our insurance did not cover sporting injuries, and he could not afford diagnosis and treatment on his $100 monthly stipend. The Rogues' behavior reopened an emotional wound. His ex-girlfriend was white and southern, and her relationship with him, an Afro-Latino, had not been acceptable to some of her friends and family. He had felt racial and cultural rejection in his skin, flesh, blood, bones, and soul. He had a keen sense of injustice, and that's why he'd perceived quickly that the referee himself was deliberately unfair. And Luis carried himself with dignity—he embodied righteous indignation when necessary and knew when to leave a site of injustice. That's why he'd walked off the field.

In my sensible heart I stood by my decision to stay on the field to play against the Rogues and ref and injustice, but my respect for Luis also made me wonder whether my friends had been right. The Rogues' blatant behavior opened my eyes to the more subtle workings of prejudice and injustice on campus, in Arkansas, and in *la Yunai.* I saw in the clear light of the *fútbol* field a revelation of hateful sentiments that usually lay hidden in the dark. In that sense, Luis had been ahead of me—his experiences had sharpened his sagacity. He'd understood quickly what was happening on that field and decided to wipe the dust off his feet. I was only beginning to understand it.

Today I see more clearly that Luis was familiar with various social, cultural, and political obstacles that can disrupt or entangle immigrants' lives in their new places. American philosopher Lara Trout helps me articulate this issue. Developing Charles Peirce's thought in sociopolitical directions, she calls this general category of obstacles "social secondness," that is, "socially dictated environmental resistance."[1] This is environmental resistance due to "social conventions that are largely outside of one's control."[2] Her definition is based on the category of experience that involves reaction and resistance, and that is usually associated with physical or biological environmental resistance but need not be circumscribed that way, even for Peirce. In our social milieu at that time and place, for example, social convention dictated that *everyone* should speak English in public. Speaking in a foreign language, especially in front of English speakers, was subtly censured as transgression of a social norm. Sometimes social obstacles are directed at specific groups of people. Thus, Trout defines "sociopolitical secondness" as "social secondness that is not encountered equally by all members of society … [but rather] involves constraint that is directed at non-hegemonic groups. It includes prejudice and discrimination based on factors such as economic class, race, sex, sexuality, and so on."[3] When people of a specific ethnic or economic background are denied opportunities for education or employment due to social norms or even systematic policies they are experiencing "sociopolitical secondness."[4] In other words, these are the difficulties and roadblocks that members of oppressed groups face due to social norms and conditions, while members of other groups do not face them. They may even be unaware that such obstacles exist because they don't experience them personally. As an Afro-Latino, for example, Luis had had to confront subtle censure and insidious rejection in order to date a white girl from Arkansas. As a team of Latino *fútbol* players in a southern college tournament, we faced a hostile team and a collaborating referee who were determined to keep us from winning on the football field *because* we were Latinos. Sporting competition involves playing your best and, in so doing, aiming to win as a consequence. But the Rogues were not aiming to play their best; they were trying to defeat the Latino kids at all costs.

The question for us at that time was how to confront injustice rooted in prejudice. I wanted to stay on the field, play on, beat those jerks—especially that hack on defense—or at least lose knowing we were losing to only the referee and not to them. But Luis, *El Catracho*, and others decided it was better to walk away with dignity. No rivalry on the field could ever justify those *gringos'* conduct, and as the referee was himself an agent of injustice, it was better to leave that place. It was not essential to fight the good fight there and then. Were my friends wiser than I was? Prudential reason today tells me yes; it was only a game in a far-off field in the South. The game was becoming violent, and we stood the greater chances of suffering the harsher injuries, since we were players and not hackers. But my sensible heart is still playing on that field, fighting on. It has never walked away. In articulating this nowadays, I appeal to Charles Peirce's ethical sentimentalism, that is, "the doctrine that great respect should be paid to the natural judgments of the sensible heart."[5] My heart is an organ of affective perception—of perceiving and interpreting situations of vital importance and of guiding my conduct in such matters—that freely offers me its counsel. I should be attuned to and respect that counsel, even if sometimes other reasons may lead me along a different course of action. In terms of my concrete experience, I felt in my innermost core that I needed to stay on the field and play. My heart told me that, and I felt it in my body. The hearts of Luis and *el Catracho* had different sentiments; they felt they must walk away. I should have respected that. But it was just as important that I respected my own sentiment to stay on the field and play against the Rogues.

I never got a chance to discuss any of this with my friends, however. The team died. *El Catracho* never again spoke to me. We were together at the college for three more years, and he never did once care to acknowledge me. It was as if by calling him a coward I had injured his manhood irreparably. He appeared so hermetically sealed off from me that I never saw a chance to apologize. I should have tried anyway; I should have created the chance. I felt the impulse to seek forgiveness and reconciliation, but failed to follow through. I dug into my own stubborn hubris, thinking myself to be above his silly *machismo*. I never knew, then, what he thought of the episode with the Rogues or what his conclusions were. A friendship that had begun for play had ended in strife. We had reacted differently to adversity, and in this case our own immaturity, pride, and pettiness got in the way. I failed to sow seeds of loveliness in the hateful.

That must have been the last game of the season because I cannot remember any other matches after that one. The team disappeared. The following year there were no *Kickers*. Noel, Luis, and Ricardo had graduated, and I, now a junior, went away to study in Florence. That pause was healthy; I forgot about rednecks in "soccer" fields, as I'd begun to think of those *gringo* boys.

During my senior year Lenny, the gentle redhead, invited me to play with a club he had started. He'd left the Rogues. I don't know if it was because he was fed up with their attitude or because he didn't play much. He wanted a more balanced, level-headed team, and I agreed to play. I cannot remember the name of the club. It wasn't important to me. It was not dear to my heart, like the Kickers had been. I just played left full-back and enjoyed it. We were not very good, had no competitive ambition, and as a result were much more relaxed and playful. We even played against the Rogues and lost. But even that mattered little to me. My struggle had begun—hateful seeds had been sown on our college's smooth, green field, and I longed for grace.

Yet, though I did not care for their team, I saw that "Maradona" Brian had developed into a well-balanced defensive and attacking full-back along the right sideline, while Brian P. continued to play fine *fútbol* on midfield with even more discerning vision than before. Then, at the end of the year, a final and tacit reconciliation happened, at least for me. We were all seniors. For graduation, my parents came to Arkansas for the first and only time during my years as student in the United States. One evening, we went out to dinner at a local restaurant, and on our way out I saw both Brians dining together with some friends. I approached and greeted them, and I introduced my parents to them. As southern gentlemen, they stood up, smiled, and talked to us. They did not speak Spanish and my parents little English. But I translated the brief, friendly exchange. Then we left. That was the last time I ever saw them, smiling at my parents who'd come to visit from Central America. In the end they were respectful to us, and that gesture helped me to forgive completely. I have at times in my life been very painfully aware of the need to be forgiven when I can offer no reparation, and for that reason I also have tried to offer forgiveness even when it has not been requested. I never told my parents what had happened two years earlier with "them Brians" on the football pitch. It was past, and there was grace. After strife, we could find seeds of loveliness.

HARDSHIP AND FRIENDSHIP WITH THE
BENITO CAMELAS FÚTBOL CLUB

The experiences in Arkansas had opened nonconscious affective wounds that grew deeper and more painful over the years that followed, however. After graduating from college in Arkansas, I accepted an assistantship to pursue graduate studies in Pennsylvania. I moved north because I wanted to live in a new region of *la Yunai*. I earned a master's degree in statistics and then worked for a software company. On Sundays, for fun, I played in an amateur "soccer" league with the Philipsburg Strikers, a team from Central Pennsylvania. As far as I could tell, Sunday was the only time during the week most of my teammates played a sport or exercised. They were middle-aged, married, and had children, so playing with the Strikers gave them an excuse to get away on Sunday afternoons, play a game, and then have beer and pizza at one of the local pubs. The pub was the team's "sponsor" because the guys knew the pub's owner and were regular patrons. So the pub bought us the jerseys and provided us with a few pizzas each Sunday after the game; we bought a couple pitchers of beer, and everyone was happy—so happy that I actually suspected the guys enjoyed the beer and pizza afterward more than the games themselves; we were awful on the pitch due to poor physical shape and lost most of the games.

With the Strikers, though, I was capable of enjoying the fellowship of *fútbol* games. During the work week I looked forward to seeing those guys for a *mejenga*, a pint, and a slice. On Sunday afternoons I'd drive along the beautiful forested mountains of Central Pennsylvania, vibrating with the anticipation of entering the field, playing as well as we could—even if that wasn't much—and then heading to the pub to talk about the match, sports, and the town. In such conversations glimpses of my teammates' lives emerged—I'd see them as husbands, parents, uncles, friends, teachers, hunters, workers; I'd hear of people they loved, difficulties they confronted, hopes they cherished, friends they missed. It mattered very little, then, that I'd grown up so far from there, loving people, confronting difficulties, and cherishing hopes so different from theirs. It was enough to play together and then have our own kind of symposium before they went home to their families in town and I drove back on the winding roads along the same mountains and forests at dusk.

During most of my two years at the software company, I was the only foreign worker. And I was the only foreign Striker. As far as I knew I was nearly the only foreigner in the whole league, except for a team made up of migrant agricultural workers who harvested crops in Central and Eastern Pennsylvania. The Strikers played against them once. There were many Mexicans and also several Central Americans, especially Nicaraguans, on the team. They did not play very well; we actually won that game. But they had fun together, and it had been a relief for me to hear and speak Spanish with them in a *cancha* in rural Pennsylvania. After the game I stayed on the field talking as long as possible—even as the sun descended on the horizon and the coolness of autumn amid the mountains began to bite—asking them as much as I could about their peoples and places at home and leaving unspoken our reasons for being in *la Yunai*. A *nica* midfielder, who probably was a great baseball outfielder, and I spoke of eating *tamales* and *gallo pinto*, of savoring *guayabas*, of listening to *marimbas*, and my heart beat to the rhythm of nostalgia. Perhaps a sense of cultural isolation was beginning to weigh on me more than I could consciously ponder.

When I enrolled in graduate school again, I most earnestly sought the company of Latin American students, and this was true on and off the *fútbol* fields. Even before returning, I had met some *latinoamericanos* at pick-up games at the university. One late afternoon, playing at a rugby field turned *cancha de fútbol*, I met Ariel. He was tall, thick-set, and had long black hair and a scruffy beard in the style of 1980s rock stars and Argentinean *futbolistas*. For some reason I have never understood, Argentinean football players are stuck in a bad time warp—they like to look like members of hair-bands from the 1980s, and Ariel had just that look. By his style and gestures I guessed he was an Argentine, but I was not sure as I could not identify his mellifluous accent. It turned out that he was from Córdoba, not Buenos Aires, and spoke in the characteristic musical way of a *cordobés*, almost singing the last syllable of each word. Later I'd find out he was a fantastic guitar player and singer. So *fútbol*, music, Argentine style—all these elements explained his look.

Another time, playing a one-day tournament at the university, I had met Martín, from Peru. Also tall, but thin and dark-skinned, he was a fine left-footed forward. We somehow had been recruited to play on the same team, and we made a fine pair playing along the left side of the field. Perhaps it was cultural footballing affinity. Peruvians have an elegant way of playing by controlling the ball and moving it around with short, precise passes, building the play carefully until they create an opportunity to score; Costa Ricans, in our own measure, often aspire to this style also, and I thought Martín and I had attempted to play in just this way. Our team lost, but we understood each other on the field.

When I officially re-entered school, I ran into Ariel and Martín again at a regular pick-up game (I called it a *mejenga*, Ariel a *picadito*, Martín a *pichanguita*) every Saturday morning at the high school field near the university. In those weekly games I soon met Fernando, Gerardo, César, and *Meque*, all from Argentina, and one year later, Manuel from Uruguay. Fernando was a tough defensive midfielder with a lot of *maña*; César, a quick, fast-dribbling forward who could double as right-winger; Gerardo a fine goalkeeper who made up for slowing reflexes with good positioning and play anticipation; *Meque* a disciplined, effective offensive midfielder; and Manuel, in my opinion the best *futbolista* of all of us, an intelligent, elegant *zurdo* who could control the midfield with clean marking and precise passing or anchor the team and organize it from central defense with the whole field in front of him. Playing together on Saturday mornings, with many other graduate students from *la Yunai* and all over the world, we began to forge friendships.

A few weeks into that first fall semester, we decided to form a team for the university's intramural tournament. It was to be played on small outdoor fields, seven on seven. Gerardo, Ariel, Fernando, Martín, *Meque*, César, and I could field a team, but we needed a few more members. The rules allowed for unlimited substitutions, so we needed to have enough players to rotate and keep up the intensity of play, especially because we were all graduate students and we'd be playing mainly against undergraduates with better physical fitness. From our Saturday *mejengas* we invited Ralph, a German friend with a Latin American heart; Danny, an Englishman who played fine and firm defense; and two United Statesians, Bryan and Brandon. Bryan was a steady runner and a good sport, though not a very skilled player. Brandon, however, was a fantastic center forward—he had a fine vision for finding gaps and moving into them with speed, a quick short dribble to get out of defensive jams and create angles for shooting or passing, and a strong shot from close range.

We had our team. But we needed a name. When a few of us went to the organizational meeting for the tournament, where rules would be explained and teams signed-up, we did not know what to name the team. Then Fernando suggested "Benito Camelas." We burst out laughing at the well-known, saucy play on words, based on the use in most of Central America as well as Argentina and Uruguay of the pronoun "*vos*" instead of "*tú*." At first we thought we couldn't, but as the meeting came to an end and we filled up the sheet with all the players' information, we couldn't come up with a different team name. We tried to search for other names, but laughter didn't let us think, and we drew a blank. Finally we let it be our inside joke: English speakers would probably think of Benito Camelas as a proper name and would never hear it in *español centroamericano* or *rioplatense* as "*vení tocámelas.*" It was an immature male joke, but we used it to mark the team's character as a group of friends—mostly students sharing a common culture and language and the experience of being foreign—trying to have fun together and make life away from home a bit lighter and more joyful.

At least that was the intention. But we also wanted to play *fútbol* well and win, and we each understood these ends—joyful play and competitive winning—a bit differently from one another. Fernando wanted to win using *maña*—toughness, disguised fouling, subtle provocation, breaking of concentration, and the like—alongside talent and skill. César wanted to be a purist of the beautiful game and of fairness; in discourse he defended the highest ideals of the best conception of our sport, but in the field he was not above resorting to the same *mañas* as Fernando to aid our victory. In thought I defended the ancient ideals of beauty and goodness and the virtue of self-control but also contradicted myself in action by resorting to strategic defensive fouling and roughness when provoked to it. *Meque* was half-Swiss and wanted to play strictly by the written rules, without tricks to fool referees or arguments with the opponents. Martín, as a quintessential Peruvian, concerned himself with offense exclusively and did not worry much about defense. It would take us a while, then, to find our team's ethos.

In the days before the first game, we behaved like children, dreaming of playing for a big championship. We spent quite a bit of time imagining and discussing how we'd play together. We even practiced a bit in the midst of our studies. Though we strategized together we needed a leader to make some decisions, especially the tough ones of who would start and get most playing time. We named Fernando team captain, and in the end this set the tone for the *Benito Camelas F.C.* Over time we developed an ethos *rioplatense*; we played to win based on skill and technique, aiming mostly for offensive team play, but were not above resorting to defensive toughness and tactical *mañas* to get the job done.

When the first game finally came, we were excited and a bit nervous. I had played with far more organized teams in more serious tournaments, but this time the nervous anticipation felt more intense than ever before. I don't know why it should have been so. Perhaps because I felt more connected by friendship to these guys than I had to prior teammates? Perhaps because they'd decided I should play as creative midfielder, the Benito's number 10, a position I had never played before? When the game started, though, nervousness turned to joy, expectation to action, and dreaming to imaginative performance. We played fine, not great, but won. Afterward, we analyzed everything, discussed what we should do to improve, but also joked about our boneheaded mistakes.

The *gringos* Brandon and Bryan probably thought we were crazy, but Bryan tolerated us, and Brandon actually enjoyed our ways. He'd use his basic Spanish to talk, argue, and joke with us before, during, and after the games. Ralph, however, soon grew tired of us. He did not find our humor, our pre-game talks, our half-time arguments, and our post-game joking, teasing, and "analyses" amusing. And he particularly objected to the tactical *mañas* that our captain Fernando advocated. So, after a couple of games, he did not return to play. And Danny, who had completed his PhD, soon got a job and moved away.

We kept playing, though, and for the level of that intramural league, we played well. We won mostly by skill, technique, and a bit of shrewdness, even though usually the other teams were more physically fit. Along the way to the playoff rounds, we played a couple of closely contested games. One was against a team of Spanish and Latin American undergraduate students. They were as *mañosos* as we were, but much to their chagrin we outplayed them. In the end they were sore losers and sought a scuffle, but there was no arguing with the score. We could simply walk away. A rivalry emerged, but it was mostly a sporting one. The other game was against a fine club of *gringo* players. We knew their captain, Josh, from our Saturday *mejengas*, and so we called them *the Joshes*. They had played "soccer" for their high schools throughout Pennsylvania and had put together a fine team for the intramural tournament. We played a hard, intense but fair match against them, with some *maña* but without violence on either side. This was all fine—teams playing intensely, trying their best, testing each other's skills, even challenging each other's wits, coolness, and level-headedness.

There were also mean and ugly situations, however, and they usually arose unprovoked from less skilled teams primarily made up of frat boys. I can't remember anymore the order or timing of the nasty episodes; I just have a strong affective memory of the anger they caused. Once we were a few minutes late for a game, and the rivals chided, "In America we start on time!" As we proceeded to trash them by playing, they talked trash about us to each other. Another time it was the familiar and repetitive talking like "Speedy González" to each other: *Ándale, ándale, arriba, arriba.* Another time it was a "Go home!" yelled in frustration from the sidelines, just like the Rogues years before.

Some of my friends could laugh with scorn; others kept their heads cool and above the fray. For my part, in that first tournament I kept my marking strictly clean, did not argue, and simply played my best; however, a mix of angry indignation and dread, planted in my heart over the years on *fútbol* fields in *la Yunai*, continued to grow. I demanded respect and won it efficiently on the pitch, but I also felt increasing dread at being surrounded everywhere, not only on the field, by bullies who came to epitomize my idea of a *gringo*.

Over the next couple of years—as Brandon's graduation left us without our best goal scorer, Manuel arrived to anchor the team; I failed as creative midfielder and moved back to play defense alongside Ariel; Fernando moved up from defense to defensive midfield; Gerardo finished his postdoctoral research and returned to Argentina; Doug replaced him in the goal; César moved to a teaching position in Ohio; and my Ivorian friend Senin, a strong, thick-set forward who controlled the ball with ease, keeping it seemingly tied to his foot as he dribbled, and who shot on goal with strength and precision, joined us—the *Benito Camelas F.C.* played fine intramural *fútbol*, reached every championship match, and lost every single one of them in the second half due to lack of fitness. *Fuimos eternos subcampeones.* We were comparatively old and getting older, though not necessarily wiser.

As *gringo* stupidity continued, I grew more indignant, lost my temper more easily, and fouled violently more often. After each violent confrontation, regret would overcome me, and I'd aim for self-control again. Until finally, on a clear, crisp night when a whole team imitated *Speedy González* and one of its forwards spent the entire game trash-talking, I lost self-control and launched feet first into the nastiest play of my life.

As all of this happened, my conflict with *gringo* culture increasingly vexed me. Why shouldn't I identify this culture, on the *fútbol* field and off, with my friends Brandon, Brian, and Doug rather than with nameless frat boy jerks? Take Doug, for example—born and raised in a small New England town among tough, hard-working folks; educated in the liberal arts and philosophy; a kind teacher capable of engaging the mind and heart of his students; and a runner, basketballer, baseballer, aspiring *futbolista*, and all around sportsperson—he was the paragon of a reasonable and sensible American. Or consider Brandon—he was a military man, a member of the R.O.T.C. on campus who aspired to be a Navy pilot, but I knew him as a friendly, smart guy with a curiosity for foreign languages and cultures. Why couldn't I let them, rather than a horde of bullies, be the exemplars of United Statesian "soccer" in my mind? Try as I did to appease my heart with such reflections, why did the angry indignation burn ever more intensely in my blood and bones so as to overcome me? Perhaps I was not open to the possibility of finding seeds of loveliness in the hateful—not only in the hatefulness of *gringo* prejudice but in the hardness of my own heart.

In the midst of all this conflict, my friendship with the "Benitos" provided me not only with refuge but even with joy. I knew equilibrium, prudence, and self-mastery should ultimately come from within. While I struggled to achieve them, it was a consolation to have a social context in which confrontation, whether subtle or strident, and its consequent defensiveness, were not the norm. As I interpret it now, *philia* helped to protect my heart from encroaching hardness.

Though our friendship sprang initially from our love of *fútbol*, it was fostered by our personal experiences and affinities. It began *en la cancha*, first playing *mejengas*, then founding a *fútbol club* for the sake of youthful joy, and finally developing an ethos for our team while sporting, competing, winning, losing, arguing, disagreeing, dreaming, and joking.

This ethos of mutual support, conversation, debate, and playful fellowship developed off the field as well. Soon after we became friends and founded the club, someone suggested we should get a satellite dish together to watch professional matches on weekends. Martín, who was always efficient at getting things done, found packages with sport channels, prices, and so on. Though we lived on graduate student stipends, we could all pitch in a few bucks and get the service. Our real problem: Who'd host the sessions? Spouses, partners, and girlfriends did not want any part of hosting a bunch of *hinchas* every Sunday afternoon. So it'd have to be one of the single guys hosting, and we ended up setting up the dish at Manuel *el Yorugua*'s apartment. His Argentinean roommate, *El Armenio* Vartanessian, a gentle-hearted engineer who did not care at all for *fútbol*, knew us well and liked us, so he agreed. So every Sunday afternoon we'd get together, usually to watch Argentinean matches narrated in *porteño* accent. Everything was fine at the club's headquarters for a while. Then Manuel got married in Uruguay. M came to Pennsylvania and moved in with him. Poor girl. Poor newlyweds. We should have respected the honeymoon year and offered to move the club's Sunday sessions elsewhere, but we had nowhere else to go. And so we said nothing, stayed put, and waited to be told to take our game-watching sessions away. Somehow they tolerated us, though, even to the point that sometimes they'd spend Sunday afternoons away from *their* apartment and let us stay watching.

We'd also have dinner together almost every weekend. *Las Benitas*—as we came to call our spouses and girlfriends when our enthusiasm for the team was a bit out of control—would be with us, sometimes along with other friends, mostly Latin-Americans and Spaniards. Ariel, we discovered over many dinners at his and Ana's apartment, had great talent in the kitchen and loved to cook anything from *empanadas* to gourmet dishes to *asado* on the grill, always accompanied by wines from Mendoza, usually a Malbec. Other times we'd enjoy Peruvian *ají de gallina* and *pizco* at Martín's place, or K's *cajun* dishes—jambalayas and gumbos especially—which brought an original touch from Louisiana to our culinary experiences.

As these dinners became symposia, our friendship grew. We shared experiences with each other. Ariel, driving on a weekend night, was stopped at a police roadblock for a routine sobriety test. He was stone-cold sober but, being flatfooted and becoming very nervous, managed to stumble while walking and ended up at the police station for a blood test. The results were negative, but should he get some official statement from the police? A graduate student concerned for his visa and his academic and personal future had to think about such things. César got a job offer in Ohio and pondered whether he should go. Martín's girlfriend would be coming from Peru to join him and study as well. My grandmother Dora died—the third painful death in my family, after my grandfather Enrique and my uncle Yique, since I'd left Costa Rica. César's father became ill. I pondered whether I should move from mathematics into philosophy. And so our stories went.

As international students in Central Pennsylvania, we shared some of our good and bad, significant and trivial, experiences of adaptation to *la Yunai*. Being from Latin America, we'd go to restaurants for deliberate eating and drinking and long *tertulias de sobremesa*—after-dinner conversations—often to find tasteless food and hurried, disgruntled service. One time at the Deli, a popular restaurant near the university, a waitress —probably a student herself—became so distressed that we spoke Spanish to one another and did not pay attention to her but to our conversation that she hit the table a few times with her hand and yelled to get our attention. This was so puzzling as to make us laugh and ponder if perhaps she had never been around many foreigners who behaved a bit differently and did not speak to each other in English. Sometime afterward at Faccia Luna Trattoria, while recalling this event, Ariel made some observations in English about life in the United States. He wondered why people were so resistant to learning, even hearing, other languages and why they seemed to know or care so little for learning about the world. Since K was a teacher, this led to a conversation about the deficiencies of the public education system. In a voice intended to be well heard, a man who was eavesdropping at a nearby table said to his wife, "Why don't they just go home?" I did not lose my cool this time, but I did not stay silent, and I addressed him directly: "We are just wondering, not attacking anything." His wife was horrified at my comment, probably considering me the rude one, but the man kept quiet. Another time we wanted to play our usual Saturday morning game with all our other football friends, mostly foreigners, at the local high school field. As we were beginning to play, a *gringo* came and told us we could not play because he would be using the field with some local kids. When we asked what gave him authority to decide, he said: "Because I pay taxes." The ignorant jackass did not know that foreign students paid all the same federal, state, and local taxes on their stipends as well. And thus continued the ugly rifts and annoying frustrations.

But we also met fine, gentle people in town, at games, or traveling together. Sometimes we'd drive on sunny afternoons during spring to visit Amish towns in Central Pennsylvania and admire their fine craftsmanship with wood at their shops, or on glorious summer days we'd grill *asados* at any

of the beautiful state parks. On a cool autumn weekend some of us traveled
to Tioga County to see the mountains, waterfalls, river, and forests at Pine
Creek Gorge, known as the Pennsylvania Grand Canyon. Along the way, we
ate good ole' hamburgers at a classic, authentic roadside diner. In Wellsboro,
near the gorge, we stayed at a family inn where the owners hosted us with
care and were happy to see students from far away visit their neck of the
Northern Pennsylvania woods. And as we walked in the woods, breathed the
crisp air, and heard the water running deep in the heart of the canyon, I felt
peace alongside people I loved.

Another weekend, we drove to Southwestern Pennsylvania to see *Falling
Water*, the beautiful house designed for the Kaufmann's by the American
architect Frank Lloyd Wright. I never have aspired to nor cared for wealth,
but at that house, looking at the creek and falls and woods as the water rushed
underneath, I felt such a tranquil joy—the sense of organic equilibrium, of
integration of the inward with the outward, that I was striving for in my
heart— that I thought if in a hypothetical world I were to become wealthy, it
would be to enjoy such a place for contemplating, reading, writing, walking,
and, mostly, loving and living. That sense of balanced joy stayed with me the
following day, when we drove from Bear Run to Pittsburgh to see the three
mighty rivers converging, the cityscape rising among them, and the Pirates
play baseball against my Cardinals. Many years after my first game in Saint
Louis, I saw the Cards play again, and again I felt joy to be in *la Yunai* with
people I cherished.

Besides experiences of rift or harmony in the land of the Yankees, we all
shared ideas, principles, dreams, and ideals. Between all of us, guys and girls,
Benitos and *Benitas*, there were sociologists, political scientists, economists,
historians, philosophers, literary critics, chemists, agronomists, engineers,
and biologists, and so we'd talk about our projects, our interests, our goals.
We also made fun of each other, or at least the guys, as the girls were exempt
from our relentless *choteo*—Fer stunk of cows and dung; Manolo chased
otters up and down rivers in the wilderness; César behaved as an ethical
sportsperson only on paper, not on the field; Martín was progressive only
in theory but aspired to the comforts of the aristocracy. We often talked and
argued about culture and politics and life in Argentina, Peru, Uruguay, Costa
Rica, and *la Yunai*. Some wanted to stay in *gringolandia*, others to return
home, everyone to contribute something, even a little bit, to our societies in
the form of science or letters or teaching or, quite simply, work and life. Some
were progressives, others liberals, one a conservative, others simply contrar-
ians, just as some were *hinchas* of *Boca Juniors*, while others rooted for *River
Plate* or *Rácing, Alianza Lima, Peñarol, Saprissa*.

What mattered—what really made a difference as we lived away from
home and family and friends—was our friendship: *philia* born of sporting

together but fostered by sympathy—literally "feeling-with" each other—and strengthened by true affinity or commonality of ends and goals and purposes. In the midst of those years as foreign students in *la Yunai*, this friendship sustained all of us in different ways.

AGAPISM AND *GRINGO* SOCCER

César was the first of us to leave the team and the university and went to teach in Ohio while finishing his thesis. Fernanda stayed to finish her degree, and then they moved together to tenure-track jobs at universities in upstate New York. The *Benito Camelas Fútbol Club* kept playing for a couple more seasons, but eventually we all graduated, moved away from Pennsylvania, and the club disappeared from the university's intramural fields, though not from our memories and hearts. Some of the club members left the United States, some stayed, some moved around. Ariel moved with Ana to Valencia, Spain, where they were offered research positions in their respective fields of atmospheric and soil chemistry. Fer went to Arizona but eventually returned to Argentina where he loved *el campo*, the countryside, in the province of Buenos Aires. Martín moved back to live in Lima and resume work as a sociologist at his research institute. Manolo went to Indiana where M studied for her doctoral degree. They moved then to Ohio and finally to research positions in wildlife management in Costa Rica. Their moving to jobs in research or teaching around the world was typical: Well-educated foreign students come to *la Yunai*, with their research and teaching keep this country's enormous system of research and higher education going, take advantage of the opportunities to learn and grow, and move on to advance science, letters, and the arts not only in *la Yunai* but all over the world. Most of the time it happens silently but persistently, while clueless frat boys get wasted weekend after weekend.

I was the last one to leave Pennsylvania. By then I felt culturally isolated in *la Yunai*, restless, and tired. Everywhere I looked, suffering from a kind of spiritual short-sightedness, I only saw *gringos*. It was time to leave for a good while. I found a research group with which I could work for a semester in Sao Paulo, Brazil, and moved.

Why did I go? In part I went for sauntering. But mostly I left because I was more wounded by all those years as an increasingly alienated foreigner in *la Yunai* than I could understand or process. Because of these wounds, I lacked peace and internal balance. Most importantly, I did not feel at home affectively. Instead of love, I felt anger—the sort of anger that, unchecked by sympathy and self-criticism, might develop from an emotional response to situations of danger or injustice into a deep-seated sentiment of hatred.[6] I did not want a sentiment of hatred to develop in my heart, but seeking distance from *la Yunai* was all that I could muster at that time to smother the growing sentiment.[7]

As my years in *gringolandia* had added up, I had grown increasingly hostile to the US national team, almost to the verge of hatred. The lowest point had come during my first years as a doctoral student. I was visiting my family in Costa Rica with K on the day of a qualifying game for the 2002 FIFA World Cup against Uncle Sam's team. My friends had invited me to watch the match at the stadium, where I could have safely, anonymously, and basely—like a goddamn Rogue—let out my anger against the *gringos*, but I decided to stay home and watch it with my family and K. I thought I could be calm and enjoy a game with my family as we had done so many times over the years when our national team played.

As the game unfolded, though, the teams remained tied 1–1 until the very last minutes. With tension mounting, I stopped seeing the actual game and began to see the Arkansas Rogues and the Pennsylvania frat boys in *gringo* jerseys on the field. I grew restless, as I wanted us to crush them. Those pretty-boy players were so smug every time they came to play in Central America, looking at our countries as if from up high, that it made me furious. Besides, with the tie Costa Rica would be virtually eliminated from the Cup.

Then, as the game wound down, Costa Rica advanced along the right wing, and a *yanqui* defender intercepted a cross inside the penalty area with his hand. The referee whistled the penalty. The *gringos* protested. But it was clearly a penalty. Then the tension and anxiety prior to the penalty kick grew. Casey Keller, the fine goalkeeper, was in top shape. But Hernán Medford, our star forward for many years, asked to shoot the penalty. He was determined to score. One could sense it in his body language. He did not look at Keller. He simply chose a target on goal to shoot at, looked to the ground, his body leaning forward to start the run and kick. At home, I was pacing back and forth. The referee whistled. I held my breath. Medford started immediately and shot hard to Keller's right. The keeper did guess the side correctly but could not get there in time. The ball flew past him, at mid-altitude, near the post, and into the net. Medford ran to celebrate. The fans in the stadium, in the homes and restaurants and bars exploded with joy. But I exploded with anger and yelled, *"Tomen hijueputas, métanselo donde les quepa."* My family was stunned. My mother asked me to calm down. But I said, *"Es que usted no vive con ellos."* She did not live with *them*, as I did. K immediately felt hurt to the core, her face grimacing. She thought she was one of *them*, as if I blamed her, as if my anger were directed at her, her family, her friends, and her people.

Regret overcame me immediately. My father said, *"Usted tiene que ser más prudente."* He was right, but I needed more than prudence. I needed *agape* for grace and forgiveness. What did it matter that I was really yelling

at the Rogues and frat boys and jerks I had met on and off the *fútbol* fields of
la Yunai? That could not take the pain of my base outburst away from K. And
that did not justify me either. In my spiritual blindness, I often failed to see
any difference between "them jerks" and any other United Statesian. I even
should have met Rogue and frat boy xenophobia with a wholesome heart, balanced and forgiving though stout, for my own sake and for the sake of K, her
family, and all our American friends. At that moment, the basest in my life, I
knew, felt in the core of my being, that I was not only intemperate and impru-
dent, but wounded, out of balance, and on the threshold of hooligan hatred.
And I had hurt the woman I loved. Without the possibility of atonement, all
I could do was ask for forgiveness, and K offered me her grace. I stood in
need of her agapic gaze, of her loving capacity to still see germs of loveliness
in the hatefulness of my outburst and its underlying conflict, and she looked
upon me with that gaze. In spite of the pain I had caused her, she forgave me.

Aside from fostering *philia* with the *Benitos* and other friends on the field,
the best I could accomplish over the next few years in order to restrain the
emerging hooliganism in my sporting heart was to cultivate an uneasy but
prudent distance from *gringos* and their "soccer." I stopped watching games
between Costa Rica and the United States because I knew my passions were
stronger than my temperance. At most, I watched alone, but usually I only
checked the score after the game. If we won, I was happy imagining the plays
from reading the newspaper accounts; if we lost, I avoided thinking about
how it happened or talking about it.

I stopped playing competitive tournaments altogether. I played only *mejengas*, and only very friendly ones, so as to avoid conflict. That was all I could
do—avoid the conflict brewing in my heart; I could not resolve it.

When I moved to Brazil, avoiding conflict became easier—I hardly ever
saw *gringos*, and I never played with them. I simply enjoyed friendly pick-
up games, especially on the beach in Santos. I rejoiced at playing in the city
where *O Rei Pelé* had played most of his career. With the breeze blowing,
the sea waving calmly, the late afternoon sun descending on the horizon until
sinking on the Atlantic, I played with gladness and essayed my best attempt
at *o jogo bonito*, the beautiful game. I relived the joy of *fútbol* from my youth
playing in minor league teams in Costa Rica. I played hard but clean defense,
marking firmly but only disputing the ball. When I controlled *el balón* I tried
to pass it effectively and elegantly. I dribbled only when necessary and shot
with control when I saw a chance. I focused entirely on the game.

As work and life unfolded, I eventually landed in Brooklyn. There had
been enough distance by then that I simply ignored *gringo* soccer. I have
never watched any US club or national team games since returning to *la
Yunai*, not even in the World Cup. If Uncle Sam wins, I try hard to be happy
for Doug, Bryan, and the memory of Brandon, the *Benito* who died, his

Navy jet crashing against the ocean while training for war. When I arrived in Brooklyn, I looked only for friendly pick-up games at Prospect Park, mostly with immigrants from the Middle East or Latin America, until a painful injury forced me to retire from the fields—*colgar los tacos* as we say in Costa Rica—and I had to grieve the loss of my footballing life. It is over.

All these years I have thought about the process lived in my *corazón de futbolista*. I often have reflected in terms of American philosopher Charles Sanders Peirce's evolutionary love. He writes of agapism as the view that "love, recognizing germs of loveliness in the hateful, gradually warms it into life, and makes it lovely."[8] I recur to it mostly as an ethical thesis about the nature of *agape* in evolving human relations, in those connections that can either draw us together or drive us apart. To love agapistically means, in part, to recognize the seeds of loveliness, gracefulness, and goodness in the hateful, disgraceful, and base and to act on the basis of that recognition in order to create, mend, recreate, and improve our relations to others.

When it comes to ugly *gringos*, for years I thought this meant recognizing the potential for gracefulness or goodness in them. In spite of our ugly bouts on the field, the last time I saw the Brians from Alabama in an Arkansas diner, they had been kind and graceful to my parents. The frat boys from Pennsylvania were capable of sympathetic bonds with each other, even if it was an exclusionary sympathy directed at group members only. The seeds of sympathy were in their hearts; they needed to learn to extend their sympathy to others, to include in the circle of their relations people unlike them.[9] I tried to appease my heart with this reflection. However, it was not enough to heal, forgive, and restore my internal wholesomeness and equilibrium. I couldn't resolve my struggle by thinking that they had the potential to be more loving. So now I try to identify *gringo* soccer with the best Americans I have known on the field. But really all I can accomplish is the same tense, guarded, cold detachment as before.

Ultimately, I have come to understand that agapism demands something different from me. I must recognize again the germs of loveliness, gracefulness, temperance, patience, and goodness in my own heart. It is in my core—in the agapistic seeds that remain alive in spite of hooligan hatefulness born of strife—where I need to find a way to love and forgive, to be wholesome and in inward and outward equilibrium again, even as I defend my dignity and demand respect. This defense is important, as my friend Luis exemplified by his conduct on campus and on the *fútbol* field in Arkansas. For grace to be effective, others must also respond to my loving demand for respect in kind, as the Brians did at that diner in Arkansas. When I look inward, though, I should search in my own heart, capable of love to overcome hatefulness, for a way to be as the child who played for my beloved *Club Deportivo Saprissa*, fair and elegant, in the fields of Costa Rica and abroad, all those years ago, before migrating.

NOTES

1. Lara Trout, *The Politics of Survival: Peirce, Affectivity, and Social Criticism* (New York: Fordham University Press, 2010), 58.

2. Ibid.

3. Ibid.

4. Ibid.

5. C. S. Peirce, "Evolutionary Love," in *The Essential Peirce: Selected Philosophical Writings*, eds. N. Houser and C. Kloesel, vol. 1 (Bloomington: Indiana University Press, 1992), 356.

6. There are forms of emotional anger that are conducive to the survival of an oppressed person and even foster their personal growth through reflective and self-critical effort. See María Lugones, "Hard-to-Handle Anger" in *Pilgrimages/*Peregrinajes*: Theorizing Coalition against Multiple Oppressions* (Lanham, MD: Rowman and Littlefield, 2003), 103–118.

7. For the sort of sympathetic and self-critical effort that is conducive to personal and ethical growth, see Lara Trout, *The Politics of Survival.*

8. Peirce, "Evolutionary Love," 354.

9. Overcoming the conscious and nonconscious habits that guide exclusionary, rather than inclusionary, sympathy is difficult but possible. In community, human beings are capable of criticizing and modifying such habits. For an account of how such ethical and social-critical work can be accomplished, see Lara Trout, *The Politics of Survival.*

Chapter 12

Churchgoing

On a hot Sunday morning at the end of my first summer in *la Yunai*, the Henry family took me to their small congregation, in inner city Houston. Former Christian missionaries in Costa Rica, the Henrys had invited me to visit them in the sprawling Texan city where they had founded a new missionary church. Most of the churchgoers were Mexican immigrant families. They were warm and welcoming people who strove to make a good life in the midst of harsh conditions, having fled poverty at home to face the social challenges of inner city life and exploitative work in Texas.

As he did every Sunday, Calvin Henry preached in Spanish. At the end of the sermon, in the usual style of a revival preacher, he invited those listeners who were present and had not yet been saved to stand up and step forward to confess before the members of the church that Jesus Christ was the Son of God and Savior, and then to be baptized. Suddenly, among dear friends and in that small church of immigrant parishioners, I felt it was time to be baptized, to mark my commitment to live a Christian life as I understood it at that age. With a sincere heart I stepped forward and confessed my belief. Immediately after the service, Calvin immersed me in the baptistery of his congregation, as the members sang in Spanish:

Redimido fui, redimido fui,
por la sangre de Él, por la sangre de Él …
mis pecados han sido lavados, redimido soy.

I had witnessed similar scenes of baptism and heard that song many times before, in a small evangelical congregation in Costa Rica, but I had never felt it was my time to be born again. After being baptized by Calvin, I felt joyful in my decision. I did not feel transformed or changed; I did not feel the

Holy Spirit had suddenly descended upon me. I simply felt that I had chosen a Christian way of life at the time and place that my heart had dictated, and I had no inkling of the path of life that lay before me.

SAN JOSÉ TO HOUSTON

While growing up in Costa Rica, I usually attended Sunday school in an evangelical congregation with my mother and sisters. As soon as the biblical lesson was over, however, I ran home to watch professional *fútbol* on television with my father, and so I never stayed for the religious service. On some Sundays my father and I would go to the stadium to watch our club, Deportivo Saprissa, play, and then I would not attend Sunday school at all. As I became a teenager, my Sunday schoolmates, obeying the influence of parents and experiencing social pressure within the congregation, began to be baptized. Being as young as thirteen or fourteen, they repented of their sins and were born again. But then they felt even more pressure to attend every Wednesday devotional and Saturday meeting in addition to the Sunday service. The heaviest responsibility of all, however, was to stay holy and not sin ever again. Though I did believe then in the stories of the Old and New Testament as examples of how one must live, and though I did internalize the notion of disobeying the holy scriptures as sin, I never really believed in the need for church membership and service attendance in order to live a Christian life, nor did I seek to be part of the social group within the congregation. I just didn't like to sit still while listening to sermons or attending meetings or to resign my every activity to the church.

As I turned sixteen and seventeen, I attended Sunday school less and less. Sometimes I played *fútbol* games with my high school and club teams on Sundays, and other times I went to the stadium with my buddies to watch *mi amado* Saprissa play. Then the pastors of the church became alarmed, and every time they saw me they insisted that I should not abandon the church but be baptized and become a member in full fellowship with the redeemed. On one occasion one of the pastors, Minor, a man from Nicaragua, came unannounced to visit me at home to persuade me to convert. Out of courtesy, I sat for almost a whole afternoon listening to his arguments, based on his interpretations of the New Testament, while I insisted that I did not yet feel it was time. It was the truth. It was also true, however, that while he talked I was missing that afternoon's *mejenga* in the street with my neighbors. I felt eager to be done and run outside to play *fútbol*. Defeated and concerned for my rejection of baptism, Minor gave up.

I didn't get baptized while I lived in Costa Rica, even though my own neighborhood friends, who were all Catholic, used to tease me by calling me "*San* Daniel" because I was the only evangelical Christian in the block. I attended Bible school on Sundays, while they all attended Saturday night mass at the Catholic Church. *Don* Carlos, a good-natured man in his forties, was the first one to call me *San* Daniel. Then his sons and other friends from my street started calling me a saint as well, always with a laugh. I thought it was funny, though I was quite conscious that they had no idea, really, of what happened in a Sunday bible school. As social Catholics, they didn't even read the Bible, ever. And it would have been pointless to try to explain that I was not a member of the church and not a saint because I had not been baptized. The whole thing would have been bewildering to them, and it was not important enough to me to explain it. We played *fútbol* and baseball, rode bicycles, went to movies, and hung out at the street corner together, and that was enough for me.

When I arrived in the United States, however, my perspective changed. I had left my home and my country and thought that, to some extent, I was now on my own. In spite of the silent pain I carried within me from M's death, I felt thankful for everything I had lived in Costa Rica and hopeful for the experiences that were to come. Over the course of my first summer school term in *la Yunai*, I saw that a lot of the southern students had been baptized, were church members, and seemed sincere in their devotion to God. I began to feel that perhaps it was time to be baptized. I did not have very clear ideas as to the theological significance of this ritual, though I knew that for the congregations I had attended it literally represented the definitive step for salvation. For me it symbolized, in a practical way, a desire to make the Christian principle of love the central value in my life. This desire, however, was mixed with a great confusion as to the nature of sin and its forgiveness by grace, as I thought sin meant the transgression of rules written in the biblical scriptures and interpreted by the church, and as I thought of God as an omniscient, omnipresent, conscious person that would one day judge everything I did. The risk of literal damnation and the promise of literal salvation in another life, all depending on my earnest attempt to observe the rules ordained by God and revealed through the inspired writing of holy men, still seemed real to me. With this mixture of candid desire to love and dogmatic confusion, I traveled to Houston, to visit the Henrys, at the end of that first summer.

When I was a kid, Calvin and Linda had been sent, along with their young daughters, Michelle and Darla, to found a new congregation in Costa Rica. When they arrived from Texas, there was already in the country another missionary family, the Bynums—Ray, Elizabeth, and their children—who had come from Kansas to Costa Rica in the late 1960s. My mother had converted from Catholicism by being baptized during a missionary campaign, in the style of revival meetings, when I was around four years old. It had been a time of emotional need and spiritual search for her, and the promise of grace and her faith that in the gospels she could find a way to live with hope led her to baptism. In a black and white picture of that day, she stands in front of the river, a young, lean woman in her mid-twenties, smiling, her long, black hair dancing in the breeze. Her grandmother Betsabé, her mother Luz, her aunts Carmen and Nelly, stand near her among other women, all of them smiling. The river in which they would be immersed to be baptized flows behind them.

After my mother's conversion, the Bynums had helped her to read and interpret the message of Christianity, as written in the gospels and epistles of the apostles and according to a theological perspective born of the Restoration Movement in the United States. More importantly, they had been supportive and loving. My father, a nominal Catholic, understanding her search for a hopeful way to live, had supported her and shielded her from the merciless criticism of people around us, even our extended family. Some of his relatives had tried to attack her conversion as a cultural scandal and religious heresy, and he had shut them up immediately. That was not easy in Costa Rica then, as nominal Catholicism was culturally enforced by all means possible. In our very conservative Catholic country, my father's relatives perceived becoming an evangelical Christian as entering a cult and seeking social ostracism. However, my father never allowed anyone anywhere to criticize my mother or us, even though he never converted or joined a protestant or evangelical church. Meanwhile, the Bynums had encouraged my mother's own search by reading the Bible with her. They were earnest and sincere in their faith and respectful of my mother's own queries.

When the Henrys arrived in Costa Rica a few years later, they also provided encouragement to my mother's faith. In her friendship with Linda, my mother discovered new ways of thinking and living. My father, meanwhile, who generally was aloof and had few friends, had allowed an approximation with the Henrys, and a friendship developed over time. My parents often invited them over for dinner, and they would come with their children. Calvin, especially, loved Costa Rican food and culture and had adapted himself quite smoothly to life in our country. A big, tall Californian, he loved to tell jokes and laugh out loud. As he told them, his light-colored eyes would get the spark and slant of a mischievous boy. Calvin and my father became unlikely friends, being so different, the former outgoing and earnest, the latter more stern. They enjoyed, however, comparing notes and observations on United Statesian and Costa Rican culture. I became friends with Michelle, who was exactly my age. Michelle and Darla and, later, Trey—a third child who was born in Costa Rica—spoke Spanish like Costa Ricans. They had adapted well to our way of life. They spoke like *ticos* and ate our food and laughed at our jokes. I never sensed in any of them any aloofness, much less any sense of cultural superiority. Nor did I ever feel it around the Bynums. I thought of all of them as friends of our family.

When I arrived in Arkansas as a college student years later, the Henrys had returned to live in Houston. During my first visit to their home, they received me like a family member, with care and joy. Now we spoke mostly in English, even though I still could not express myself fluently. They took me to see the NASA Space Center, the zoo, and the University of Houston's campus. On a Saturday morning, we walked along the massive, though personless, downtown, and I felt dumbfounded—it was my first encounter with the impressive, but lifeless, centers of younger cities in *la Yunai*. Downtown Houston's tall buildings seemed to be "glass without feet," as philosopher John McDermott calls them, to indicate that they are not grounded in the lives and vital practices of local communities.[1] On a weekend, when a city like San José would be bustling, Houston's downtown felt devoid of life, a ghost town. Fortunately, Chicanos, *mexicanos*, and *texanos* infused it with vitality elsewhere. One day for lunch, Calvin took me to eat local Tex-Mex food at a hole-in-the-wall joint owned and run by a Chicano family. The syncretic flavors surprised my palate. Another day, he took me to eat thick, dripping, good ole' Texan hamburgers in a small diner-style joint—my first time to try an authentic American burger in its proper setting, not the junk sold by United Statesian food chains in San José.

Before the end of my trip, I rode with Calvin to take Michelle to her college in Abilene. Together we moved her things into her freshman dorm room. Then I saw him cry when he embraced her and left her there to start her college life. He knew that she probably had left home for good, and I realized this to be the case for many middle- and upper-class university students in *la Yunai*.

Before Michelle left for Abilene, the Henrys took me to their congregation, in inner city Houston, where they communed with Mexican immigrant families. Calvin and Linda continued to work earnestly for their mission. On that hot Sunday morning in late August, after the end of Calvin's sermon, among dear friends and in a small church of *inmigrantes*, I was immersed in clear, cleansing water and baptized. When I emerged from the water, I heard the congregation sing in Spanish: *"Redimido fui ..."* And as I stepped out of the baptistery, the church members came to embrace me, even in my wet white robe, and to greet me. Men, women, and even children blessed me. Most of them had come to Houston from Mexico. As Calvin had explained, their lives in the inner city were not easy—men and women worked very hard, earned low wages, and lived in difficult social conditions as undocumented immigrants. But they were joyful and mutually supportive, and they offered sincere fellowship in their small congregation. To me that felt like the simple heart of the matter—the core of a life of love, grace, and solidarity—and the best setting for me to mark a desire to live such a life.

AMID THE SAINTS IN ARKANSAS

During my freshman year, I tried, for the first time in my life, to be a committed churchgoer. On a Sunday morning during my first fall semester in Arkansas, soon after being baptized in Houston, I rose to go to church with my friend Benjamín. I had no suit to wear, so I put on a white, button-up shirt; a pair of khaki pants I had just bought at a local store downtown; and my well-shined, brown leather shoes. Benjamín prided himself in being a sharp dresser. He was wearing a slick black suit, silky white shirt, a light-blue silk tie, and a fine leather belt with matching black shoes. He studied business and already looked like a dandy banker.

As we walked from campus to church, I looked at all the students walking along with us. That morning, like every Sunday morning, the young saints had risen early and congregated to praise the Lord and partake of communion. Boys and girls gathered at the campus cafeteria for breakfast and then walked to church together. The girls wore long, flowing dresses, usually flower-patterned. Their modest garments covered well their chests and shoulders, hung loose on their bodies, and descended well below the knee, often to their ankles. The girls wore minimal or no make-up and often tied-up their long hair. Instead of purses, they carried their bibles as they walked from campus to church. Their smiles and hopeful looks made their modesty endearing. They were young and beautiful and seemingly happy. The guys dressed up as well. Some wore dark suits and sharp ties, like Benjamín, but most of them wore the good ole' boy uniform consisting of a navy-blue jacket with golden plastic buttons; light-blue, button-up, Oxford shirt; khaki pants; sometimes a leather belt; and dirty, un-shined brown shoes.

There were several churches in town, and they were all packed on the Christian day of rest. The largest and most popular was the College Church, on the main avenue near campus. Thousands of students, several professors and college administrators, and many people from the small town gathered there. The fairly young, energetic, and charismatic preacher knew how to inspire young souls to live the righteous life and do the good work. A bit farther away was the Downtown Church, not too far from the old town center and its jewel, the county's Courthouse. One could walk there, but everyone who attended drove or got a ride. A bit farther away from campus in the opposite direction, near the local Walmart, there was another church that provided vans on Sunday mornings so that students without rides could attend their service. There was, then, absolutely no reason why one couldn't go to church. They were everywhere and accessible, and nearly all students attended.

The sober services consisted of singing traditional hymns a cappella without even clapping, reading the holy scriptures, praying jointly, partaking in communion by breaking the unleavened bread and drinking grape juice—no wine allowed, as it may lead to temptation and drunkenness, and listening to the main sermon. Depending on the preacher, the sermon emphasized the blessings and the love promised for the children of God in this life, or the risk of fire, brimstone, and eternal damnation threatened by the Almighty Lord for the next, eternally painful life. Either way, the sermon always ended with an invitation for repentance, confession, baptism, and salvation. Hardly ever did anyone respond; everyone had already been baptized and saved. There were no musical instruments, no ornaments, no art, and no images anywhere in the church building. Only a pulpit, benches, hymn books, bibles, and people. Everyone behaved quietly; the elder men adopted stern attitudes. Everybody was composed as they listened to the prayers or sermon; no one ever shouted an "Amen!" or a "Praise Jesus!" Married men occasionally embraced their wives. The young couples did not touch each other, however; at most, they held hands discreetly.

On that particular morning, I went with Benjamín to the College Church. He liked the atmosphere of the popular church with the cool preacher and the awesome harmonies during hymn-singing. Benjamín sang well and enjoyed it. I wished I could sing well but actually sang like a tone-deaf parrot. Though I enjoyed listening to the harmonies, I felt uncomfortable during the whole service, wondering what was so cool and glamorous about that popular church. It felt to me like an elaborate show. After the service, people greeted each other, smiled, chit-chatted, and got on their merry way without much sincere fellowship.

Along with most students, Benjamín and I returned to the cafeteria on campus for lunch. When we entered the cafeteria, it was time to see how dressed up and tidy everyone really looked. It was a cafeteria full of straight-laced saints, talkative and relaxed after communion and worship, their holiness reaffirmed. Just about the only people wearing jeans and t-shirts were either the Central American scholars who did not attend church and did not care to pretend they did, or the African-American athletes who were in that college on scholarship to win football or basketball games, or run in track meets, instead of being there to remain steadfast in their faith and find a spouse within the church. For yet some others, post-service lunch provided a chance to admire the best-looking boys and girls, or to be admired as such.

Though the experience at the College Church disappointed me, I sought for other ways to participate with my peers in the weekly ritual of churchgoing. I thought that it would be helpful to me for living a life of love and grace. This desire was not devoid of confusion about my own beliefs or free from other motivations. Just as for many of my mates, churchgoing for me became a way to socialize, to fit into my environment. Having grown up as *"San* Daniel" in my own San José neighborhood, I did not find evangelical churchgoing to be culturally bewildering, as it was to some of the Central American scholars at our college who were Catholic. Instead, attending church services became a natural way to interact with friends and peers. In the early fall of my freshman year especially, it became one of the ways to be with Pam.

I met Pam during the orientation sessions for freshmen right before the semester started. A sweet, cute girl from Fort Smith with a lovely Arkansas accent, she had a great sense of humor. During those days we spent a lot of time talking and doing things together, like going for walks on campus, to the movies, or for frozen yogurt in the hot, late summer evenings. Once she drove to a camp just north of town, and we hiked in the trails in the woods to some rocky cliffs overlooking the lush forest and the tranquil Little Red River. One evening, after several dates, while sitting together in the swings in the main lawn on campus, I kissed her. Afterward, she laughed at me and said she had wondered how long it would take me to do it. "Hey, I am shy!" I said. We also went to some evening devotionals—small, informal meetings where someone read some Bible verses and shared a simple reflection on them, someone else led a prayer, and everyone sung simple songs of worship, less elaborate and lyrical than traditional hymns but with catchier melodies.

Naturally in that context, then, we started going to church together on Sundays. Pam's roommate Carolyn, the shy girl from Walla Walla, also came with us, along with other friends. Pam drove us to a church a few miles away from campus. More people from town and fewer students attended church there than at the College Church, and their attitude seemed more genuine and less flashy than that of the students. I had just arrived in Arkansas with half a duffle bag of clothes and felt far more comfortable at that church than at the Christian fashion parade near campus. I would sit next to Pam, enjoying her proximity as we prayed, sang, listened to the sermon, or gave a humble offering during collection. After the service, we would return to campus, have lunch at the cafeteria, and then Pam and I would spend some time together. One lovely September afternoon a few weeks into the semester, when the summer heat was no longer oppressive and the warmth and soft sunlight felt glorious, we stayed on the lawn just outside her dorm for hours. When I returned to my dorm room, it was time for dinner. Though I was trying to be a churchgoer, I could not bring myself to attend church again in the evening, as so many students did. I went to the library instead.

My regular library-going, in fact, brought about the demise of my relationship with Pam. It seemed to Pam I was quite devoted to it. As the fall semester advanced, I started to spend almost every evening during the week in the library, while Pam did not. She once told me, not in complaint but in sincere befuddlement, that she had the only boyfriend who was studying all the time. Apparently, all the freshmen on campus were busy going to movies, on walks, to devotionals, or out to eat. During the week, Pam and I always had dinner together but at the cafeteria on campus, as I had no money, not even for the cheap diner in town. All I had was my on-campus meal plan. After dinner, I would spend the evening studying. I did enjoy our weekend dates and looked forward to them. But that was not enough for her, and I felt her dissatisfaction and my own. One evening late in the semester, as finals approached, I told her we needed to talk. She came to meet me at the library, and I explained that I thought we should break up. She sighed and said she had told her friends she was coming to the library "to get dumped." I'd never heard that expression before, and it seemed so ugly and harsh. I tried to console her. But you can't console the person you have just "dumped." To top it all, I had been such an insensitive moron that I broke up with her in the library steps. What a clueless fool! But the insensitive mistake was made; I couldn't take it back.

After I broke up with Pam, I needed to find a different church because I wanted to give her space. I continued my attempt at sustained churchgoing by going downtown. I wanted to grow spiritually, though I still was confused as to what that meant. I did not think I had to earn blessedness by going to church—salvation did not come by works but by grace. But my effort to go was born of the belief that one had to strive to obey the rules, the "dos and don'ts" of doctrine. I still came too close to the ritualistic religious commerce that Khalil Gibran describes, in the voice of a dejected Sage, in his poem "Of Religion" in *The Procession*:

Religion is a well-tilled field,
Planted and watered by desire
Of one who longed for Paradise,
Of one who dreaded Hell and Fire.
Aye, were it but for reckoning
At Resurrection, they had not
Worshipped God, nor did repent,
Except to gain a better lot—
As though religion were a phase
Of commerce in their daily trade;
Should they neglect it they would lose—
Or persevering would be paid.[2]

I did not feel that by going to church I traded in tickets to heaven or hell, yet there was an element of commerce in thinking that spiritual business was best transacted on Sundays at church. I did not come close to the inner freedom and call for original faith that one hears in the voice of the Youth, who responds to the Sage in the same poem:

In the wild there is no Credo
Nor a hideous disbelief;

Song-birds never are assertive
Of the Truth, the Bliss, or Grief.
People's creeds come forth, then perish
Like the shadows in the night.
No faith stood out after Taha's
And the Christ to shed its light.[3]

In other ways, though, my search felt less commercial; it wasn't like going
to market. On campus, I tried participating in devotionals with small groups
of friends. Five or ten of us gathered on a midweek evening by the lily pool,
in front of the Administration Auditorium on campus, to sing a few songs of
praise, listen to a short meditation drawn from Scripture, pray together, and
talk. The auditorium—a red-brick building with a Greek Revival portico on
the frieze of which the college's name was etched—oddly framed the stage
with its air of scholarly refinement harking back at once to the Hellenic
classical era and to English universities. The thick oak trees on the main
lawn—their branches swaying and their leaves rustling in the cool evening
breeze—reminded us that we were in the South. The sound of flowing water
from the lily pool's fountain created an atmosphere of tranquility. In that
context of serenity and intimacy we sang, listened, prayed, and conversed.
For me those experiences approached a more genuine sense of community
and fellowship than any ritualistic churchgoing.

TROUBLING SIGNS

Though in the church I met nice people who greeted me every Sunday, some
from town and some from the college, we never got past that greeting point in
conversation. I began to feel that I didn't quite belong in that world. Gradually, I came to see and hear things that troubled me.

   Some of the disquieting signs were theological, or rather, doctrinal in
character. At the time I agreed with the principle of interpretation of biblical
texts as the first guide to belief. But even then I surmised, without being able
to articulate it in philosophical terms, that critical common sense, sentiment,
and reflection upon experience should inform that interpretation to make it
discerning, insightful, and livable. I guessed that life experience could disrupt
our received ways of understanding Christianity and demand reflection and
reinterpretation.[4] So I wondered at the folly of some prominent churchgoers
thinking themselves to be the defenders of *the* true interpretation of the New
Testament, as if their knowledge and experience exhausted the possibilities
for insight. I was also perplexed by their conviction that their congregations
were *the* best restoration of the first-century church, even if I agreed with

their view that congregations ought to be independent and autonomous from each other, without an institutional power structure and an ecclesiastical hierarchy dictating doctrine and policies from the top downward. I did not want to be dictated beliefs and orders from above all the way to me—a struggling churchgoer with a pseudo-anarchist bent. Indeed, reading Thoreau's *Walden* planted a seed of his brand of anarchism in my heart—of looking away from the mores of social institutions and searching for my own experimental way of living on principle. But I didn't know yet how to let that seed germinate freely.

There were more menial issues that led to tragically comical dissensions, enmities, and divisions among beloved brethren. Congregations sometimes split over issues such as whether instead of strictly a cappella singing there could also be clapping during services. Instrumental accompaniment was out of the question, even if some adduced David playing the lyre in worship and praise, as that was *Old* Testament evidence. For that same "old" reason, even if David danced before the Lord,[5] Christians could not dance. These attitudes spilled from the church onto campus. While popular dancing seemed not to be all that important to the cultural life of churchgoing wasps and thus was easy for them to renounce it as sinful, it was a major part of Central American culture. I had learned to dance Caribbean rhythms like *salsa cubana, merengue dominicano,* and *cumbia colombiana,* with my mother and sisters at home, and while growing up I had always danced for fun at family reunions and at parties with friends. There was no malice in any of it. So in Arkansas I could simply ignore the righteous judges, young and old, who prophesied damnation to dancers like me.

I did not drink any alcohol the first two years of college, and the last two years hardly any, because my father didn't drink either and I never had a desire to do it. But I did not think there was anything bad, much less sinful, about those who enjoyed beer, wine, or this or that other spirit. I thought the zealous condemnation of drinking led to such bewildering ideas as a "dry county." Indeed, our college was located in a county where no establishment—no store or restaurant or market—could sell alcoholic beverages. There were no bars in town or in the entire county. The result was that everyone who wanted to drink, student or townie, drove out of the county. They'd drink at the bars elsewhere and then drunk-drive back into the county. That was a brilliant idea. A safer alternative, though, was to make a trip to the liquor store that stood exactly outside the county line on the road to Memphis. Its billboard read: "Last stop to White County." People coming back into the county would often stop to buy their booze, or even drive all the way there just to buy it.

Other "Christian" attitudes troubled me by then far more than the condemnation of dancing or drinking. Once a speaker on the Lecture Series of the university's American Studies Institute, who was a law professor at a prominent university in Malibu, California, claimed in his speech that AIDS was an illness that only afflicted homosexuals, implying that it was a punishment from God. I was stunned by his claim, which scientific evidence disproved already in those years, but even more by the seeming agreement of the audience, or at least their quiescence. It was supposed to be an academic talk. A few days later, I was relieved to read, on the student newspaper, a letter to the editor by a biology professor who challenged the appalling scientific ignorance behind that claim and hinted at its bigotry, which perhaps she could not denounce openly without consequences from the conservative administration.

Significantly, the biologist who challenged the mighty professor was a woman. The same law professor had claimed in the very same speech—a gem of scholarly wisdom—that women should be silent before men at church and subservient in the family, in agreement with church doctrine. As I listened I thought of my two younger sisters, who had recently left their church in Costa Rica precisely for feeling oppressed for that reason. I asked him in the question and answer session how the church could ordain such silence and subservience to women who were just as educated and smart as men, including the female university students present there in the auditorium. He cited a biblical verse of Pauline origin that I have forgotten and do not want to look up, with no nuance of interpretation so as to historical time, place, and cultural context. I did not accept it, nor did I insist, but *seemingly* all my female college mates agreed or acquiesced. Today I think it is more likely that those who disagreed found it futile to object in that context. For me, at any rate, those sundry bits of dogmatism and hypocrisy heralded trouble.

EROS ACROSS EUROPE[6]

With other attitudes, I was as confused as my peers. With regard to premarital sex, I had internalized the belief that it was wrong in the eyes of God without examining the reasons. Even if it had been wrong, why was it so? I had no idea. Even in retrospect, I can't identify the precise source of that belief. Surely I adopted it by letting an external authority determine the habitual beliefs that guided my actions, my actual living.[7] But which authority? My parents hadn't instilled in me any belief that sexuality could be sinful. Perhaps it was the conservatism of Costa Rican culture? Or the conservatism of the evangelical churches I had frequented, even if I wasn't a member? I wanted to have sex as much as any other young guy, but the righteous thing to do according to Christian social mores was to follow the rules and deny one's desires—not to discern, guide, and act on them prudently so as to enjoy them safely and lovingly.

Then I met B—an intelligent, culturally sensitive girl from Bentonville. We were away from Arkansas, juniors on a study abroad program in Europe. When we met on a train from Amsterdam to Frankfurt, she had asked me about Costa Rica and had spoken with passion about her wanderlust. She had been a student in Vienna and had traveled around some places in Europe. She especially loved Eastern Europe, since the Iron Curtain had just fallen and everything there was in flux and very different from the West. I immediately found her attractive and felt drawn to her. She was petite and fit like a runner; her dark brown, curly hair fell below her shoulders; her light brown eyes had a joyful shine that occasionally turned wistful when she became pensive; her smile had an endearing shyness about it; and her cinnamon skin seemed soft and tender. She also had a witty sense of humor and loved to make fun of me—of my awkwardness in conversation (which mostly was nervous shyness around her), of my weird way of wearing regular jeans, t-shirts, and canvas shoes along with hand-crafted, leather bracelets from Costa Rica and *Rasta* hats from the Caribbean; and especially of my romantic fancies which I did not hide from her, as when I fell in love with the sculpture of a bather in Florence's *Palazzo Pitti*, noting especially her delicate ears. She drew a cartoon sculpture with a legend in a bubble which read, "I am a pretty sculpture with beautiful ears!"

Yet she also seemed to like my quiet way of being and my careful way of approaching her. At the Tuscan villa near Florence where our group stayed, we talked a lot while others played cards or listened to music. We looked for each other on walks around Florence, Siena, and San Gimignano. She had laughed at my story after I told her I had been detained by the border police and deported from France for trying to enter the country without a visa. But after the semester ended and I had to fly from Italy to Spain to avoid entering France where "people like you are not wanted," a consular officer had told me in Turin after my deportation—B and our mutual friend Mandy had come to meet me at the Barcelona airport. As we left, we took a moving walkway and she was facing backward, toward Mandy and me. We were all distracted and, when we came to the end of the walkway, she fell on her butt. We all laughed so hard that our stomachs hurt, and she turned bright red, like a ripe tomato. We were still laughing when we had *tortilla española* for lunch at the market, walked from *Plaza Cataluña* down to the Columbus Monument along the lively, crowded *Rambla*, and later took a night train to Seville. In our train compartment, we had two bunk beds. Mandy took the lower one; B and I took the upper one. I embraced her and we fell asleep but woke in the middle of the night. Then I kissed her for the first time. It felt soft and tender.

We spent the day with Mandy walking through Seville, visiting the Torre de Oro on the Guadalquivir River, the massive cathedral with its bell tower, La Giralda, the Alcázar, and the Plaza de España. At the terrace of a bohemian *bodega*, in a cobble-stoned street near the university, we had some wine and *tapas* as we listened to live flamenco music. Then we took a crowded overnight train to Madrid. B and I didn't speak of the night before. The next day, in the capital, we met other students from our group, and we hung out as usual, visiting the Museo del Prado. But she and I decided to go to Lisbon, and that night we took another train. This time we did not have a compartment to ourselves, and we simply slept next to each other in our chairs. When we arrived, Lisbon was foggy, cold, and overcast. We ambled through the city, passing by the fountains on the Praça Dom Pedro IV in front of the National Theater, talking, and walking close to each other. We roamed through the narrow alleyways of the old town and the Alfama, and without planning it, we ended up later at the *São Jorge* castle. We could not see anything when we arrived. But then the fog lifted and, as we stood near the castle's walls overlooking the city and the Tagus River, I kissed her again. It felt nice and tender, and I fell for her.

As night fell upon Lisbon, we walked back to the train station. All we had were our rail passes and no money for lodging, so that very night we took a night train back to Madrid. The next day we met our group again, and everyone parted. It was late November. Some wanted to go to Ireland, Scotland, and England. Others returned to Amsterdam to fly back to Atlanta. B took a train to Vienna, where she would spend almost a month visiting friends. I stayed in Spain, as I wanted to go south to Andalucía. But B and I planned to meet again in Vienna, and nine days before Christmas, I arrived on an overnight train. She was staying at a residential apartment in her former school, within walking distance of Stephansdom, just across the bridge from Schwedenplatz. I found the address and walked up the wide stairs of the old building. When I saw her, my heart started racing and I felt nervous. She smiled. At her friends' apartment, I left my backpack in the living room, grabbed some clean clothes from it, and took a cleansing, warm shower. At night, B and I went out to have a drink and when we returned, her friends were sleeping in their rooms. Though I thought I'd sleep in the couch, I came into her room, and we talked for a long time in bed until we fell asleep together.

Over the next few days, I spent a lot of time sauntering through Vienna, mostly on my own during the day time. Every night I met B, and we went out, often with her friends. One night I got us tickets to listen to the Vienna Symphonic Orchestra play Beethoven's *Symphony Number 6*. I felt increasing emotional tension and wanted artistic release, but the symphony's pastoral airs did not help me to sublimate and release that tension. Afterward, though, as I tried to philosophize about the performance, B laughed at me and her lighter touch relaxed me. We had slept together in bed a few nights, just holding each other, before the moment arose naturally, without further hesitation. I was drawn personally to her, in heart and body, and we made love. Tenderness grew and desire rose in me as I felt her close, closer.

We brought joy and passion and care to the experience, the result of a process of growing intimacy. And yet, the next day, I felt ambivalent, as if I had done something wrong—though I didn't exactly know what was wrong with it, since I liked her and felt so drawn to her. She also said she felt ambivalent about it. And yet we were attracted to each other. Our days in Vienna passed by quickly, and when she flew to Arkansas and I took a train to Switzerland, where I had arranged to work at a hotel in exchange for lodging and food, our parting felt bittersweet. I did not know what would happen. Emotionally, I felt unprepared to deal with the uncertainty while I knew I had let a significant bond emerge in my heart. I thought about her for weeks.

When we saw each other again in Arkansas, just before the spring semester started, we felt just as drawn to each other. For a few more days, I felt the joy of being with her. But our time together didn't last. When school started, she went back to her boyfriend, and I became very sad. She felt confused, as I think she felt legitimately split between him and me. I was also confused as to what I should do about my feelings for B. Had I asked them, my wise peers would have said that the sadness and pain at our distancing were the wages of my sin, I guess. The official line of any leader of the church would have been that I had sinned and must repent. But what did "sinning" and "repenting" mean in sensible and reasonable terms? I had no idea, though everyone could have quoted biblical verses to me. I felt I had lived an experience that expressed naturally what had grown in my heart over several months. Yet, I felt torn between that sense of naturalness and guilt induced by religious mores.

For the churchgoing students, similar experiences of desire, passion, love, joy, sadness, or guilt, happened mostly in silence, in the dark, hidden from public view, even if sometimes they became subject of public gossip. In the midst of this environment, I remained silent. If I heard gossip about someone having sinful premarital sex, I walked away but didn't challenge it. I couldn't make up my mind about the whole thing. It took years of life experience and maturing before I could see just how unhealthy and misguided were the naive denial and condemnation of passions and emotions on campus and in the church. Today I wonder why we couldn't have talked about the relationship between sex and emotions, of passion and love, of pleasure conducive to joy or sadness, to suffering or well-being, in personal and sensible terms, letting us reach our own conclusions, instead of hearing priestly threats about sin and its wages. I don't think I have now an infallible ethical view on sex—on when, how, and under what circumstances it leads to well-being. I do think, however, that open, earnest dialogue, the sharing of concerns and experiences without passing judgment—open-ended, sympathetic, communal inquiry, to put it in Peircean philosophical terms—leads to greater well-being than hiding our confusions and struggles in the dark and pretending that we conform to external norms on sexuality. At that age, at any rate, I was all confused by the reigning mores around me, as much as most of my peers and friends.

GOOD COUNTRY PEOPLE SELLING BIBLES

Meanwhile, we were surrounded on campus by an unofficial contest—namely, to be recognized as the Most Outstanding Young Christian. Perhaps the most important contest was among the preacher wannabes from the Bible and Ministry School as there was no Theology Department. They were often invited to give the pseudo-sermon at the chapel service. As far as I could tell, each aimed to be the hippest, funniest proto-preacher on campus. There was a guy from Australia, Rich, who seemed to be winning due to two factors. He had a "different" accent which he made sure to exploit during his wise sermons to charm the attentive flock, telling anecdotes about his efforts to buy "rubbers" at the bookstore; yet, as he was a native English-speaker, for the *gringos* he was not as foreign as the other foreigners. But he could also be seriously spiritual, as when he admonished all of us sleepy chapelgoers, in a voice at once stern and concerned, "not to be a River Phoenix." I had no idea who River Phoenix was, or how he had lived or died—it was one more sign that I was in the midst of a cultural world where I did not belong—but I gathered it was a hot issue in the *gringo* media at the time. Some famous guy had appeared to be one way but had lived and died in another way. The sermon, at any rate, meant we should not be hypocrites. I wondered about Rich—was he, in all his wisdom, a River Phoenix?

It was probably unfair to suspect this guy, but he reminded me of Flannery O'Connor's story "Good Country People."[8] One day a young man shows up at Mrs. Hopewell's home, somewhere in the rural South, carrying a seemingly heavy case. After exchanging pleasantries, she gets to the point and asks what he is selling. He tells her he sells bibles and offers her one, as he can see she has none in the parlor. But she refuses it, lying that she keeps hers by her bedside, though she kept it in the attic. The narrator reveals that "Mrs. Hopewell could not say, 'My daughter is an atheist and won't let me keep the bible in the parlor.'"[9] In a good ole' country accent, the witty salesman replies, "Lady … for a Chrustian, the word of God ought to be in every room in the house besides in his heart."[10] And when she still refuses, he plays his role, saying "Well lady, I'll tell you the truth—not many people want to buy one nowadays and besides, I know I'm real simple. I don't know how to say a thing but to say it. I'm just a country boy. … People like you don't like to fool with country people like me."[11] Mrs. Hopewell takes the bait, as now she becomes eager to show she doesn't disdain his folk: "Why! ... good country people are the salt of the earth."[12]

From this point onward, the story turns. Mrs. Hopewell's atheist daughter, who legally has changed her name from Joy to Hulga, has a PhD. In her thirties, she is sickly and wears a prosthesis in one leg, so instead of pursuing an academic career she has had to return home. Her mother still thinks of her as a child and does not understand her: "The girl had taken the Ph.D. in philosophy and this left Mrs. Hopewell at a complete loss. You could say, 'My daughter is a nurse,' or 'My daughter is a school teacher,' or even, 'My daughter is a chemical engineer.' You could not say, 'My daughter is a philosopher.'"[13] Noticing her vulnerabilities without revealing it, the Bible salesman finds a way to win her confidence and ask her out. The intelligent atheist fancies she will seduce a good country boy. It is the boy, however, who fools her in the cruelest of manners. When she discovers the deception, she *hisses*, "You're a fine Christian! You're just like them all—say one thing and do another. You're a perfect Christian, you're ..."[14] In many ways, my growing indignation with churchgoers around me may have been just like Hulga's hissing. But here comes the twist, in the words of the narrator: "The boy's mouth was set angrily. 'I hope you don't think,' he said in a lofty and indignant tone, 'that I believe in that crap! I may sell Bibles but I know which end is up and I wasn't born yesterday and I know where I'm going!'"[15]

I sometimes pondered whether the preacher wannabes were good ole' country boys selling bibles. Then I'd think, however, of Thoreau going to Walden Pond to avoid the hustle and gossip of town, to simplify life and imbibe its bone marrow, and I'd strive to cultivate the same inward spirit and mind my own affairs, letting them be as simple as possible.

FRUSTRATING SKIRMISHES

Over time, the combination of hubris, ignorance, and religious conviction that led so many of my acquaintances and even friends to think of their nation as culturally superior to any other, gradually took its toll on me. The hypocrisy of the Rogues—and of their churchgoing friends, college boys and girls, who celebrated roguish taunts in the *fútbol* field—had brought about my first outward clash with the reality of cultural prejudice. Had I read at that time Frederick Douglass's condemnation of the "American Church"—that is, of the great mass of religious organizations of this country which supported the Fugitive Slave Act in his time[16]—and keeping in mind the historical and ethical distance with the gravity of the acts that Douglass denounced, I would have felt that these words applied to the Rogues: "The church regards religion

This became my Sunday ritual. I slept late; showered; went out for a stroll on the train tracks or to the smooth, verdant *fútbol* field; and then I joined *mis compas centroamericanos*—many of whom were nominal Catholics—in the cafeteria to eat and speak in Spanish. We all wore casual clothes—t-shirts, jeans or shorts, and sneakers—disrupting, and even defying, the Christian catwalk. I was beginning to find my rhythm.

RURAL CHURCHGOING IN ARKANSAS

In Arkansas, though, I had one more churchgoing experience that remains dear to my heart. I no longer went for religious guidance or spiritual enlightenment. I went for the loving companionship of country folk. *Oklahoma* Jason, who had been the leader of a spring break missionary trip to his home state, invited me to attend a small, rural church with a group of students on a Sunday afternoon. I thought that would be perfect. I could sleep in, walk, eat, talk to my friends, and go to church away from town in the late afternoon. So I accepted the invitation. Late one Sunday afternoon I met him and a couple other students on campus, and he drove us to a tiny, single-room church building somewhere off of a lost country road in Central Arkansas.

The wooden church-room had great dignity in its austerity. Stilts raised it above the flat ground, and we had to walk up a few wooden steps to enter the room through its double-paned door. There were no windows on the façade or the back of the church; a single window on each side let light in. No bell tower or cupola crowned the tin gable roof. The exterior had once been painted white, but the paint must have begun to chip away so that eventually it had been sanded down to expose the natural color of the wood again. The interior had never been painted. A few wooden benches, probably crafted by the church members themselves, sat one behind the other in two files on either side of the single isle. A simple pulpit—also the work of a farmer-carpenter aiming for functional minimalism—stood at the front of the isle. No images. No ornaments. Only the faithful people, with their bibles and old hymn books, turned the thrifty room into a church.

Indeed, we were greeted by a congregation of elderly farmers—white-haired, wrinkled, gray-eyed men and women smiled at us and welcomed us into their church. Over the course of several Sundays I got to know them a bit. They were children of the Great Depression and survivors of the World War who had toiled as small farmers for decades as they raised their children, taught them to farm as they encouraged their education, and then saw them leave the farms and move to towns and cities in the state and, a few, across state lines throughout the increasingly urban South. The couples had been married since youth, but some members were now widows or widowers. They'd been raised as rural churchgoers and had remained churchgoers all their lives. So every Sunday they gathered to pray, praise, and partake of the Lord's Supper. Even as the congregation aged and was bound for disappearance, they welcomed us young *fellers* to join them for worship. They always received us with warmth and thanksgiving, probably happy to have some young people spend time with them. The presence of even just a few of us nearly doubled the congregation. There was no pastor for such a small one, so usually the men took turns preaching to their brothers and sisters, their lifelong friends. When we visited, though, *Oklahoma* Jason often preached— more in the style of a conversation with a few people sitting near him, than in the style of a sermon delivered to distant audience from a pulpit. His sincerity assuaged my skepticism and sarcasm about preacher wannabes from our campus. Hymn-singing, though poor in its harmonies, also felt earnest regardless of how it sounded. At church, our hosts were happy.

And so I loved our Sunday rides to get there, off highway into country road, along farms and woods, to an open patch of land where the austere churchroom stood. Inside, people enlivened it with fellowship and love just as the afternoon light slanted into it to brighten the room. In that church, I always found *agape*, welcoming and cherishing love—never politics or prejudice, even as its members shared the culture of the Bible Belt. Perhaps, had I dug and inquired, I could have found theological rigidity and some prejudices, but they never came to find me and slap me in the face. During the months I attended, I felt welcome and more a caring saunterer than a churchgoer—at home in a far-off territory among foreign peoples.

Somehow, though, my sauntering churchgoing ended. Jason graduated or other things came up for him, and without a ride I could not return to that small country church. Afterward, churchgoing at the college town became duller and seemed even more hypocritical to me. I felt that churchgoing did not contribute anything to the cultivation of my struggling inward life.

READING "CHURCH GOING" WITH PROFESSOR ORGAN

During my senior year, I took an English literature course with Professor Organ, a thin, tall, and reserved man who taught with a restrained passion. His love for life expressed through literature underran his sober and serious demeanor during lectures and discussions. Though my experiences in *la Yunai* had drawn me to American literature most forcefully, Professor Organ—*caballero de triste figura*—had led me to discover the beauty and elegance of various English, Scottish, Welsh, and Irish traditions. Instinctively, at the level of raw heart, I mostly identified with the ideals, passions, and language of Romantics like Keats and Shelley and of the oddball neoromantic Dylan Thomas. However, the most striking reading experience for me came when we encountered Philip Larkin´s "Church Going." Even as I fell away from churchgoing in the United Statesian Bible Belt, so far away from postwar England, Larkin's poem moved me by addressing the very struggle I confronted in my religious life. I read the poem as if it spoke directly to my heart, as if it were meant to express the personal religious struggle of a *muchacho* in the Bible Belt rather than the cultural transformations confronted by Englishmen after the war. In our class discussion, perhaps Professor Organ perceived that something deeply personal was at stake for me in grappling with the poem; at any rate, he was receptive and responsive to my attempt at approaching it through personal response.

After imagining the silent and musty scene inside an Anglican church of the opening stanzas, these verses struck me like a kick in the gut. The poet stands there perplexed,

Wondering what to look for; wondering, too,
When churches fall completely out of use
What we shall turn them into ... .[20]

Why did I go to church, when the experience felt increasingly so empty? What was I searching for in those stern buildings where I often felt as lonely among the many members as if I were in an empty church in the English countryside, or even worse, when I witnessed the gracelessness that passed for doctrinal steadfastness? What would *I* turn into if I stopped going? Could I live a meaningful inward life outside the church? How?

I did not know how to answer. Larkin's poem did not lead me to an epiphany, but raised questions to which I have often returned since that first reading with Professor Organ. Even after all these years away from the Bible Belt, after my conclusion that the weekly churchgoing ritual did not fit with my way of cultivating an inward life, I have no definitive answers. I do not expect ever to have them. There will always be questions and my experiential and reflective attempts at essaying fallible answers.

Yet, I do go sometimes to sit, midweek, in the silence of Grace Church on Broadway, near Union Square, in New York City. I first regard its gray, stony *façade*, contrasting it with its green gardens, and I look up its neo-Gothic tower as it points high up to heaven, before I walk through the pointed arch gates. I often find myself alone in the elegant interior, and as I look at the intricately ribbed vaulted ceilings high above the nave and then observe the altar and the elaborate, bright, stained glass behind it, I still feel the inner hunger of which Larkin writes in the closing verses of the poem.

The magnificence and elaborate ornamentation of this building, suggestive perhaps of the hierarchical nature of the Episcopalian church, is very different from the sparse, modest buildings where I once attended services at nonhierarchical congregations. And yet, when I am standing inside Grace Church alone and in silence, I often think of that small congregation of immigrants in downtown Houston where Calvin Henry baptized me and of that small rural church in Central Arkansas where I found warmth and a heartfelt welcome. And then I hope I may still find ways to foster fellowship and communion, in society outside churches, with sincerely agapistic churchgoers in *la Yunai*. Cultivating my sense of being at home in this country depends largely on the possibility to experience solidarity and fraternity with them, outside of church walls and roofs, in the open air of social communion.

NOTES

1. See John McDermott, "Glass without Feet," in *The Drama of Possibility: Experience as Philosophy of Culture*, ed. Douglas Anderson (New York: Fordham University Press, 2007), 204–218.

2. Khalil Gibran, *The Procession* (New York: Philosophical Library, 1958), 44. For the influence of Ralph Waldo Emerson and Henry David Thoreau's transcendentalism on Gibran's *The Procession*, see Ahmad Majdoubeh, "Gibran's The Procession in the Transcendentalist Context," *Arabica* 49, no. 4 (2002): 477–493.

3. Gibran, *The Procession*, 46.

4. Philosophically, this can be articulated on the basis of Charles Peirce's philosophy. For one account of this critical, reflective process with regards to religion, see Douglas Anderson, "Peirce's Common Sense Marriage of Religion and Science," in *The Cambridge Companion to Peirce*, ed. Cheryl Misak (Cambridge: Cambridge University Press, 2004), 175–192.

5. "And David danced before Jehovah with all his might; and David was girded with a linen ephod. So David and all the house of Israel brought up the ark of Jehovah with shouting, and with the sound of the trumpet. And it was so, as the ark of Jehovah came into the city of David, that Michal the daughter of Saul looked out at the window, and saw king David leaping and dancing before Jehovah; and she despised him in her heart." 2 Sam. 6:14–16 (Holy Bible: American Standard Version).

6. This section is particularly self-revealing. I wrote it for younger people in the midst of some struggles similar to ones I confronted. I find that cross-cultural attitudes regarding sex, often influenced by religion, are a source of struggle for my students, especially for those who come from elsewhere to New York, where attitudes toward sex *seem* to be so liberal. So I am taking the risk of revealing my own struggles, tensions, and self-contradictions as a Central American in the Southern United States in this regard. I think this may bother stricter philosopher-readers, especially those who have forgotten what youthful confusion felt like. I think, however, that it may show to some younger readers that others have been just as confused as they are, and that

philosophical reflection upon personal experience, and open dialogue about it, may be a helpful way to work through their confusions.

7. This is what Charles Peirce calls the "method of authority," one of the four methods by which we tend to establish the beliefs or dispositions that habitually guide our actions. See Charles Peirce, "The Fixation of Belief," in *The Essential Peirce: Selected Philosophical Writings*, eds. N. Houser and C. Kloesel, vol. 1 (Bloomington: Indiana University Press, 1992), 109–123.

8. Flannery O'Connor, "Good Country People," in *A Good Man is Hard to Find and Other Stories* (New York: Harcourt Brace Jovanovich), 167–195.

9. Ibid., 177.

10. Ibid.

11. Ibid.

12. Ibid.

13. Ibid., 174–175.

14. Ibid., 193.

15. Ibid.

16. Frederick Douglass, "Oration, Delivered in Corinthian Hall, Rochester, July 5, 1852," in *American Philosophies: An Anthology*, eds. Leonard Harris, Scott Pratt and Anne Harris (Oxford: Blackwell, 2002), 337–346.

17. Ibid., 343.

18. This was a remnant of the once pervasive view among many United Statesians that in Latin America, and perhaps elsewhere, people are politically oppressed because of their own cultural incapacity for democracy. See Victor Raul Haya de la Torre, "Is Latin America Ready for Democracy?," in *Latin American Philosophy: An Introduction with Readings,* eds. Susana Nuccetelli and Gary Seay (Upper Saddle River, New Jersey: Pearson Prentice Hall, 2003), 138–142.

19. Bill Berry, Peter Buck, Mike Mills, and Michael Stipe, "Losing my Religion" in R.E.M., *Out of Time* (Warner Brothers, 1991), compact disc.

20. Philip Larkin, "Church Going," in *The Less Deceived* (New York: St. Martin's Press, 1965), 28.

Chapter 13

Finding a Loving Home among Friends

As my college acquaintances left or shifted and as I became more self-aware regarding my inner life, I gradually learned to cultivate a few friendships grounded in affinity and not circumstance. Among loving friends, I found an affective home.

Churchgoing, chapel-going, and even devotionals did not help me to cultivate my inward life. Such rituals did not suit my solitary, introspective, and Thoreauvian anarchist tendencies. I felt more encouraged, genuine, and free in intimate conversations with friends, far away from ecclesiastical hierarchies, social posturing, and passive head-nodding at sermons among strangers. Caring friendship and reasonable and sensible affinities with people close to me counterbalanced my loss of interest in churchgoing.

VISITING THE HALFWAY HOUSE WITH SHANNON

I felt more at home, emotionally and spiritually, visiting a halfway house in town than at church. In the fall semester of my senior year, my friend Shannon took me to a house where she volunteered. It was an old, wooden house raised on stilts, with an ample porch and many rooms, located a few blocks from campus. Shannon had used drugs during her high school years, and though I did not know to what extent, it seemed to me that it had been a problem. She had made a courageous personal effort, with the help of others, and had stopped. So she liked to spend time at the house for former drug users, some of whom had been convicted for drug possession and were then taking steps toward a new beginning in society. Shannon was loving, understanding, and truly empathetic with them. When we met, I started visiting the house with her, and I got to know well some of the guys who lived there. One of them, especially, became my friend. Ron was a tall, strong, African-American man in his late thirties or early forties. He had the frame of an athlete and the size to play power forward on the basketball court. He had been quite a good basketball player. Sometimes we'd go play to the court near the house along with some of the other guys. Ron displayed the best skill on the court. In contrast, I was awful. Everything I did stunk—dribbling, passing, and especially shooting. Ron always laughed but not at me, just out of enjoyment, and he tried to help me become better, giving me some pointers on fundamental skills and basic tactics. Even something as simple as the pick-and-roll had been a mystery to me before his explanations, but with his help I understood how to execute the play. He could have been a coach and a teacher.

I only saw Ron and the other guys at the house, but I felt he appreciated and trusted me. They all loved Shannon, as she had sought them out of loving solidarity. Shannon seemed more engaged with assisting at the house than with flashy churchgoing, and I found that to be a more genuine enactment of *agape*—of the cherishing love that accepts others just as they are and tends to their growth and well-being in their own terms.[1]

I also got to know a bit the man who ran the halfway house. He was a churchgoer, but he was no preacher or elder wannabe. Practical and reasonable in his running of the house, he knew when and how to be sensible and when and how to be tough. Sometimes I judged him, in all my *naïveté*, to be too inflexible, even unmerciful, especially when he had to expel from the house those who had started using drugs again. It seemed too cold. Later, through a painful realization, I understood he needed to keep the house in order. He began to give warnings to Ron about house rules and to have some tough conversations with him, tough I did not know why. His attitude toward my friend became increasingly stern. In misguided sympathy, I did not ask Ron what was happening but simply agreed when he assured me he was being wronged. I offered him my help if he needed it and gave him my phone number on campus.

One evening, when I returned from the library to my dorm room, there was a message in my answering machine. I began to listen to it nonchalantly but immediately became attentive when I heard Ron's voice mumbling. He had tried to tell me something, but his speech was incoherent. Yet his tone sounded pained and fearful, and I sensed his call to be a cry for help. But I got the message after curfew, both at the dorm and at the halfway house, and there was nothing I could do but call Shannon to let her know. We waited.

The following morning we walked over to the house, skipping chapel on campus, to discover that Ron had been kicked out because he had been using drugs again. It must have been crack, which scourged *la Yunai* at that time. Shannon and I felt devastated. We didn't know where to search for him. We guessed he must have taken a bus or hitched a ride away from town. But we didn't know his hometown, and it was unlikely there would be some place he could consider home. We never heard from Ron again. We hoped for news and prepared to help by looking for alternatives to the house, but he did not call a second time. For a while, I even took to reading in my room so I wouldn't miss his call if the phone rang. Until I accepted, with grief, that he was gone. Even today, I wonder about him. Is he well? Is he suffering? Is he dead? After Ron was expelled, I continued to visit the house, but it seemed a bit emptier of friendship to me. I admired even more, however, those who persevered in their efforts to recover. Shannon also remained steadfast in her commitment to helping the people at the halfway house. She visited them, listened to them, helped them with job searches, and made them feel as if there were a hearth for them in town and the world if they kept striving to find it. Through her example, I understood better the suffering that the house tried to alleviate, or rather, that caring people like Shannon tried to alleviate by their work at the house.

A ROMAN SAUNTER

Tennessee Jason offered me another friendship that helped me feel at home everywhere we walked, drove, or hung out. I met him during our study abroad trip to Italy in the fall of my junior year. One night during a group trip to Rome, I wandered through the Eternal City's contorted streets while fascinated with its mixture of the ancient and the modern, of classical elegance and contemporary coolness and a bit of chaos. I arrived at the Spanish Steps, where young Romans and Italian and foreign tourists gathered on the cool evening to talk a while before going for dinner or drinks. As I walked up the steps, searching for a spot to stay still and absorb the scene, I saw Jason sitting by himself, quietly observing people. We had been traveling with a large group of students and teachers for a few days straight, and we both had decided to wander away from the group and roam the city alone. Tall and thin, he had been a track and field athlete up to his freshman year in college. He had long, curly, brown hair, and melancholy, observant eyes to match his thoughtful, laconic disposition. He also seemed sensitive to nuanced differences between people's culture and character. Up to that moment, I'd had a few casual conversations with him in passing. Mostly we'd been together with the entire group, but I had noticed that Jason did not trample over customs and local ways of being wherever we had gone, unlike some of the more extroverted, unaware *gringos* in the group. When I saw him at the Spanish Steps, I gladly approached him. Though I did not know it then, my solitary Roman saunter had led me to the beginning of a lifelong friendship. He greeted me with a smile and we started talking.

We stayed at the Steps for a while, watching people and commenting on the things we'd seen that evening in Rome. The sky grew overcast as we talked, and then rain began to fall. The crowds dispersed quickly, each group seeking a bar, *café*, or *ristorante* to continue experiencing the Roman night. Jason and I started a spontaneous joint walk about the city. As the rain fell on the cobbled streets, we ambled deliberately, stopping to see the window displays of bookstores, art galleries, and other stores. At some point, when the rain fell hardest, we stopped at a traditional bar near Piazza Navona and ordered *café*. The dark, thick-bodied, aromatic espresso energized us for the final stretch of late night walk, back to the hotel across the Tiber, near the Vatican. Along the way, I began to know more about Jason's youth in Nashville, his scientific intelligence, his literary and musical sensibility, and his cultural openness. He struck me as a Tennessee-raised American bound for the world. For the rest of the semester, as we traveled with our group around Italy and to Greece, hung out at our university's villa outside Florence, or explored that beautiful city of the Renaissance, our friendship emerged. Then we continued it upon our return to Arkansas in the spring.

That return was marked by a shared sense of disillusionment. The time spent in Italy had provided Jason with perspective on some of the contradictions in the mixture of institutionalized religion, economic privilege, moral conservatism, and cultural arrogance that pervaded the life of our college in close connection with the church. For me, the time away from campus—after two years spent mostly on it—sharpened my awareness of some of its alienating aspects—alienating in the sense of isolating me from the mainstream beliefs on campus and of distorting many students' sense of social reality and adult life. We saw that while both college and church purported to defend "Christian love," effective and conscientious engagement with social justice seemed to be surrendered in favor of the *appearance* of defending "moral values"—that is, church-condoned mores. Even the academic mission of the college appeared to be secondary to perpetuating the *mirage* of so-called "Christian life" among the morally outstanding student body. Jason and I loved studying English, for instance, but while our college's library had nearly stopped buying literary scholarship since the 1970s, the president— a quintessential academic administrator—was busy planting flowers in the campus' greens before alumni homecomings so their money would keep flowing to build buildings.

The Business School was well-funded—the college had a duty to graduate managers and marketers so they could keep the world of business and money and capital going in moral, Christian ways. But the president's top priority was the new Bible building under construction. Ah yes, the college had an even greater duty to graduate preachers and missionaries so they could lead the world toward Restoration. Vice-presidents, deans, and perhaps professors must be comfortable at a new building while doing the good work of training the young preachers. Meanwhile, seeing a new work in literature or sociology or philosophy at the library seemed like a miracle.

From our own weird funk, Jason and I sought ways for idealist rebellion. We were not above making an occasional trip to the county line to buy booze. One Friday night, we wanted to drink. We were sad Romantics in Arkansas missing our days of backpacking in Florence and Rome. I was over twenty-one years old, but Jason was not. He usually drove, but his car was at the shop. So he asked a friend of his, a freshman, to drive us to the liquor store. We bought a bottle of rum, our desired spirit. Then our well-meaning, dim-witted driver decided to speed back. The state trooper we *had seen* on the way out of the county was *still* there on the way back into the county. Lo and behold, he stopped us. When he asked our genius friend what he was doing driving so fast, our friend volunteered the information that we were driving from the liquor store back to campus. He was a minor. So was Jason. I was legally an adult and had bought booze with minors, and it was in the car. My heart sunk. My throat dried. I thought I'd be charged and expelled from the college. Thankfully, the state trooper was a merciful angel. He only gave our driver a warning and let us go. "Amazing grace, how sweet the sound that saved a wretch like me," I sang in my mind.

Dissatisfied with the hypocrisy of our college's Christian image, in the spring of my senior year Jason and I had an idea for a prank—one we hoped would send a message, even if a lone cry in the desert. On a Saturday afternoon we drove to Walmart—the town's market place—and bought spray paint and rope. Back on campus, I checked out of my dorm to stay at his on-campus apartment—this was allowed on Saturday nights— so I wouldn't have to be back by curfew at midnight. Late that night, we took an old, thick white sheet to a secluded parking lot and spray painted on it, in big thick capital letters, the opening dictum from the book of Ecclesiastes: "VANITY OF VANITIES! ALL IS VANITY."[2] We tied the ropes through holes we'd made on the sheet's corners. Well past midnight we drove to the Bible building's construction site. Dim lights illuminated the quiet, deserted streets on campus.

Jason parked on a side street, at a darker spot where a tree shaded the lamp light. He stayed in the car with the banner. I got out and hurried to the building, and I walked around the fence to identify a place to break in. We had no intention—or the talent—to create graffiti art or paint messages, much less did we want to steal anything. We just planned to climb to the second level of the construction, where a large lobby seemed to be planned, and hang the banner front and center, so it'd be visible on Sunday morning, as students walked to breakfast and then church services.

Just as I approached a dark corner of a side parking lot to check if we could climb the fence, guards on a campus security patrol car spotted me and drove into the lot. "Darn it!" Several times before then, when I had felt wired and restless in my dorm room after curfew, I had gone to the restroom on the first floor of my hall and snuck out the window for a quiet, late night walk on campus. I had always managed to avoid the patrols, but precisely that night of the prank I got caught.

As the patrol approached and stopped next to me, I turned to face it. The young, white, overweight cop sitting on the passenger's seat lowered the window, looked at me with an awkward smile that I supposed was meant to be a menacing grin, and asked what I was doing. I said the only thing I could think of: "I am out for a walk." "Yeah right. And you are walking toward a fence on a dark corner of a parking lot next to a construction site," I thought *el tombo* would reply. He looked at me for a couple of seconds, letting me know he had spotted me and could recognize me. To my surprise, however, he only told me to go on with my walk. So I walked away slowly and serenely in the opposite direction, away from the building and from Jason's car. The patrol drove away, the cop still grinning at me as they passed me once again. I walked around the block. When I got back to the car, Jason had been waiting a while. He'd watched the scene, but had no idea what had happened. Fortunately for me nothing had happened, except that now we obviously couldn't continue with our prank. Oh well, nobody would've understood it anyway, and perhaps it was plain silly. Heeding the psalmist, we could have asked God to "teach us to number our days, that we may gain a heart of wisdom."[3] We indeed realized our failure at planning and executing a simple break into a construction site. As graffiti artists, we would have been awfully ineffective, and not just for lack of talent, but for plain lack of good ole' common sense. *Scout the site first, dimwits.*

Our naive attempt at a prank, though silly, reflected one of the reasons why I admired Jason and valued his friendship. He wanted to do away in his own life with vanity, pretension, and meaninglessness pursuits of popularity or money or recognition—even that recognition that resulted from posturing as a self-righteous, churchgoing, chapel-singing young Christian on our campus or at our stern churches. He cared for people, for friendship, for earnest though fallible love of neighbor, for grace, for simplicity, and for learning also.

Moreover, he proved to be a supportive friend when, for most of my senior year, I lost K. In spite of our mutual attraction and literary affinity, when we were sophomores and juniors K had avoided or resisted my romantic interest in her. We were close friends, but she avoided intimacy in subtle ways. One night in Rome, when we were junior exchange students, we ran into each other at *Piazza San Pietro* in the Vatican. Happenstance brought about our first moment alone in Europe. As the sun descended and dusk settled upon the square, we sat together at the base of a Doric column in the colonnade. We started to talk about William Styron's *Lie Down in Darkness*, which she had lent me to read.[4] Our natural affinity for themes of love, loss, and suffering in literature drew us into an intimate conversation. Then, just as I was getting closer and trying to sense whether I could kiss her, she got up in a hurry, said she must go, and returned to our cohort's hotel nearby, walking as fast as possible. I just watched her go. We played out variations in this scene several times.

Disillusioned, I gave up, or so I thought. In Seville, Lisbon, and Vienna, I fell for B instead. When B returned to her boyfriend in Arkansas, though, I felt heartbroken. I felt very confused by these two different, conflicting attractions. After I recovered from that heartbreak, however, K gave me a chance. Some miraculous work by Aphrodite made her change her mind. Or perhaps she had felt a mutual attraction earlier, but had not wanted or allowed herself to give it a chance. When I kissed her for the first time at a playground in our college town, I thought it was the sweetest kiss I had ever felt on my lips— soft, tentative, tender. A couple of times per week we started going to movies, for walks, for hikes at the woods near the Little Red River. I felt happy. Then I pressed too hard. I wanted to see her more often, and she wanted to keep things moving slowly. Dejected, I became annoyingly demanding. K broke up with me for good reason, and for a while during my senior year, I was pining again for lost love.

Jason saw all of this unfold. The most patient of friends, he supported me while even I felt and thought: "Enough with the pining already, for goodness' sake!" Jason listened to me, hung out with me, gave me rides to run errands, bought me medicine when I was sick, took me to the dentist, invited me to go home to Nashville during a break—in short, he took care of me. One night in the midst of my renewed lamentations for K, he even lent me his car to drive out to Greers Ferry Lake. I snuck out of my dorm, walked to the parking lot, and drove away among winding roads to the lake shore near Heber Springs. A foolish Shelley or Keats, I sought solace in the sight of the calm lake under moonlight and the sound of waters lapping on rocks. On my way back, a state trooper pulled me over. I froze. I did not know what I had done wrong. He walked to my window and shone at flashlight on my face. "What are you doing?," he asked. "I can't sleep so I came out for a drive," I said, sparing him the sappy reasons why I couldn't sleep. "OK, I just wanted to check what someone is doing driving around here at 4 am in the morning. Go on," he said. I suppose he saw I was just a lonesome college kid. When I gave Jason his keys back in the morning before chapel and told him the story, he laughed. I felt comforted by that laughter.

After I graduated from college, I moved to Pennsylvania to pursue a graduate degree. For his part, Jason transferred from our waspy college to Tennessee State, a predominantly African-American university. He felt more at ease
and happier there. K, meanwhile, stayed for her last semester at our college
to finish her English degree. It was then, after I had given up, said good bye,
and moved away, that she realized she loved me and did not want to lose me,
somewhat in the dramatic style of the film *Reality Bites*, the very film that had
encouraged me to tell her I still loved her as I graduated and moved away.[5]
To complicate matters, K had her epiphany in Dubna, Russia, while on a missionary trip. She couldn't call me or reach me by email. So she wrote me a
letter and mailed it. It took weeks to reach me. When I read it, my heart beat
hard and fast with joy, but I couldn't call K either. So I told Jason, my good
friend, the cheerful news. He felt genuine gladness at my romantic twist of
fate, and I felt delighted at sharing a happy moment in my life with a caring
and supportive friend.

FRIENDSHIP AS CARE

Shannon's and Jason's friendship provided me with an affective home. Our
reasonable and sensible affinities counterbalanced my disappointment with
rote churchgoing and offered me a loving community. They fulfilled the
promise that I had found in Kahlil Gibran's *The Prophet*:

Your friend is your needs answered.
He is your field you sow with love
and reap with thanksgiving.
And he is your board and your fireside.
For you come to him with your hunger,
and you seek him for peace.[6]

Today, I understand my experience of their friendship in terms of the ethics of care. According to these ethics, as articulated by American philosopher
Virginia Held, persons are "relational and interdependent"—that is, our social
relations, including relations of interdependence such as friendship, are con-
stitutive of our identity, of who we are.[7] Thus, people who are "motivated by
the ethics of care would seek to become more admirable relational persons in
better caring relations."[8] Shannon and Jason sought to relate to their friends in
ways that helped us along, encouraged us, tended to our needs, and fostered our
growth and progress toward our goals. They were agapistic caretakers with us.

When I think of them nowadays, I can agree with Held in understanding their care in terms of caring relations. In such relations, care is as both

practice and value. First, care is a "practice involving the work of care-giving and the standards by which the practices of care can be evaluated. Care must concern itself with the effectiveness of its efforts to meet needs, but also with the motives with which care is provided. It seeks good caring relations."[9] A "practice" is an activity sustained over time that incorporates values by which to guide and evaluate it.[10] Shannon, for instance, cared for our friends at the halfway house by meeting their needs, such as being listened to or assisted in job searches, through ethically commendable motives—solidarity and love. Second, "for actual practices of care we need care as a value to pick out the appropriate cluster of moral considerations, such as sensitivity, trust, and mutual concern, with which to evaluate such practices."[11] Jason and Shannon, as friends, enacted these values. They were attentive, sensitive, and responsive, as ethical care requires.[12] They cared for me. They cared for people. Their friendship consisted in caring, and their care helped me feel at home in *la Yunai*.

NOTES

1. See Charles Peirce, "Evolutionary Love," in *The Essential Peirce: Selected Philosophical Writings*, eds. N. Houser and C. Kloesel, vol. 1 (Bloomington: Indiana University Press, 1992), 352–371.

2. Eccles. 1:2 (Holy Bible: American Standard Version).

3. Ps. 90:12 (Holy Bible: New International Version).

4. William Styron, *Lie Down in Darkness* (New York: Vintage, 1992).

5. See *Reality Bites*. Directed by Ben Stiller. (Los Angeles: Universal Pictures, 1994), film.

6. Kahlil Gibran, "The Prophet" in *The Collected Works* (New York: Everyman's Library, 2007), 135.

7. Virginia Held, *The Ethics of Care* (New York: Oxford University Press, 2006), 13.

8. Ibid., 14.

9. Ibid., 36.

10. Ibid., 37.

11. Ibid., 38.

12. Ibid., 39.

Chapter 14

Dancing Out of the Labyrinth

From Solitude to Communion

I dined for the first time at *El Pollo Rancherito* during my first winter in Brooklyn. On that Friday night, I had just walked over half an hour in the cold from the Brooklyn College campus in Midwood to my neighborhood, Kensington, and I was starving. I did not want to delay eating by spending time cooking at home. So, when I arrived at the corner of Ditmas Avenue and East Third Street, I sought the Mexican couple who sold *tamales*, *tostadas*, and *tacos* out of food containers that they carried in a shopping cart. But the winds blowing up from the Atlantic swept and froze the Kensington streets that night, and the *tamaleros* were not there. I decided to eat at *El Pollo Rancherito* instead.

I had bought take-home *tacos* and *enchiladas* there a few times, but I had never stayed for dining. When I arrived that night, the tall, overweight African-American bouncer who worked at the door on Friday and Saturday nights was already there. The front windows were covered from the inside by condensation, so I could not see in the room. When I walked in, I discovered the tiny, cramped dining room was crowded to capacity. The eight or ten tables were all occupied by young and middle-aged Mexican and Central American men. I could recognize their origin by their Spanish accents. Sometimes before, when I had walked in to pick up food, I had even heard men speaking to each other in Amerindian languages that I guessed were of *Náhuatl* origin from Central Mexico, but not that evening. They certainly were listening to music in Spanish; the stereo played *norteñas* about lost loves and longing for home. The tiny television set on top of the cashier's counter toward the back of the room showed a *fútbol* game. Some of the men watched it, even as they talked loudly over the music. The two waitresses brought fresh, warm food and beer to the tables. They wore short-sleeved red blouses, tight-fitting black miniskirts, black aprons, and low-heeled black shoes. They had brown-sugared skin and night-black hair, just like the men, so by outward appearances I stuck out quite a bit. But it didn't matter. I approached a table and asked the three dining men if I could sit at the fourth chair. They seemed a bit surprised for a second. I didn't know if it was due to my request or because they had taken me, perhaps, for a Russian or Polish neighbor walking in to pick up food and take it away. But after a brief hesitation they said yes, and I sat down with them.

I introduced myself, they told me their names, and we shook hands and greeted each other: "*¡Mucho gusto!*" Two of them, in their early thirties, some wrinkles already showing on their foreheads, came from Puebla, Mexico, while the youngest one, Pablo, in his early twenties I guessed, came from Quetzaltenango, Guatemala. "*¿Y vos?*," he asked me, using the second-person singular pronoun "*vos*" instead of "*tú*," which Central Americans often use. "*De Costa Rica*," I answered. "*¡Ah, sos tico!*," he said, referring to me by the name Costa Ricans are known to other Central Americans. As we started talking, a waitress asked me what I wanted to order. "*Tacos de pollo y una Negra Modelo, por favor*," I requested. Then we talked. They asked what I did, how long I had been in Brooklyn, and whether there were other Costa Ricans around, since they knew none. I found out that they were working in construction, together in the same crew for a contractor. Each one of them single, they had left behind parents, siblings, and extended families at home. They did not mention girlfriends or spouses or children. They lived in the apartment building next door to *el Rancherito*, on Ditmas Avenue. Their building rose right next to the elevated tracks for the F train, and they confirmed that it was deafeningly loud in there. I lived a block away from the elevated tracks and station, and when the train passed I could not hear the words on the radio or the music on my stereo. My apartment house even shook sometimes when two trains, going in opposite directions, passed by at once. "How much louder their place must be," I thought. From their description, I also gathered they all shared their small apartment with other mates and that they took turns sleeping. The older women who lived in their building did the laundry and many chores for the younger men, who worked as many hours as they could. I wondered about the social and economic dynamics in their building, a small community in itself, but I did not want to pry into their lives. It was Friday night, I wanted to eat, have a beer, and speak in Spanish to some fellow Latin Americans. They were done with work, were tired, and preferred to talk about *fútbol*, the current form and prospects of the national teams from Costa Rica, Mexico, and Guatemala, the historic rivalries in our region and unforgettable games and the playing styles. And so we talked mostly about *fútbol*, even as we drank our beers and ate our *tacos* and other fare.

When I had just ordered my third *birrita*, I noticed that Pablo had grown a bit quieter, more pensive. His black eyes wandered around the room but did not focus on anything in particular. At times, he fixed them on the television screen or a beer bottle on another table, but he wasn't really looking. I wondered what he was thinking. He seemed lonely to me. But our two friends from Puebla kept talking over the music, and I felt divided between continuing that conversation or engaging Pablo in a different one. As I tried to make up my mind, though, Pablo got up. A *cumbia* began to play on the sound system, and he walked up to one of the waitresses and asked her for a dance.

The tables were even closer together than usual because the staff had cleared the space in one of the corners of the dining room for dancing. Pablo took the waitress by the hand and walked with her to the open corner. He had drunk a few beers, but he still had good balance and his wits about him. So he kept his steps according to the rhythm and in sync with his dance partner, and he spun her and turned and moved around with her. He smiled and a spark of joy lit up his dark eyes. The waitress also smiled as she danced, though a bit more soberly. When the *cumbia* ended, Pablo bowed and thanked her and tipped her one dollar. As she returned to the counter to pick up a couple of bottles for patrons at a nearby table, Pablo walked back to our table, sat down smiling, not saying anything, and took a sip from his beer. "¡*Bailás bien!*," I said, complimenting him on his dancing. He smiled and took another sip. I stayed a while longer, still divided between the ongoing *fútbol* conversation with the two *poblanos* and Pablo's pensiveness. As he drank a couple more beers, though, he became more taciturn. When an upbeat *norteña* with a lively accordion melody started to play, he got up again and asked the second waitress to dance. But he had lost a bit of his balance, and he did not keep his step to the Mexican rhythm, so their dancing seemed belabored. His partner focused on protecting him and herself from a misstep or a fall rather than on enjoying the dance. From the very corner, the disk jockey, who doubled as a bouncer, observed them carefully. The waitress succeeded in avoiding mishaps, though. The *norteña* ended, and Pablo thanked and tipped her also. He walked back to our table as she accepted a dance with another patron.

Pablo sat down and ordered another *cerveza*. I wondered if that was a good idea, but I didn't say anything. I didn't ask him if he wanted more food rather than another drink, or if he didn't need to go home and get some rest. I didn't say a word, and his two friends did not seem worried. Instead, I paid my check, including a round of beers, thanked them, shook their hands, and went home. Even as I shook Pablo's hand, I thought I should at least get his contact information to stay in touch. But I didn't do that either. I bundled up and walked across the steamy room to the door, looked at the waitresses dancing another northern Mexican tune and thought how nice it would be to dance with them for joy—not for tips—if I knew how to dance *norteñas*, and stepped outside into the cold Brooklyn winter. As I walked home, I thought of Pablo's loneliness and his effort to assuage it by dancing, and I remembered many hours and days during my first years in *la Yunai* when an intense sadness accompanied solitude.

DANCING *EL PUNTO GUANACASTECO* IN THE BIBLE BELT

An unsettling feeling of disconnection from the peoples and cultures of Latin America and a longing to reconnect with them pervaded my college years in Arkansas even as I explored *la Yunai*. By the time I was a senior, the sense of isolation and the longing for communion had become very intense. As far as I could tell, the few Central American students on campus constituted the only Latin community in our small town and perhaps in all of Central Arkansas. In my walks and Southern road-trips, I had never seen a restaurant from, say, Mexico, El Salvador, or Peru, or a Dominican dance joint, or Colombian food market. Except for the members of the small church in inner city Houston where I had been baptized, I had not had any significant contact with Latinos. I had looked, but outside of campus I had not found anyone or any place for re-connection.

So it was up to us as students to create a community, and we devised some strategies spontaneously from a desire to enjoy our cultures. During my first fall in Arkansas, I discovered, along with my new Central American friends, our yearning to share our cultural bonds among ourselves and with others. We seized on the fifteenth of September, Central America's Independence Day from Spain, as the first occasion to celebrate and share together. The senior students—Abraham, a very serious but gentle guy from Costa Rica; María, the road-tripping traveler from Nicaragua; and others—took the initiative to organize a small *feria*, a food and crafts fair. We invited our friends—fellow students from Arkansas, Oklahoma, Tennessee, Louisiana, Missouri, Texas, and beyond—to come to our fair on a Saturday afternoon at the main student center on campus. The visiting students from each of the five countries that celebrated their independence on September 15—Guatemala, Honduras, El Salvador, Nicaragua, and Costa Rica—brought regional crafts for display. But the scholars from Panama and Belize participated also, even though their countries had different dates and a different history of independence: Panama from Colombia and Belize from the United Kingdom. That first year I had not brought any artisan crafts from Costa Rica in my half-empty duffle bag. But Abraham; Alonso, my redheaded friend; and Luis, my *fútbol* mate, had some wooden crafts from Sarchí, a town in Cordillera Central famous for its woodworking artisans. I enjoyed discovering the styles, materials, and patterns of crafts from the rest of Central America. Prior to our fair, I had only seen some indigenous textiles from Panama—bright and colorful animal figures, such as turtles, fish, and birds, embroidered on a background of black or red cotton. My maternal great-aunt Daisy had been married to a man from *Ciudad de Panamá* and had presented some artful textiles to my maternal great-grandparents. As a child, I had seen the embroidered fabrics displayed at their house in San José. At our student fair, my friend Diana explained that these crafts, created by the Kuna people of San Blas, were called *molas*. I also saw for the first time Salvadoran and Honduran crafts, but I was most struck by the colorful, carefully woven textiles of the Guatemalan and Belizean Mayans. The patterns of the textiles had cultural meanings that my *mestizo* friends from Guatemala could not decipher, and so we were all mystified.

Most of us lived in residence halls on campus and could not cook, but a few senior students lived in on-campus apartments. In their kitchens we managed to prepare some traditional dishes from each country to share among ourselves and with our visiting friends at the *feria*. It was impossible at that time in Arkansas to find yucca or plantains—the only two items of Costa Rican fare that I could think of cooking as a freshman—at the local grocery stores. But César and Abraham had thought of bringing soft, thin corn tortillas from their last summer trip to Costa Rica. We could not find black beans at the grocery store, but we found red ones and improvised a red version of *frijoles molidos* to be eaten with tortillas. The Salvadorans, however, had brought *maza de maíz* (cornmeal dough) from their land, and they prepared fresh *pupusas*—thicker and crunchier than Costa Rican tortillas—filled with cheese, refried beans, and pork. I enjoyed eating a *pupusa* for the first time in my life. So did Pam, the Southern girl I had just started to date, who came to the fair at my invitation. I felt delighted to share food and admire crafts from Central America with her, even as I discovered them myself. My fellow students also enjoyed sharing with their friends from the South and elsewhere in *la Yunai*. Our little *feria* allowed us to create a community, to recreate our bonds to our lands and our peoples, even as we shared them with Anglo-American friends. We broke from the routine of attending classes, studying at the library, daily chapel-going, Sunday churchgoing, eating tasteless cafeteria food, and negotiating the quotidian aspects of our relation to Southern culture by celebrating our own *feria*, in our cultural terms, along with friends.

During my sophomore year, we organized our Independence Day *Feria* again. That year I prepared for it: I returned from my summer trip to Costa Rica with several wooden crafts by Sarchí artisans and some small baked-clay vases by indigenous *Chorotega* potters who varnished the vases dark-brown and then traced bone-white animal figures for traditional decoration. Like many of my fellow students, I wanted to share these small samples of local art and culture with our American friends. That year we added some cultural presentations to the fair's program. We, the *ticos*, sang a folk song entitled "*De la caña se hace el guaro*"—a story about a man who drowns his sorrows of lost love by drinking *guaro*, a strong spirit made from sugar cane. We did not consider the fact that we were singing about drinking for Southern Christian Restoration students on a conservative campus located in a dry county. We simply sang for good fun, struggling to keep the melody and harmonize our voices as we played the tune from a cassette tape. After the fair, David, the director of our scholarship program, remarked to me that I seemed to have enjoyed myself a lot while singing about drinking. He laughed and let it go. The *feria* again had allowed us to create and recreate bonds of friendship and community among Americans from the central and northern regions of the continent.

Two years later, however, during my senior year, I realized that our culture perhaps was under greater scrutiny than I had realized. Our Central American *Feria de Independencia* had become tradition. We looked forward to the display of crafts, sharing of food, telling of historical tales, and poorly rehearsed but joyful cultural presentations. We *ticos* did not plan our cultural presentation very well that year, so a couple of days before the fair we decided to sing again "*De la caña se hace el guaro.*" We had a good time doing it, but the new director of our scholarship program inquired into the lyrics of the song, since our improvised choreography suggested people drinking themselves to oblivion in a bar room. His secretary, a woman from Honduras who very much believed in Restoration-brand Christianity, found our song offensive and tattled on us. On Monday morning, the director summoned us *ticos* to his office. With a grave voice and stern face, he said he must investigate the lyrics of the song so as not to compromise the good reputation of the scholarship program on campus. He asked us to bring him the cassette tape with the song. Roy, Marcos, Henry, and the others looked at each other and remained silent. I felt so indignant, however, and my blood boiled so quickly, that without deliberation I looked at him and said that the tape was mine but I would not bring it to his office and that if he wanted it, he could come to my dorm room anytime to borrow it or send his secretary to pick it up. Then I walked out of the room. That was melodramatic, perhaps foolish, even arrogant and haughty. But I felt so incensed that a folkloric song from our country should be a matter for the Christian Inquisition on campus that I acted on my sentiment of indignation. The director never came to borrow the tape; as for the secretary, women were not allowed in men's residence halls anyway.

The episode sparked our desire, with some tinges of revenge, to gain a wider audience for our cultural presentations. Serendipity presented us with an opportunity later during my senior year. By channels I cannot recall, the Central American students were invited to put on a presentation for chapel service during a week dedicated to celebrating international cultures on campus. We seized upon the chance. María, a senior from Nicaragua and a good friend of mine throughout the years on campus, played guitar very well and had a beautiful voice with a very warm timbre. So she prepared to sing, along with a chorus of the better voices among the students, a repertoire of popular songs from Central America and Spain. Some others, including me, rehearsed a dance to "*El punto guanacasteco*," a folkloric composition from northwestern Costa Rica. Over my four years in Arkansas, I had brought several tapes of folkloric music from various regions of *Tiquicia*, as Costa Rica is fondly called. I had enough tapes that we could select from among many rhythms and compositions. As a kindergarten and elementary school kid, I had learned how to dance and choreograph some classic pieces from Guanacaste with several classmates in order to present them for school festivities. Other Costa Rican students had also learned several dances in their schools, so we could call upon our "vast" experience as schoolchildren. Meanwhile, our friends from other countries wanted to learn the choreography and have a good time dancing in the process. All of them could listen to and move in sync with the rhythm of *marimbas*, the main instrument—a wooden percussion idiophone of South African origin and Central American evolution—in folkloric orchestras from Guanacaste, which often also include guitars, brass such as trumpets and trombones, and other percussion instruments such as *maracas* and *güiros*. We discovered *marimba* percussion to be a common musical reference for all of us, from Guatemala through Central America all the way to *Ciudad de Panamá*. And very importantly, we could all move to its rhythm. So after listening to several pieces and trying to choreograph them, we collectively chose *El punto guanacasteco* for our presentation.

We started to rehearse *El punto* in earnest in the evenings after dinner at the cafeteria. Someone brought a tape player, I brought my cassette with an orchestral version, and we set to dancing. *El punto guanacasteco* is danced in couples, and all the couples dance as a coordinated group. So we had to choose partners, and I lost no time in finagling my way to matching up with Liliana, a lively and very smart student from Honduras. *Muchacha sonriente*, her smile always beaming, she carried a joyful energy along with her, and we always had engaging and fun conversations when we saw each other around campus or at the "Latinos' table" at the cafeteria. I felt she and I could transform our "good vibe" into joyful dancing. I also got a sense that Liliana enjoyed dancing with me. But it would have been just as fun for me to dance with Diana, my Sino-Panamanian friend, or Ángela *la chapina*, or any of the girls, as it would have been for Liliana to dance with Julio *el canalero*, or Roy or Marcos, my *tico* buddies. All match-ups would have been fine, for we all wanted to have fun dancing together and then to share that joy with our Anglo-American friends. So in the evenings we gathered in an empty classroom; listened to *El punto* on the cassette player, pausing it often to learn its sections; and choreographed each of these, teaching one another the steps and adding our own flare, variations, and innovations, especially when we didn't quite know what the moves should be.

In addition to relishing the music and dance, I silently delighted in our choreographing and rehearsing as a cultural subversion—a rebellion carried out in joyful spirit and for good ole' fun. Our *tico* folk song about *guaro de caña* had been censured and gotten us threatened with punishment by our petty inquisitors as being contrary to good Christian mores. In the context of the Bible Belt, for many people on campus dancing amounted to sinning. So I wanted to delight in our "sinful" culture of dancing for fun anytime, anywhere, with anyone.

In Costa Rica, July 25 is a national holiday commemorating the Annexation of Guanacaste, and children learn to choreograph various *guanacasteca* folk tunes for the celebratory acts at school. I am not sure if my parents volunteered me or if my teacher asked them, but I joined the "dance troupe." I learned simple choreography with seven classmates, including Alicia, the first girl I ever liked, and Carlitos, my best friend for playing. In the pictures that my father must have taken with his old Canon camera, I am wearing a hilarious imitation of male folkloric dress: a *chonete* (a narrow-brimmed, flat-topped white canvas hat) with a *guaria morada*—Costa Rica's national flower, a deep-purple orchid—printed on it; a long-sleeved, button-up shirt of white synthetic fiber imprinted with small figures that are too blurry in the photograph to make them out; bell-bottom blue jeans with brown-leather patches at the knees, a bit large for me and tied to my waist with a thick, black leather belt; black leather boots technically designed for orthopedic correction; two red bandanas, one knotted around my neck and another hung at my right hip from my belt; and a small machete—the agricultural laborer's main tool for farm work—in a leather sleeve hung at my left hip. Come to think of it, I chuckle imagining the ruckus that would ensue nowadays in *la Yunai* if a Latino kid, or any kid, showed up to a dance performance at his kindergarten with a machete hanging from his belt. But at that time and place, wearing a machete to represent an authentic farm worker must have seemed innocent enough to my principal and my teacher to allow it, just as it must have seemed cute to paint with coal a black mustache, in stark contrast with my childish, white face and my blond hair. In the pictures, Alicia also wears an eclectic but much cuter approximation of women's folkloric dress: a white cotton blouse held up at her tiny shoulders with a single ruffled pleat folded over her chest and embroidered in red and blue lines that run the length of it; a long, wide, flowing skirt without pleats, falling to her ankles, made of lime-green cotton fabric with red roses printed on it; and black, low-heeled shoes from our school's daily uniform. A pink carnation is pinned to her short dark-brown hair, and a white-beaded necklace contrasts with her golden-honey skin. In some photographs, I am dancing with a girl with shy moss-green eyes and a timid smile, whose blond hair is braided and tied with red ribbons, while in others I am dancing with Alicia. In one of those photos, I am looking straight

at the camera with a broad smile and bright, happy eyes while raising a bandana just as Alicia looks at me with her dark-roast coffee eyes and laughs
while drawing up her skirt above her ankles.

We all seem happy in those photographs. And that must have been the
main feeling—childish delight at the simple pleasure of moving to the
rhythm of *marimbas* and dancing with friends. I have more lucid memories
of that simple, innocent joy of dancing to the same folkloric music during
elementary school, with friends like Miguel, Marcos, Robert, Laura, Carolina, Carmen, and Marielos. We were children living some of the delightful
experiences that would remain in our hearts and affective memories for life.
I felt that same joy learning to dance popular rhythms, like *merengue*, *salsa*,
and *cumbia*, with my mother and sisters at home, playing music on the stereo in our living room in the afternoons after school, and dancing with my
extended family—great-grandparents, great-aunts and uncles, grandparents,
parents, sisters, aunts, uncles, and cousins—during gatherings for birthdays
and weddings and New Year's Eves.

Dancing had been such a spontaneous and innocent source of delight for
me while growing up that I had difficulty grasping why it should be consid-
ered sinful by so many people at churches and on campus in Arkansas. Sinful
they found it, however, and punishable. Students on campus were not allowed
to organize dance parties or go out dancing to clubs, under risk of expulsion
from the college. So the students who did organize parties or go to clubs
danced in rebellion, "sinning" to defy the Inquisition, and not in fun to be out
in the open and for the sake of pure and simple joy. Had they been allowed
to dance from childhood, perhaps they would have danced their whole lives
from wholehearted happiness, just as David rejoiced as he brought the ark of
the god he adored into his city: "Wearing a linen ephod, David was dancing
before the Lord with all his might, while he and all Israel were bringing up
the ark of the Lord with shouts and the sound of trumpets."[1] But their parents
and overseers must have censured these rebellious kids for wanting to have
fun, for desiring to dance, as being not only against the predominant mores of
the conservative culture but also sinful. Their parents, preachers, elders, and
meddling busybodies were the moral descendants of Michal, the daughter of
Saul: "As the ark of the Lord was entering the City of David, Michal daughter of Saul watched from a window. And when she saw King David leaping
and dancing before the Lord, she despised him in her heart."[2] So they did not
dance in the spirit of David.

I could understand, however, the rebellious dancers' subversive impulse,
and I empathized with it. I felt eager to seize my chance to subvert fire and
brimstone condemnations of dancing, though in a joyful and playful spirit, by
performing during chapel service on our conservative campus. For my friends

perhaps there wasn't that subversive element, but at any rate we all rehearsed in Davidic playful delight.

We continued to rehearse until, on the evening before our presentation, we wanted to gather at the main auditorium on campus, where chapel service was held daily, and practice on the stage. But we couldn't work it out. All the same we rehearsed our choreography several times at the usual classroom. We were excited, even giggly, and laughed a lot together. Then the morning of the presentation arrived. For once, I got up very early, had breakfast at the cafeteria, and met my friends in front of the auditorium well before the 9 am chapel service. Once inside, we put on our folk-dancing costumes. They were actually an eclectic mixture from all over Central America, since each of us had to wear the garments and accessories we had brought over the years from each of our countries.

I donned a *chonete*, a long-sleeved, button-up white shirt, white pants, and rustic leather sandals open at the toes, cross-strapped over the insteps, and single-strapped at the heels. I tied a red bandana around my neck, and I wore a wide, red, shiny *cincha* or cummerbund as a belt. I also tucked into the belt line of my pants, hidden by the *cincha*, the tips of two more red bandanas, in such a way that each one hung from one of my hips. I carried no machete in a leather sleeve. My *compas* wore similar costumes, but with variations in the style of the hats—wide-brimmed or round-topped; sandals—finer, darker leather or strapped in different ways; *cinchas*—cotton or wool, some narrower, some handwoven; or the pattern of colors—blue bandanas, blue jeans, and bone-white *cinchas* decorated with clay-red geometric patterns.

Liliana wore a white cotton blouse, held at the edge of each shoulder by a thin, very short sleeve in such a way that her olive-skinned neck, shoulders, and arms revealed her youthful freshness and vitality. She emphasized her neckline with a tight, black ribbon. Her blouse had a single fold that pleated over the shoulders and across her chest, and the pleat was embroidered with flowers. Her long, white cotton skirt fell to her ankles and over her feet, cascading in several pleats also embroidered in red and blue lines. Her delicate feet, wearing leather sandals, hid beneath her skirt. She tied her black hair up in a bun and wore a flower on her ear. The other girls dressed similarly, but again with variations—some of their blouses were double-pleated; sometimes their shiny-fabric skirts were bright-colored, the cascading triple-pleats being red-black-yellow or green-yellow-red or blue-white-red in succession (this represented the more traditional Costa Rican dress); some wore necklaces instead of ribbons and braided their hair or let it fall freely to their shoulders if long or ornamented it with pinned-in flowers if short.

Many of us were urban kids from San Salvador, Tegucigalpa, or Managua; others were small-town or rural kids from Peréz Zeledón, David, or Chichicastenango—or even coastal kids from the vicinity of Belmopan or from the

Bay Islands of Honduras. We wore an eclectic mix of Central American folk-loric dress. And we were about to choreograph, for an audience of Southern kids, a traditional dance from Guanacaste. In some ways, we were inventing for them a romantic past from a region of Mesoamerica none of us came from, even though I did genuinely love it from childhood. But none of those seeming inconsistencies mattered; the true heart of the matter was our desire to share our culture and joy among ourselves and with others, even if in many ways that culture was really a spontaneous recreation and invention.

Then the time came to announce the dance and perform it. We were all standing off stage, just to the side of the entrance, hidden by the long, drawn curtains. Each couple had lined up in succession, the men on the left, the women on the right. Liliana and I, the shortest ones, were first in line. I was also in charge of explaining a bit about *El punto guanacasteco* to the audience before we performed it. When the university's president, who presided over our daily chapel service, announced the presentation, I walked to the pulpit to explain it. I spoke of its origins in Guanacaste and its history in Costa Rica, and then I hinted at the meaning of the choreography as a courting game, as men wooing women and women playfully resisting until giving in to the courtship. Then I told everyone that they should be attentive and watch carefully because, at the end, the women finally agree to kiss the men discreetly. When I announced kissing on stage, calling it the "best part," the audience laughed, delighted at the thought of couples "making out," but the president turned his head to look at me in disbelief. I still wonder what he thought. I only caught a glimpse of him with my peripheral vision, so I could not tell if there was disapproval in his look or just perplexity. But even at that moment, seconds before our performance, his look did not ruffle me because the students had laughed, and I felt giddy. I walked back to the line and saw Liliana smiling at me.

As we walked onto the stage, we immediately realized that we had made a huge mistake. We had always rehearsed the dance moving clockwise in a wide circle. But because of the position of the pulpit near the entrance, we had to walk onto the stage counterclockwise. That inverted everything. But we had no time to think or adjust or turn around and change direction because the sound producer in the booth began to play *El punto* as soon as the circle of couples had closed. So we had to roll with it.

Liliana and I led the circle, dancing as a couple, and each couple followed behind us, keeping the rhythm and moving counterclockwise in coordination. She led me, and I followed after her as if I were gallantly chasing her and she were playfully fleeing. Our feet stepped in sync: right-left-right, left-right-left. I took the bandana from my hip with my right hand and made it spin in circles over her head. She held her pleated skirt at her hips and made it flow in and out. Her small feet stepped right-left-right as her right hand waved her skirt out-in-out. At the second right step in each sequence, she turned her torso and head slightly to look at me over her right shoulder, and I leaned over close to it to meet her playful eyes and smile at her. Then she stepped left-right-left as she waved her skirt out-in-out. Left-right-*left* and she turned her torso and head to look at me smiling over her left shoulder, and I would lean over close to it to meet her beautiful eyes, falling in love.

Then a change in rhythm and a change in step and direction, as each couple moved toward the center of the circle. Still standing behind Liliana, I stepped sideways and inward, in sync with her: left-right-stop, left-right-stop. She looked left and inward over her shoulder, and I looked at her face—her high, soft cheekbone and small, slightly rounded nose—in profile. We converged with all the couples at the center of the circle, and each of us turned on our own axis toward our left in three steps. Then we reversed direction outwards, returning to our original position in the circumference: right-left-stop, right-left-stop. Liliana now looked right and outward over her shoulder, and still behind her I looked at her other lovely cheekbone, melting with tenderness. Even though the steps and turns for this sequence were completely reversed with respect to our rehearsals, we all succeeded in our spontaneous adjustments.

The melody and rhythm then guided us to repeat the two sequences. First, we moved around the circle counterclockwise, each boy chasing and wooing his girl. Then the music led us into the center of the circle and out from it, but this second time, the couples faced each other, in more overt flirtation. Liliana looked at me with her lovely expression as she danced, and I kept in sync, enamored with her, as we came to the climactic moment in the choreography.

Liliana made half a turn toward her left and I half a turn toward my right so that we came to be back to back, feeling our bodies touch and anticipating a sweet kiss. Then we took our preparatory steps: Liliana swayed right-left-right on her spot as I marched left-right-left on mine. As I stepped, I took a tip of the bandana with my left hand and prepared to unfold it completely. Then I raised the passion-red bandana gently over my right shoulder, and I looked right also, expecting to meet Liliana for a furtive kiss over our shoulders. However when I looked over my right shoulder, Liliana looked over *her* right shoulder also, so our faces did not meet for our kiss. The bandana was meant to hide us from view so we could kiss furtively, but we were turned around with respect to our rehearsal, and *I* did not adjust. Our first kiss failed. The audience burst out laughing. So did Liliana, as I felt her body shake against my back. And so I laughed at myself. But on the second chance I adjusted, and after the three-step sequence, I looked left just as Liliana looked right. This time our faces met, hidden from view by my bandana, and we "kissed." As the sequence repeated itself, I had the glorious joy of "kissing" her twice more on stage.

The original composition afforded yet another sequence for chasing and wooing along the circumference, flirting in and out of the center of the circle, and kissing at the end out the courting game. But we had agreed with the producers to end the choreography at the first kissing session. On that exceptional day during chapel service we could dance folkloric music and even smuggle some "kisses" into the act before the Inquisition could react and ban public displays of affection and punish us.

When our choreography ended, Liliana and I were still laughing, and the audience cheered. The other couples had not seen my mistake, so they didn't know why people had laughed, but they were also exultant. The audience, which must have included hundreds of our friends and acquaintances, clapped and so did our university's president. In the end, our "kissing" proved sweet, tender, and sinless. Meanwhile we, a group of playful students from Central America sojourning in Central Arkansas, had danced a bit and enjoyed it a lot. We hugged offstage, talked a bit, and quickly changed clothes to go our respective ways.

Only fifteen minutes later I was already sitting in my abstract algebra class, probably trying to focus on such things as theories of rings and fields. But I couldn't concentrate; I kept reliving the performance in my mind, cherishing the way it had felt and making sense of it, perhaps already interpreting and recreating the experience in imperceptible ways. Liliana had gone to attend one of her business courses, and everyone else had gone on with their daily routine, chipping away again at the goal of learning and earning a degree. But we all felt happy. We had shared a bit of ourselves, people had appreciated our presentation, and we felt a bit more at home. We had broken from our ordinary state of estrangement in order to delight in midmorning dancing, a type of *fiesta* that felt like a homecoming.

In the days that followed, I sensed that moment, that event, to have been significant, even though I couldn't articulate why. My heart felt unabated delight as I recalled the rehearsals and performance with *amigas* and *compas*—with Liliana, María, Julio, Roy, Diana and the others—and with buddies like Anthony, the football player, and Tim, who had learned enough Spanish while growing up in San Antonio to talk to his Mexican friends there and who loved cultures from south of the *Río Bravo*. Even my acquaintances seemed a bit more like good "neighbors" in the sense of persons close to me in sentiment, close in "life and feeling."[3] Nowadays, with the help of Mexican poet Octavio Paz, I articulate the sense and vital importance of that dancing experience for me in terms of a dialectic movement from solitude into communion.

THE DIALECTIC OF SOLITUDE

Dancing *El punto guanacasteco* together had been a creative way for us to transform our vital and cultural solitude into a search for communion with friends and neighbors. For philosophical poet Octavio Paz, solitude is the existential condition of human beings. But it involves a dialectic. It engenders a search for communion with others in order to escape from our solitude. In "The Dialectic of Solitude" Paz writes,

> Solitude is the profoundest fact of the human condition. Man is the only being who knows he is alone, and the only one who seeks out another. His nature ... consists in longing to realize himself in another. Man is nostalgia and a search for communion. Therefore, when he is aware of himself he is aware of his lack of another, that is, of his solitude.[4]

This way of articulating our basic condition strikes me as too strong nowadays. I understand ourselves to be *relational* beings rather than solitary ones by constitution. As I conceive of it, we are persons constituted not only by our affects—such as solitude or love—and our guiding *telos* or aims—what we strive to be in the future—but by our core relations to peoples and places. These are core relations even in the sense that they are part of our hearts—our hearts are connected to people we cherish and places where we have felt at home. However, I think that when some of our core relations to those peoples and places are severed or threatened, a sense of solitude as a deep-seated sentiment—a characteristic or habitual affect—settles in our hearts. Paz captures poetically our experience in "the labyrinth of solitude": when important relations are severed or curtailed, a deep sentiment of solitude spurs a search for communion; we seek to recreate our personal wholeness by restoring, reforming, or re-configuring our relations to others. In one of its manifestations, I interpret the labyrinth of solitude to be a situation in which we are distanced or separated from people who share our most intimate hopes, sentiments, goals, and ways of living—a situation in which we feel these ways of living to be threatened. In Arkansas, my friends and I felt distant from Central America, from our lands and our peoples. Even as we tried to integrate ourselves to life on campus and in *la Yunai*, we wanted to share our foods, our music, and our dancing rhythms with each other and with our friends from the South and the world.

As I recall the way we felt, I can understand Paz's ideas when he writes:

> All our forces strive to abolish our solitude. Hence the feeling that we are alone has a double significance: on the one hand it is self-awareness, and on the other it is a longing to escape from ourselves. Solitude—the very condition of our lives—appears to us as a test and a purgation, at the conclusion of which our anguish and instability will vanish. At the exit from the labyrinth of solitude we will find reunion ... and plenitude, and harmony with the world.[5]

I can make sense of this passage as a description of how I sought to achieve personal wholeness by cultivating relations to others in *la Yunai* and thus restoring a sense of communion. Dancing with Liliana, Julio, María, and the others, and talking about it with Tim, for example, I restored my sense of being at connected with others in the South. I also can make sense of this passage as a regulatory hope, as the aim I hoped to achieve through various practices—through road-tripping and playing *fútbol* with *compas*, attending a small rural church in Arkansas, visiting a halfway house in town with Shannon, and rehearsing and performing a folkloric dance with friends.

Paz describes various ways in which the dialectic between solitude and communion is at work in contemporary society. He finds expressions of it popular language when it identifies solitude with suffering: "The pangs of love are pangs of solitude. Communion and solitude are opposite and complementary. The redemptive power of solitude clarifies our obscure but vivid sense of guilt: the solitary man is 'forsaken by the hand of God.' Solitude is both a sentence and an expiation."[6]

Paz's example illustrates the popular view that solitude as suffering ensues when one is abandoned by or separated from God. When I read this passage, however, I think mostly of popular music from Mexico and Latin America. "*Historia de un amor*," the *bolero* composed by the Panamanian songwriter Carlos Eleta Almarán, resonates with Paz but carves much deeper wounds into the godless suffering of lost love. The singing voice asks why God made him love his woman, only to take her away and so to make him suffer:

Ya no estás más a mi lado, Corazón.
En el alma sólo tengo soledad y si ya no puedo verte,
¿por qué Dios me hizo quererte para hacerme sufrir más?[7]

His beloved, his *Corazón*, is no longer by his side, and in his soul there is only solitude. She had always been his reason for being. Adoring her was his religion. Their unequaled love, like the fruit from the tree in the Garden of Eden, led him to understand all good and all evil. It illuminated his life, but then it obscured it.

When I listen to the version of this *bolero* by the Mexican trio *Los Panchos*, three guitars and three voices with a full orchestra, I remember the music my maternal grandparents listened to during family parties at their home.[8] These were the experiences of solitary suffering from lost love that I absorbed from music, as did so many of my friends in Costa Rica, before I lived them in my heart, flesh, and bones. I came to fully apprehend the sentiment behind the *bolero* in Arkansas, only after M had died in Costa Rica and I had run away from silent grief by moving to the South of *la Yunai*. There must have been something graspable but ineffable about the commonality of feeling—about how we all suffer from lost love sometime in our lives—because years later I learned that the Panamanian songwriter had written this *bolero* for his brother after his brother's wife had passed away. Moreover, as a college student in Arkansas, when I listened to REM's

"Losing my Religion," I understood Michael Stipe to be singing in the same affective vein of Eleta Almarán's *bolero* interpreted by *Los Panchos*. He sang about losing one's religion by losing one's love, about finding oneself lost.[9] I sensed there to be a commonality of sentiment among *solitarios* suffering from lost love from Panama through Mexico to college bars in Athens, Georgia, and in between.

Thinking along with Paz, a cosmopolitan writer from the heart of Mexico, makes me think of Mexican songsmiths in particular. They have written some of the best, most enduring, and most heart-wrenching *boleros* and *baladas* in Latin America that identify solitude with suffering. Armando Manzanero's "*Esta tarde vi llover*" is among my favorites.[10] In the song, the solitary *bolerista* saw rain falling and people running in the afternoon, a blue star shinning in the evening, autumn arriving, birds in love kissing, the sea singing, but *she* was not there. He does not know if she misses or betrays him; he only knows that he saw the rain falling and people running in the afternoon, but she was not there. At moments when I pined for Pam, the sweet Arkansas girl from Fort Smith, with whom I broke up as a freshman only to regret it as a sophomore, and later when I bemoaned that B had returned to her boyfriend after our study abroad in Europe, I accompanied my nostalgic, solitary lamentations by listening to this *bolero* on my stereo in my dorm room.

When Paz points out that the dialectic of solitude is expressed in popular language, I mostly trace it through popular music. But the dialectic is also expressed and at work through other avenues. Paz writes of the erotic love of couples who must shun social mores to be with each other[11] and of the lives of heroes, saints, and redeemers—such as Saint Paul, Buddha, or Muhammad—who break with an old world and retire into solitude in order to return afterward and create a new world.[12] Insightfully, though, he brings the dialectic from the heroic or saintly into the ordinary. He remarks that "all of us in our own lives, and within our limitations, have lived in solitude and retirement, in order to purify ourselves and then return to the world."[13] During my years as a student in Arkansas, I did not undertake any protracted period of meditative solitude or attempt an experiment in living such as Thoreau's at Walden Pond. However, in the midst of the quotidian routine of college life, I often sought secluded places on campus or in town where I could have periods of silence and quietude. During my first summer, I had discovered how to climb to the roof of the main gymnasium on campus. So once in a while, on a random evening, I crossed the road and the train tracks at the south end of campus, approached the gym, climbed up to its roof, and lay there watching the stars of the Southern sky. I had the roof to myself as a place to think and feel before returning to my residence hall at curfew. My saunters around town, to the courthouse at the town's main square or elsewhere, also provided me with moments of solitary contemplation. In these unheroic and unsaintly ways, I underwent the dialectic of solitude and communion that Paz points to in his writing.[14]

From my perspective, though, Paz is most illuminating when he writes about *fiestas* as experiences that move people along the path from solitude into communion. Through *fiestas*—mythical and religious rites, declamation and performance of poetry, love-making, theater, and epic—human beings emerge from the labyrinth of solitude to find each other in communion. For the Mexican poet, when we are solitary, longing for places and people we cherish, we feel exiled and thrown into "the underground mazes of the labyrinth."[15] We have lost our place, our home in the world, and are estranged in it. We have also lost our primal sense of time. We are trapped in chronometric time, counting the succession of seconds, minutes, hours, days, and years of our exile from communion and of our solitary struggles and labors. To understand the character of this experience, Paz distinguishes between original, mythological time and chronometric, historiographic time.[16] There is an original time that is not "succession and transition, but rather the perpetual source of a fixed present in which all times, past and future, are contained."[17] In this original situation, time and space form a unity: the present is here; here is the present. This is our experience in the womb and during play in early childhood. The rupture or separation of time and space, however, results in chronometric time, in the succession of yesterday, today, and tomorrow that does not correspond to the experienced flow of present reality.[18] We experience this rupture as we grow older and realize that the same historiographic time passes in other places for other people, regardless of their particular situation—for example, I surmise, regardless of whether a man celebrates his daughter's *fiesta de quinceañera* in Puebla or labors as a migrant worker in a farm in Pennsylvania or a construction site in New York.

Through *fiestas*, though, we restore our communion and recreate our proper sense of place and time. He writes: "A fiesta is more than a date or annivsary. It does not celebrate an event: it *reproduces* it. Chronometric time is destroyed and the eternal present—for a brief but immeasurable period—is reinstated. The fiesta becomes the creator of time."[19] He refers to mythical and religious celebrations, such as Catholic processions during Holy Week in many regions of Latin America, I gather. But he also regards love and poetry as capable of recreating our sense of original time, and he paraphrases Juan Ramón Jiménez on the eternity of the poetic instant: "More time is not more eternity."[20] The writing, reading, declaiming, or performing of a poem recreates our original, primal sense of time. These acts are *poietic*; that is, they create realities.[21] Paz's interpretation of love and poetry as *fiestas* provides us with another way to understand the distinction between original and chronometric time.[22] Through enacting love and poetry we infuse time with our particular affects, desires, and hopes, with our longings for encounters and their realization, and we experience time as ours, as a personal present that is continuous with the flow of our communal experience. We find ourselves together in our own place and time.

As my life in *la Yunai* continued beyond my college years in Arkansas, dancing to Latin music became one of the main ways through which I sought to escape personal solitude and cultural isolation. Dancing afforded the possibility of participating in a poetic *fiesta*. Moving in sync with dance partners to the rhythm of *salsa, merengue, cumbia,* and *bolero,* for instance, I sought to connect with other people in the flow of present time and place. Moving our bodies and letting our hearts beat to the rhythm of the music created realities apt for delightful communion, for sharing a "here and now together." By seeking out moments and places to dance, I strove to connect with other people in contexts that welcomed a bit of Latin American culture in *la Yunai*. Along the way I encountered obstacles, even deep personal grief, but on the whole I found communion.

PENNSYLVANIA SOLITUDE: STRUGGLING, DANCING, AND FALLING AWAY FROM K

Upset but smiling, I walked into the bar pretending, in front of my friends, that I felt fine. My heart was sinking like a sharp, thick shard of ice from my chest down into my stomach, cutting and freezing me inside at once. Yet I walked up to Sebastián from Rosario and Hugo from Chihuahua and shook their hands. Then I greeted Carolina, my Uruguayan friend from Salta, kissing her right cheek once, just as I kissed Gabriela from Buenos Aires and Marilú and Blanca, Mexican friends from the Federal District and Morelia respectively. We were all graduate students at the state university, and on that evening, we were out for a bit of fun at the end of the long week.

They were a bit surprised to see me, since I did not usually go dancing at the Silver Screen Grille, the only bar in our college town that played Latin music, once a week, on Fridays from 6 to 8 pm. They welcomed me all the same, and I sat at their table while we waited for the band to start playing. Then someone asked me about K. I lied and said she was busy and couldn't come out that evening. The truth was that K had not wanted to go dancing at the Silver Screen with me. Only after a very upsetting and tense conversation, in which I had tried to persuade her to go out dancing and she had insisted that we stay home, had we agreed that I would go out alone while she would stay at home. It had been one more instance of a struggle that had become habitual—I had wanted us to enjoy a *fiesta* together with Latin American friends in the only place we could dance in town, and she had preferred to stay home resting, avoiding social interaction in that festive space. Unwise and lacking foresight, I had fled the conflict without resolving it by suggesting that she stay home to rest and I go alone.

When I arrived at the bar, I needed to hide my loneliness and dejection from my friends. I could not bring myself to say much, but I pretended that I was listening to their banter and even laughed at stories and jokes I had not really paid attention to. I could not focus on their conversation. Tense body, sunken heart, busy mind, I felt anxious to dance to release the tension.

Finally the band started playing. The musicians were mostly amateurs—teachers, researchers, and graduate students who had formed a band to play Latin and Caribbean rhythms such as *salsa*, *soca*, and *reggae*. But they played with heart and energy, and they could get people moving in their chairs and jumping onto the dance floor. Our group did not waste time to start dancing. As soon as they opened with a Trinidadian beat, Caro, Gabi, and all the rest jumped onto the dance floor together. For me it seemed easier, less risky, to dance with a group in a circle, swaying and jumping and cavorting with everyone. That way, if K asked me later with whom I had danced, I could just say that we had danced all together and I had not danced with anyone in particular.

For that was our bind, the emotional and relational morass in which we found ourselves. By then, I had lived for so many years in *la Yunai*, and mostly in Anglo contexts, that a sentiment of cultural solitude had settled in my heart. So I wanted, even needed, to search for places in which I could connect with people who shared or loved Latin American culture—with friends and strangers who enjoyed eating Latin food, speaking Spanish, or dancing Latin music. And I wanted and needed K to come along with me. We had met in Arkansas, in a waspy college in the core of the Bible Belt; I had met her family and friends and fellow churchgoers in southern Louisiana, and I had adapted to those environments without assimilating. But I needed her to participate in my culture, and dancing with my friends was particularly important to me. I liked to dance for enjoyment and re-connection and communion with them. K enjoyed all varieties of Latin food, loved to travel to Latin America with me, and had worked hard at learning Spanish. She even enjoyed dining with the "Benitos," my *fútbol* friends, and their wives. But for reasons I was too blind to grasp and too immature to know how to address wisely, she resisted contexts in which I would mingle with larger groups of Latin American friends, especially if people danced. She did everything she could, overtly or covertly, to keep us from such *fiestas*. When I suggested that we go, a stressful negotiation always ensued. She resisted, her body uptight and uneasy. Then I insisted, trying to be calm but unable to hide the growing frustration in my frowning expression and my grave voice. Afterward either we'd go and she'd feel dis-tressed, or we'd stay home and I'd feel isolated from personal relations and cultural connections that I needed to cultivate. Or I'd go out alone, feeling dejected, while she would stay home, avoiding distress and perhaps hiding from her fears. If I went out alone, I was careful not to dance with any one female friend in particular, as I gathered that part of her fear stemmed from insecurity, from fear that I would like someone else, a Latina, better than her. But in attending to her fear, I began to lose my sense of spontaneity and liberty to be myself.

So as the band played *soca*, I danced and jumped in our circle, released physical and emotional tension, and let the rhythm guide me along the way to re-connection and communion with people and places dear to my heart. Moving to the beat of the music, I relaxed and enjoyed my friends' presence and companionship, even as I missed K and wanted her to share the experience with me.

That evening, when the band switched from a *soca* to a *salsa* set, I asked Arelys to dance with me. A middle-aged Costa Rican woman who had married a retired man from Pennsylvania, she often organized Latin parties at her house and provided a space to create a bit of a Latin community in our overwhelmingly Anglo-American town in Central Pennsylvania. She also frequented the weekly Latin music session at the Silver Screen. I knew I could dance with her—K knew her, she was married, and she had a teenage son and two lovely girls. She danced all rhythms well and enjoyed every one of them. She danced *salsa* much better than I did, but she let me lead her with ease, always stepping to the tempo—one-two-three-stop, five-six-seven-stop—again and again, through various positions. Though I could not turn her in complex sequences, we both moved in a familiar way, a Costa Rican way, of dancing *salsa*—the man stepping smoothly but moving his torso soberly, not competing in sensuality with the woman, but rather leading her and allowing her all the flare. Arelys and I danced a few songs and chatted. She also asked about K, and I lied again, but by then dancing had relaxed me, and, I am loathe to admit, I lied with relative ease.

When the Latin jam had ended, however, sadness began to crawl back into my chest. I no longer felt it like a cutting shard of ice, but rather like a heavy rock stuck at the junction of my esophagus with my stomach. I chatted only a while longer with my friends. They were going to have dinner at the Allen Street Grill at the old hotel across the street from the main entrance to campus. It was still relatively early for a Friday night, since the Latin music had ended at 8 pm. They asked me to come along, but I excused myself, shook hands and kissed cheeks goodbye, and walked home alone. I walked slowly and deliberately, trying not to think, uneasy about seeing K after the party and maybe having a second round to our bout. As I got closer to home, I started to feel as if a smaller rock had gotten stuck in my throat. What would I say? How could I even speak? When I arrived, however, she had already gone to sleep. I looked at her breathing rhythmically from our bedroom's door, but I did not walk in to caress her. I walked back to our living room, played Mercedes Sosa on the stereo, and lay on the futon, feeling the rock lying there inside me and trying not to think. The dancing *fiesta* had given me a moment of communion, but I felt lost in the labyrinth. Lost and solitary, estranged from the woman I loved in the midst of a culture I had cherished as much as my own, focused on breathing so as not to think, I fell asleep in the futon.

PENNSYLVANIA WINTER

Low-hanging, dark clouds had settled over Happy Valley amid the peaks of the surrounding Appalachian foothills. Winter had swept in harshly. Having just landed in town after returning from break in Costa Rica, shivering from the cold, I walked into our half-empty townhouse. A few pictures still hung on the walls, but many bare hooks revealed the barrenness of a house without love. So did the half-bare bookshelves and CD towers. K had already moved out; only my things remained. My mind numb, my heart beating heavily, I recited the opening verses of Robert Lowell's "No Hearing" to myself:

Belief in God is an inclination to listen,
but as we grow older and our freedom hardens
we hardly even want to hear ourselves ...
the silent universe our auditor—[23]

But I also said to myself the most painful verses, the ones that acutely portrayed the emptiness of a broken relationship:

White clapboards, black window, white clapboards, black
window, white clapboards—
my house is empty. In our yard, the grass straggles . ...
I stand face to face with lost Love—my breath
is life, the rough, the smooth, the bright, the drear.[24]

I walked into our house only to pack my things and load them into a truck. As I stood in our cheerless living room, I wondered about K. What had she felt as she moved out? That same numbness of the mind? That heaviness in the heart? We would never speak of it.

About a year earlier, all the "Benitos," my closest friends, had graduated and moved away from town to live elsewhere in *la Yunai*, return to Peru and Argentina, or migrate to Spain. Having lost my main group for cultural communion, I had tried to cultivate friendships with other Latino/as. K had felt even more threatened, though, and our crisis deepened. I realized that my conflicts with United Statesian oppression against Latinos had affected her trust in our capacity to live a transcultural relationship. My occasional but misplaced and deeply hurtful reactions against that oppression, as when I had shouted nasty words against *gringos* while watching a *fútbol* game, severely weakened her trust. I had tried to atone for it by cultivating our mutual love for literature, film, music, and travel. And I had tried to make her feel that I wanted her to come along with me to Latin American cultural spaces— picnics, festivals, dinners, parties. Occasionally she had agreed, but mostly she had wanted me to remain her Latino partner in Anglo contexts—among her teaching peers in Pennsylvania, her family, and her friends in Louisiana.

I had not seen deeply enough into the fear beneath her resistance or known how to assuage it. Perhaps it wasn't simply fear that I'd prefer a Latina and leave her, or that I'd reject Anglo culture and society wholesale, leaving her behind. Perhaps it was a much deeper fear that she could not belong in a Latin American "world"—a context pervaded by Latin American cultural habits, expectations, behaviors, ideals, and affectivities.[25] Culturally sensitive and open to alternative experiences, perhaps K had felt comfortable in Latin contexts where being Anglo was admired, as when she had visited Costa Rica and traveled around with me to cities, small towns, and country side, to mountains, beaches, rivers, and volcanoes. But in the particular context of Latin American graduate students creating a community in *la Yunai* she had felt inadequate, threatened. As philosopher María Lugones would help me understand many years later, "traveling" to "worlds" in which a person feels or is in fact threatened demands flexibility, adaptability, and tremendous efforts and skills of self-transformation to survive and thrive without giving in, without relenting a sense of self-worth and agency.[26] Perhaps K had even perceived that Latin American "world" to be a context in which desirable ideals of physical beauty were different from those to which she was otherwise accustomed. Sometimes, when she compared herself to other girls physically, I had sensed that K had internalized an idea that olive-skinned, dark-eyed, petite, voluptuous women were more desirable, in a stereotypical Latin world, than light-skinned, green-eyed, tall brunettes and that women who moved to the beat of *salsa* or *merengue* with ease were more desirable than women who could not or were only learning to do so. I had tried to ease her fears, to let her know that I loved her, but I failed. Perhaps the fears were not for me to assuage but for her to resolve. But these are all guesses.

At the time, I did not know how to articulate all these questions, let alone address all these issues. I fell into an emotional standstill that became a low-grade depression. I went about my studies and my work. I continued in my relationship with K while these conflicts brewed in my heart and mind. I left emotionally, without even being aware that I was doing so. I lived my affective turmoil in silence while agreeing to a tacit "truce" with K that had deepened the cracks in our relationship, turning them into crevices and gaps: I went to Latino *fiestas* alone while she stayed away. As this arrangement continued, we had not known how to keep the gaps from becoming chasms. And when the chasms had been carved, we had not known how to bridge them. I found myself vitally and culturally solitary in an affective maze.

K and I separated late in the fall as the cold weather swept into Central Pennsylvania. I bore the responsibility of ending our relationship. I had lost my intimate connection to the person I had most cherished and loved in *la Yunai*. My very self, my person, felt torn asunder. Then it took me several seasons of minute-to-minute crawling, *tanteando*, groping for an exit as if in the dark, to find my way out of the maze.

DANCING RENAISSANCE IN PENNSYLVANIA

I asked Leila to dance with me to Celia Cruz's "*La vida es un carnaval*," the first tune of the evening at the Big Easy.[27] As the joyful music filled the bar-room-turned-dance-club with good vibes, the hopeful lyrics carried by Celia's tropical-hot voice warmed our hearts. Leila and I danced it as a *salsa*, moving to the tempo: one-two-three-stop, five-six-seven-stop. Back and forth; sideways; diagonal; she turns; I turn; she turns; back and forth. Having both been raised in Costa Rica to the rhythm of such music, our bodies moved in sync. The melody and beat of the music and Celia's words flowed through our bodyminds in very similar ways.[28] I felt free and loose dancing with Leila, and I just let the music move me as I sang the lyrics wholeheartedly. I sang with Celia as if to imbibe the spirit of the song. Life is not *desigual*—not more sadness than happiness, not more ugliness then beauty, I guessed; it is rather *una hermosura*, a beauty, and it must be lived. If we think we are alone and doing badly, we must know that it is not so—nobody is alone; there's always somebody. We mustn't cry: life is a carnival; it is more beautiful to live life singing, as singing soothes our woes. Life is not always cruel; there are only bad moments, and then everything passes away. If we think nothing will ever change, we must know that it isn't so—everything changes.

I danced feeling as if I were escaping the labyrinth after having been in lost in its windings during a long, cold, solitary winter. It had been over a year since K and I had lost each other. I was in the Big Easy dancing *salsa* and singing along with Celia in order to crawl farther out of my affective maze.

Every Wednesday night during that second spring without K, I danced with friends at the Big Easy in search of communion. Leila, one of those friends, had come from Costa Rica to Central Pennsylvania to pursue her PhD in anthropology at the state university. Joyful and energetic, she danced and danced and danced. David, also from my hometown of San José, had come to do his PhD in Rural Sociology. A disciplined triathlete, he also enjoyed dancing for fun. We had become good friends, even as he had just started his studies while I was striving to finish my dissertation and move on with my life. I also enjoyed dancing with Luz Marina, *una chica colombiana*. She danced *salsa*, *merengue*, and *cumbia* with a different style that came from Bogotá. Since I could do only basic steps, I could not lead her around the dance floor as she wanted, but she smiled and had fun with me anyway. María, an extroverted literature student from Argentina, had taken *salsa* lessons and took over the dance floor with flair. Andrés, her Colombian boyfriend and the most elegant dancer among our *compas*, led her with ease. Luis Daniel, a physicist from Mexico and a friendly guy, danced with flair but not as elegantly. All the same, he danced much better than I could. I could see that Alma, an intelligent biologist also from Mexico who had a springy touch to her style, and Magda, a chemist from Colombia who danced more soberly, and all the other women had a blast dancing with Luis Daniel. Joshua, *el gringo*, had learned to dance salsa and speak Spanish in Mexico. Tall, lanky, dirty-blond haired and bearded, and brown-eyed, he kept the rhythm very well and could spin his partners around effortlessly, even if he moved a bit mechanically. He spoke Spanish flawlessly, with a noticeable Mexican accent. Soft-spoken, he enjoyed being around Latin music and people, and we enjoyed his kind presence. Sharon, a blond, blue-eyed Texan, also liked to come out with us. She had learned to dance at the salsa club on campus, and her movements were a bit "ballroomy" for my taste. But she always flashed an endearing smile while dancing that revealed genuine delight.

The group as a whole, I thought, constituted an American dancing community. Every one of us danced a bit differently; our bodyminds felt the music and moved to its rhythm in slightly different ways. But we all felt relaxed, joyful, and together for two hours every Wednesday night.

On that evening when dancing began with "*La vida es un carnaval*," the DJ had to stop playing and we had to clear the dance floor around 10:30 pm, like every Wednesday, in order to make the barroom available for all the Anglo frat boys and sorority girls that came to drink until closing time. We had enjoyed our dancing all the same, however. After the last bit of conversation with Leila, David, and others, I shook hands, kissed cheeks, and walked home slowly and deliberately—my body relaxed and loose, my heart peaceful and happy.

When I arrived at my apartment, I turned on my computer and kept writing my dissertation at my desk until the early hours of morning. In the sentiment of communion brought about by dancing with friends, I found clarity of thought and a joyful spirit for writing. I strove to finish my work by summer's end, knowing I would then leave friends and a community behind, carrying them, nonetheless, in my healing heart.

DANCING IN NEW YORK CITY: ESCAPE
FROM THE LABYRINTH

Escape One

I take Val onto the dance floor as soon as the Williamsburg Salsa Orchestra starts playing. It is rainy and cold outside Subrosa, a cool Latin dance club in Manhattan's Meatpacking District, but inside it is cozy and about to get hot. Val, a Brazilian woman who immigrated to New York as an adolescent the very same year I went to Arkansas as a student, knows Solange, the Argentinean singer of the orchestra. Val is a psychology graduate student. With chestnut-brown eyes, brown-sugar skin, long, brown, curly hair, and a powerful athletic build, she dances *salsa* like a *puertorriqueña* and *samba* like a *brasileira*. Solange is a professional singer who trained at fine conservatories. With curly red hair, light skin, freckled face, and a long, slim figure, she sings *salsa* like a *Nuyorican* and *Nueva Trova* like a *rioplatense*. In South America Val and Solange might have never crossed paths, but in New York they met when Val and I went to listen to South American folk music at Beco, a Brazilian bar in Brooklyn, and Solange happened to be singing. In the tiny dining and listening room, Val knocked over Solange's microphone as she sang, and out of the apologetic conversation their friendship emerged.

Tonight, Solange's voice fills the room with warm energy while Val dances, pouring all her vitality into movement. I focus all my energy into leading her; it is a joyful effort. We smile and laugh all night. Wearing a short, white dress with printed flowers and a carnation in her hair, Solange sings and sings, in English. Felipe, my *tico* buddy, is filling in at the *timbales* for the regular *timbalero*. The Williamsburg Orchestra's *salsa* is good to listen to and even better for dancing. They play an eclectic style, arranging indie rock tunes into *salsa* and composing their own fusion numbers. The mix of people in the room is just as eclectic. Latin Americans from all over the continent, Latino/as from the United States, Anglo- and Afro-Americans, Africans, East Asians, Afro-Caribbeans—everyone has come to dance and enjoy a Latin American *fiesta*.

Escape Two

Felipe Fournier and his band, Supermambo!, start playing their musical tribute to Tito Puente as Val and I walk into the music room at the back of Barbès. This tiny bar in Park Slope, only four subway stations away from my neighborhood, has become one of my usual joints for listening to live music and dancing. For me, it functions as the sort of spot that turns a city like Brooklyn into a "personscape"—a space where persons situated in intimate relations to their urban places live and feel at home.[29] I know by heart its music room's wooden floors, unused fireplace, irregular polygon contours, and quirky decorations, including the golden sign with glowing red lights for the "Hotel D'Orsay" that hangs at the corner behind the stage. Tonight, I have asked Val to come to listen to my buddy Felipe play Puente's early compositions on the vibraphone.

Puente, a Nuyorican son of *Boricua* immigrants, grew up in Spanish Harlem, where he became a musician, later studied at Juilliard, and then went on to a creative career playing mambo and fusing musical styles into Latin jazz. The great Tito is nowadays remembered as a *timbalero*, but from Felipe I know that early on he composed for and played the vibraphone. Felipe, a Costa Rican son of a piano player, grew up in San José, studied at local conservatories, and wanted to focus on Latin percussion but found that the conservatories in Costa Rica exclusively focused on classical music. So he went to a conservatory in Puerto Rico and then moved to New York, where he now plays percussion in several bands and leads Supermambo!

Felipe plays the vibraphone with heart and finesse. A drummer, another percussionist at the *congas*, and a double bass player accompany him. His dark eyebrows and full beard appear to thicken his thinning black hair and emphasize his glowing smile as he plays. He is slender but plays the vibes with might and zest. Soon after he starts playing, he is already sweating profusely. In a quick movement, he unbuttons his dripping shirt at his hairless chest and keeps playing. Most United Statesians in the room sway as they listen, but Val and I start dancing to Supermambo!'s interpretation of Puente's music. My *brasileira* friend and I cannot simply listen to these rhythms. We have to move to them. Soon, though, other Latino/as are moving as well.

I spot Linda, my Nicaraguan friend and Supermambo!'s manager, dancing. I met her months ago, also at Barbès, while listening to Cumbiagra's Colombian rhythms. I saw her moving like a Latina among swaying hipsters and asked her to dance. We had a blast all night, and we became friends. Educated in communications and journalism in Nicaragua, she felt happy to meet a fellow Central American. So did I. I found a familiar comfort in her accent, in her way of being, in the places she had grown up, in the foods she liked. One night she introduced me to Felipe when he played *congas* for Chicha Libre at a former warehouse transformed into an art performance space in Red Hook. Tonight, when Linda sees me, we make warm eye contact and smile to each other as I continue to dance with Val.

When Supermambo! takes a break, I introduce Val to Linda, and we talk about music, about Nicaragua, Brazil, and Brooklyn, about our life stories. When Felipe and his band start playing again, Val and I dance and dance and dance again. I notice that now even the hipsters in the room are dancing to Tito Puente's music as best they can. This is an American experience. When the gig ends, Val and I walk up to Felipe. We wait in line, as people are congratulating him. Finally, we greet him. Val met Felipe on the night when he played *timbales* with Solange and the Williamsburg Salsa Orchestra at Subrosa. We embrace him and take pictures together in front of the vibraphone. We smile with joy that flows from music, dancing, and friendship—from escaping solitude to find communion.

Escape Three

El Pollo Rancherito shut down some months ago. Nowadays in its place there is an Azerbaijani club where families gather for parties and festivities. Sometimes from my apartment I hear them playing music and singing on the patio, and I imagine them dancing. I then wonder where Pablo and the two *poblanos* have gone. Are they in Brooklyn? Have they returned to Chichicastenango and Puebla? Other times, as I wonder, I play *cumbia* on my stereo and dance it *tico* style as a *swing criollo*, subtly jumping in various feet patterns to the music's rhythm. I dance alone but do not feel solitary. Moving to the rhythm of Latin music turns my Brooklyn apartment into an American home.

Escape Four

It is Monday night in the early fall. After a long teaching day, I decided to unwind by listening to live music, so I have come again to Barbès in Brooklyn. Yotoco is playing their original and very danceable fusion of *cumbia*, *merengue*, *bomba*, funk, *plena*, and other rhythms. There is a percussionist on the *timbales*, another one on the *congas*, a bass player, a male singer on the accordion, and a female singer on the *güiro* and *maracas*. I have been dancing along with the small crowd, made up mostly of Anglo hipsters and a Haitian couple. A small Monday night crowd means a lot of dancing space available, so I have been moving with ease across the floor and mingling. Everyone is dancing together. The band has played some fun arrangements of traditional songs from Colombia and elsewhere, and some of their own compositions. Then they come to an original song that strikes my attention. The front man, a dark-bearded, curly haired Colombian guy in his late twenties, plays the accordion as he sings:

Yo soy indocumentado
y no puedo ir a estudiar.
Aunque sepa más que nadie
no entro a la universidad.
Tengo que comer callado.[30]

The lyrics make me think of some of my students at the college who are undocumented immigrants. Our public university justly does not reject their admission based on their immigration status, so they can study. But they do live with the same fears of joblessness, deportation, and family separation of all people in their situation. When they graduate, they will still be excluded from full political participation in society and even from the job market. I think of my friend W, a former student. His family migrated by land from Ecuador to *la Yunai* when he was a kid. He grew up and studied in Brooklyn. Now he is also in his late twenties, like Yotoco's singer, and has earned bachelor's and master's degrees in humanities from our university. The US government's program that temporarily protects him from deportation may be discontinued, and has a sales job for which he is overqualified. I wish I could remedy the injustice of his situation in a society that continues to exclude him. I cannot. But when I listen to Yotoco's song, I realize that the band is speaking up for him and that people are listening, even these Anglo hipsters that in the past I had disdained. After the set is over, I go to talk to Yotoco's singer. His name is Sebastián, from Medellín, Colombia. I ask him about "Indocumentado," and I am surprised to learn that he is speaking from personal experience. He was once undocumented as he grew up and then went to college in Florida. But then our immigration system provided him with a way to become documented. Now he has come to New York to work as an engineer and play music. In my mind, he has been singing and speaking up on behalf of W to the crowd. And I think that, just as in this dance floor in Barbès, it is possible for sympathetic people to sing and listen and move in sync, for the growth of loving communion, in *la Yunai*.

DANCING AT HOME

Dancing to Latin music in the *Yunaited Esteits*, I have strengthened relations with friends while establishing new relations with neighbors. Many times I have shared one or two songs and a delightful moment with people also seeking the joy of dance. Friends, neighbors, and strangers as dance partners—Latinas, Anglo-Americans, Afro-Americans, and immigrants to the United States from China, Nigeria, Spain, Russia, and elsewhere—have become delightful and meaningful partners with whom to live the present. In a variety of settings—apartments, dance clubs, town squares, and public parks—I have connected with them in contexts afforded by our shared enjoyment of Latin music, an aspect of Latin American culture in *la Yunai*. Over the years, dancing has offered me meaningful companionship and infused my life as an immigrant with happiness. Dancing with others, I have felt at home again in this vast land among its diverse peoples.

NOTES

1. I Sam. 6:14 (Holy Bible: New International Version).
2. I Sam. 6:16 (NIV).
3. See Charles S. Peirce, "Evolutionary Love," in *The Essential Peirce: Selected Philosophical Writings*, eds. N. Houser and C. Kloesel, vol. 1 (Bloomington: Indiana University Press, 1992), 352–371. In Peirce's words: "'Our neighbor' … is one whom we live near, not locally perhaps, but in life and feeling," 354.
4. Octavio Paz, *The Labyrinth of Solitude*, trans. Lysander Kemp (New York: Grove Press, 1985), 195.
5. Ibid., 195–196.
6. Ibid., 196.
7. Carlos Eleta Almarán, "Historia de un amor." First recorded for the soundtrack of the movie *Historia de un amor*. Directed by Roberto Gavaldón (México: Internacional Cinematográfica, 1956), film.
8. For a similar version with a female singer, listen to Carlos Eleta Almarán, "Historia de un amor" in Eydie Gorme and Trío Los Panchos, *Personalidad* (Sony Discos, 1996), compact disc.
9. Listen to Bill Berry et al, "Losing my Religion" in R.E.M., *Out of Time* (Warner Brothers, 1991), compact disc.
10. The song was first released as a single. Armando Mazanero, "Esta tarde vi llover" (RCA Victor, 1967), 45 rpm.
11. Paz, *Labyrinth*, 197–202.
12. Ibid., 204–205.
13. Ibid., 205.
14. Indeed, from the standpoint of William James's radical empiricism, I take Paz to be *indicating an experience* that all people can undergo and identify, in different guises, in their own lives. See, for instance, William James, "A World of Pure Experience," in *The Works of William James—Essays in Radical Empiricism*, ed. Frederick Burkhart (Cambridge, MA: Harvard University Press, 1976 [1904]), 21–44.
15. Paz, *Labyrinth*, 209.
16. He presents this conceptual distinction in *The Labyrinth of Solitude*, while he describes our experience of this distinction in Octavio Paz, *In Search of the Present: Nobel Lecture.*, trans. Anthony Stanton (New York: Harvest/HBJ, 1991). I elaborate on my reading of Paz in Daniel Campos, "On Poetry and Authentic Philosophical Reflection: The American Philosophy of Octavio Paz," *Cognitio* 8, no. 2 (2007): 179–195.
17. Paz, *Labyrinth*, 209.
18. Ibid.
19. Ibid., 209–210.
20. Ibid., 210. See Juan Ramón Jiménez, "A Luis Cernuda," in *La Corriente Infinta*, ed. Francisco Garfias (Madrid: Editorial Aguilar, 1961), 171–178.
21. Paz, *Labyrinth*, 203. The English translation, however, is dissatisfactory on this point, as it says that poetic activity is "creative activity dealing with realities." Paz writes that poetic activity creates realities: "… *una actividad creadora de realidades,*

esto es, una actividad poética." See Octavio Paz, *El laberinto de la soledad y otras obras* (New York: Penguin, 1997), 236.

22. Ibid.

23. Robert Lowell, "No Hearing 3" in *Collected Poems*, eds. Frank Bidart and David Gewanter (New York: Farrar, Straus and Giroux, 2003), 638.

24. Ibid.

25. For this concept of an experiential world, see María Lugones, "Playfulness, 'World'-Traveling, and Loving Perception," in *Pilgrimages/Peregrinajes: Theorizing Coalition against Multiple Oppressions* (New York: Rowman & Littlefield, 2003), 77–100.

26. Ibid.

27. Listen to Victor Daniel, "La vida es un carnaval" in Celia Cruz, *Mi vida es cantar* (National Own / Universal, 1998), compact disc.

28. American philosopher John Dewey used the term "body-mind" to indicate that people are vitally integrated into their natural and cultural environments. People, as natural, organic, intelligent beings, are not essentially body or essentially mind, but a continuous body-mind. I have removed the hyphen to emphasize the continuity. Dancing, for example, is physical and affective and intellectual and cultural and so on. See, for instance, John Dewey, "Nature, Life and Body-Mind," in *Experience and Nature* (New York: Dover, 1958), 248–297.

29. See John McDermott, "Glass without Feet," in *The Drama of Possibility: Experience as Philosophy of Culture*, ed. Douglas Anderson (New York: Fordham University Press, 2007), 204–218.

30. Sebastián López Velásquez, "Indocumentado," 2016, live performance.

Chapter 15

Philosophical Postlude

Resilient Love

In the early spring, I take the F train from Brooklyn up to midtown Manhattan and get off at Rockefeller Center. As people around me rush to this or that urgent appointment, I stroll north along the Avenue of the Americas until I arrive at the south entrance to Central Park. I stop there to visit the monument honoring José Martí, the Cuban poet, writer, and political leader. The equestrian statue represents his courage in fighting for Cuban independence from Spain, as Martí rides a horse that charges ahead to battle. Though it portrays his military valor rather than his poetic creativity or his philosophical thoughtfulness, today his statue serves as a symbolic contrast to the luxurious coldness of the Trump Tower. Glass without heart,[1] the tower rises as a vacuous monument to spiritual and intellectual emptiness only a few blocks away, near Columbus Circle.

Nowadays, a strident politician is yelling anti-immigrant slurs from the top of his tower. He has proposed to build a wall along the entire border between *la Yunai* and Mexico and to deport eleven million immigrants, and some United Statesians have elected him to govern their nation—the imaginary, hateful nation that would be "purely white," whatever that may mean, and English-speaking. Since his presidential campaign he has spewed derogatory remarks as to the moral worthiness of Mexican immigrants—only one of his many attacks on a variety of peoples. His insignificant name matters very little to me. I might call him Mr. Rogue. As I stand observing Martí's monument, I think of how I might respond to his roguish provocations. There are several options, more or less recommendable.

There is the defiant option expressed by Mexican rock band Molotov in their song "Frijolero."[2] A vigilante from the southwestern borderland, in the very style of this New York politician, sings:

Don't call me *gringo,* you fuckin' beaner.
Stay on your side of that goddamn river.

The *mexicano* responds:

No me digas beaner, Mr. Puñetero.

This defiant form of resistance is understandable in the face of threats and
oppression. Perhaps it is even necessary. Resistance alone does not give a
way to resolve the conflict between the *gringo* and the *mexicano,* however.
It may lead to a standstill at best, where the United Statesian vigilante
remains a *pinche gringo* to the *mexicano,* and the *mexicano* a beaner to the
United Statesian. They do not recognize each other as American. A defiant attitude says, "You will not trample me." Immigrants and temporary
migrants often need to say that; we must stand our ground. As Molotov's
song portrays, however, defiance alone does not provide a way out of the
confrontation. I do find some pleasure in imagining Molotov playing "Frijolero" full blast in a concert behind Trump Tower. But I do not find this
response sufficient.

In some ways, I respond to media coverage of the haughty politician's
provocations by heeding Thoreau's advice: "Read not the Times. Read the
Eternities."[3] When my mind is in danger of becoming soiled by listening to
news of this Rogue's words, I recall what Thoreau suggests:

> Not without a slight shudder at the danger, I often perceive how near I had come
> to admitting into my mind … the news of the street; and I am astonished to
> observe how willing men are to lumber their minds with such rubbish, — to per-
> mit idle rumors and incidents of the most insignificant kind to intrude on ground
> which should be sacred to thought. Shall the mind be a public arena, where the
> affairs of the street and the gossip of the tea-table chiefly are discussed? Or shall
> it be a quarter of heaven itself …?[4]

I agree with Thoreau that I should not let my heart and mind become the
ground upon which such trash is spewed and gnawed. I strive to protect my
inward well-being against such threats. Guarding my wholeness of mind
and heart, however, should not lead me to isolation, just as Thoreau did not
go to Walden Pond to isolate himself from Concord but rather to see from
a better perspective how to engage its citizens. Inward wholeness is also
for the sake of better outward engagement. Moreover, I might disregard the
Rogue's trash-talk for the sake of my peace of mind, for a kind of Epicu-
rean *ataraxia.*[5] There are, however, hundreds of thousands, even millions of
people, who listen to him and applaud his anti-immigrant slurs in *la Yunai.*
He will soon be gone, I hope, vanished to become an ugly, crass footnote in

American history. But the sentiments, emotions, and passions of the people who support him will still be there. I do not want to write these people off and disengage them. I rather want to walk to their worlds respectfully and talk to them and have them listen to me. I also wonder what my old friends— say, Adrian, Tim, Tibor, and Jason—women I have loved—B and K—and families I have known—Jerry and Phyllis in Oklahoma, the Kinsers in Ohio, the Heffington's in Arkansas—think about all of this. I still want to talk and listen. This is agapic resilience—the habit or disposition to continue to love, while caring for one's own well-being, even in the face of adverse conditions, such as divisive politics.[6]

Toward this end, the ideas regarding relations between Anglo- and Spanish Americans that Martí expresses in his essay *"Nuestra América"*[7] afford an apt philosophical ethics from which to seek such dialogue and engagement—an ethics that may articulate, in yet another light, the form of resilient love that I have tried to develop and live by over the past few years, as I have written these essays and thought about how to live well again in *la Yunai*.

Martí published *"Nuestra América"* in *La Revista Ilustrada de Nueva York* in 1891. At the time, Cuba and Puerto Rico were the only remaining Spanish colonies in the Americas. Martí, who lived as an exile in New York, knew full well that many politicians and military leaders in *la Yunai* wanted to turn those islands into US colonies. *"Nuestra América,"* then, was an appeal to Spanish American unity—the independent nations of Spanish America should support Cuban independence and stand up, united and as equals, to the US expansionist ambitions in the Caribbean. Martí, a romantic, exhorts Spanish Americans to embrace the natural creative impulses of their authentic identity—a mixture of African, Native American and European ethnic and cultural heritage—rather than imitating the mores and lifestyles of European "civilization." The aim is to be natural and creative, not "civilized" and imitative. Toward the end of the text, Martí addresses the attitude that Spanish Americans ought to take with regard to their ambitious Anglo-American neighbors. There he sketches the principles of an ethic that may serve as a contemporary response to the provocations of anti-immigrant agitators.

Martí writes: "There can be no racial animosity, because there are no races. The theorist and feeble thinkers string together and warm over the bookshelf races which the well-disposed observer and the fair-minded traveler vainly seek in the justice of Nature where man's universal identity springs forth from triumphant love and the turbulent hunger for life. The soul, equal and eternal, emanates from bodies of different shapes and colors."[8] I find Martí's position noteworthy because he defended it in the late nineteenth century, even as he knew that the Rogues of his time thought him inferior and worthy of colonial tutelage for being Cuban. It must have stung to know that many of his Anglo-American neighbors saw him as inferior. He must have seen it in their patronizing eyes, heard it in their contemptuous tone of voice. However, he did not recommend responding to animosity with hatred or resentment, but with justice and love. From *"Nuestra América"* we can extract two ethical principles for our contemporary situation regarding immigration—namely, justice as respect for the equal worth of all human beings and love as the source of bonding, commonality, and solidarity.

As for justice, I think that behind the strident politician's anti-immigrant opinions there is arrogant disregard for the very worthiness of their human-ity—what Martí calls their equal and eternal soul. For such a rogue, Mexican immigrants should live and die in the midst of their alleged poverty and crime in their own country; that they are human beings in need of hospitality, soli-darity, compassion, and care is not our problem or ethical concern. For Martí, in contrast, the admirable perspective would be to recognize Anglo- and Latin-Americans as equal in humanity and to live and act accordingly. One aspect of their equality is their inherent creativity—their capacity to create new ways of living and being together in our world.

As for love, Martí calls it the very *spring* of our "universal identity"—that is, love is the fountain of our commonality, the source of solidarity among people. From my perspective, I interpret love in terms of Peirce's ethical agapism. Love is the impulse first to understand the needs and aims of others, and then to respond effectively, with caring actions, as if they were our very own needs and aims. I personally can extend this kind of loving care to more recent or younger immigrants—like my students at Brooklyn College. I can also offer it to those who remain undocumented and vulnerable to exploita-tion even after years of persevering toil in our society—like my friend Carlos, who fled Colombia's civil war in 1990, migrated on foot all the way from the Colombian and Venezuelan *llanos* or plains to Texas, found his way to New York, and has driven a car daily for many years to make a basic living for his son and himself in the Bronx. I can also give this love to my Anglo friends and neighbors in *la Yunai*—people I have known and people I hope yet to meet. Moreover, for Martí love is not meekness or weakness. Elsewhere in *"Nuestra América"* he makes it clear that love must be accompanied by the courage to demand respect—from my perspective, another enactment of a resilient disposition. However, love is the sentiment that offers not only respect but empathy and support. It refuses to respond to animosity with hatred. It rather seeks to create or repair bonds of cooperation.

If a single politician's anti-immigrant opinions were to blow away in the wind, an ethical rejoinder in the spirit of Martí would not be necessary. The problem is that a proportion of United Statesians agree with him and have given him power to enforce anti-immigrant policies. In this regard, however, Martí is also instructive: "One must have faith in the best in men and distrust the worst. One must allow the best to be shown so that it reveals and prevails over the worst."[9] In the spirit of Martí, Latino/as in the United States must not despair of the possibilities of dialogue or dismiss Rogues as irredeemable xenophobes. His thought recommends a response from a different ethical ground—a ground upon which to reflect together about the experiences of immigrants and our responsibilities to them. It recommends that we seek dialogue, earnest sharing and listening, thoughtful and caring engagement. We can help each other grasp that an admirable Martian ideal for all Americans would be to be the most just, most loving people to immigrants—to treat them as our equals, and to respond to their needs and foster the pursuit of their aims as if they were our own.

LISTENING TO PHILOSOPHICAL FRIENDS: LOVING SAUNTERING, *PHILOSOPHY AMERICANA*, AND "WORLD"-TRAVEL

Molotov's resistance and Martí's love suggest one way of sketching the sort of resilient love that I seek, not only in theory but in practice. In the foregoing essays, I have articulated my sense of such resilient love mostly in terms of Charles Peirce's agapism—again, the doctrine that love is really effective in the world, that it has concrete effects upon it.[10] In terms of human interaction, *agape* is unconditional love that cherishes and nurtures the well-being of the beloved persons so they can grow and thrive.[11] Ethical agapism holds at its core the belief that "growth comes only from love ... from the ardent impulse to fulfil another's highest impulse."[12] This is a "belief" in the American pragmatist sense of being a habit that guides our actions, consciously or nonconsciously.[13] It is a disposition that shapes conduct. I have tried to articulate and practice resilient love as a principled approach to my caring sauntering in America, that is, to my effort to be equally at home everywhere in the Americas, even as an immigrant in *la Yunai*. I still aim to be at home at the level of affects—feelings, emotions, and sentiments—in relations to people and places, and goals and purposes for my life. I keep trying to do so lovingly, while respecting myself and being respected by others.

The process of writing these essays over the course of eight years (2009–2016) has led me into a dynamic of recollecting and reconstructing my personal experience, reflecting upon it, trying to articulate my guiding principles and general tendencies in the flux of that experience, evaluating critically such principles and tendencies, and, as a result of self-criticism, changing or readjusting my practices. I have tried to understand, convey, criticize, and transform my ways of being and living as an immigrant in *la Yunai*, as a person who strives to love his neighbors and wants to remain engaged with them. The process has been intensely personal, often marked by self-doubt, especially by a sense that my experience is not as important as that of others, particularly of other immigrants whose loving resilience is admirable to me. In this process, though, the voices of two philosophers, as expressed in their work, have encouraged me along. They also point toward future thinking, living, and writing.

Douglas Anderson holds that *philosophy Americana*—a philosophy that is autochthonous and grows out of the Americas' environment and experience—requires listening to arguments and stories told from our own experiential homes.[14] Our experience is a place, a starting ground, from which to launch inclusive conversations. In Anderson's words,

> Personal experience does not validate or invalidate beliefs, but it is the place from which they arise and the place to which they return. ... No particular experience can include all other experiences, but in establishing one's angle of vision, one establishes the premises for reaching out toward others' experiences, for creating communication. Not a casual conversation, but a thick exchange of thought and feeling.[15]

In writing these essays and putting them forth, I have attempted to establish this ground and this angle of vision, for striking up thick affective and intellectual conversations.

One forthcoming philosophical conversation, for me, will be with the thought of Argentine immigrant-philosopher María Lugones. Her work in *Pilgrimages/Peregrinajes* draws me to listen to her experience and to engage the philosophy that arises from that experience and returns to it in practice. Moreover, her experience-based philosophy helps me to criticize my own.

Lugones describes as "world"-travel the experience of people who must live in and adapt to various social environments, especially when they move from environments in which they feel at home to environments in which they are subordinated or oppressed.[16] This is the case of women in our male-dominated society and of ethnic minorities in mainstream Anglo culture in the United States. Women of color face an even more complex tangle of oppressing environments to travel into and out of in the course of living their daily lives. I am calling environments what Lugones calls "worlds." A "world" may be an actual society "given its dominant culture's description and construction of life," including the construction of relations of power between classes, genders, and so on.[17] This may be the mainstream working "world" of all laborers in the United States, regardless of whether they are Latina women or Anglo males, for example. A "world," however, may also be that same society "given a nondominant, a resistant construction."[18] This may be the "world" of migrant agricultural workers or urban laborers who organize to gain better working conditions from their employers. A "world" must be "inhabited at present by some flesh and blood people" who experience it affectively in very tangible ways.[19] It must be a world of concrete experience. According to Lugones, for the outsider "world"-traveling requires flexibility in shifting back and forth from a mainstream construction of life to other constructions of life where she is at home.[20] For example, she writes:

> As outsiders to the mainstream, women of color in the United States practice "world"-traveling, mostly out of necessity. I affirm this practice as a skillful, creative, rich, enriching, and, given certain circumstances, loving way of being and living. I recognize that much of our traveling is done unwillingly to hostile white/Anglo "worlds." The hostility of these "worlds" and the compulsory nature of the "traveling" have obscured for us the enormous value of this aspect of our living and its connection to loving. ... I recommend that we affirm this traveling across "worlds" as partly constitutive of cross-cultural and cross-racial loving.[21]

"World"-traveling is thus loving, but it is also a resistant practice. The skill, creativity, and love involved in this practice are for the sake of surviving and thriving without giving in to assimilationist and oppressive pressures. One way to put it is that the person adapts but does not assimilate; she rather transforms the mainstream "world" in creative and loving ways while living in it.

My sense is that an immigrant's experience can be characterized in insightful ways as "world"-travel. At least for me, studying and working in English, learning mainstream social norms and discerning when and how to follow or resist them, listening to the experiences and regarding the points of view of many different people from the South to the North, expressing my own experiences and perspectives, cultivating friendships, resisting disrespect or oppression, having fun while listening to New York salsa, indie rock, and folk music, and doing my best to offer cross-cultural care to students from Brooklyn and all over the world are but a few of the aspects of my life as a "world"-traveler in *la Yunai*.

Then, Lugones' philosophical account of her experience as "world"-traveler helps me to raise a central question about my own. I have accounted for my immigrant experience as caring sauntering, that is, as the experimental attempt to make myself at home in *la Yunai* and across the Americas in terms of affects, relations to people and places, and life-goals and aims. This style of sauntering, regarded as a form of "world"-traveling, does involve skill, creativity, love, and playfulness as openness to possibility.[22] I do wonder, however, if my style of sauntering is sufficiently resistant from Lugones' point of view. According to her, "resistance is not reaction but response—thoughtful, often complex, devious, insightful response, insightful into the very intricacies of the structure of what is being resisted."[23] I interpret Lugones' "world"-traveling as loving resistance, while I have characterized my sauntering as an attempt at resilient love. I wonder if there is a significant philosophical difference in the shift in emphasis. Lugones describes "world"-traveling in some veins as subversive "trespassing," especially through politically organized resistance.[24] Is my sauntering too light and individualistic a way to tread into the oppressive world of Rogues? I do aim for my sauntering to be resilient, resistant, and transformative of mainstream "worlds," even as it remains a caring and loving practice. I strive to listen and to speak in ways conducive to being listened to by those I want to engage. I also try to act in ways that are responsive to earnest conversations and shared reflection upon experience. Lugones reminds me, at the same time, to assess the effectiveness of my attempts at adapting to and transforming "worlds" through my style of sauntering.

Moreover, Lugones warns that we cannot travel to oppressive "worlds" playfully and lovingly. Those are "worlds" that "we enter at our own risk, 'worlds' that have agon, conquest, and arrogance as the main ingredients in their ethos. These are 'worlds' that we enter out of necessity and that would be foolish to enter playfully."[25] In line with this, I do realize that I have a relative privilege in sauntering lovingly to some "worlds" where other immigrants, including many of my friends and some of my students, could only travel with great caution. I speak English, am authorized to reside in *la Yunai*, teach in a college, have many Anglo-American friends and students, and write freely. This gives me access to and a voice in social contexts, especially United Statesian ones, where other immigrants whom I know and love can only tread with risk. I hope that rather than withdrawing from such Anglo "worlds," I can use my access to bring my voice and the explicit and implicit voices of others to earnest conversations leading to reflection and transformed action. And I strive to do this through a fallible agapistic ethos.

For, as Lugones also emphasizes, "there are 'worlds' that we can travel to lovingly, and traveling to them is part of loving at least some of their inhabitants."[26] I still do want to go on walks, take road trips, play friendly *fútbol* games, read American literature with friends and students, dance, cultivate friendships, and even "go to church" in the woods, lakes, mountains, prairies, and beaches of *la Yunai*, from Arkansas and Louisiana, through Oklahoma, Tennessee, and Kentucky, to Ohio, Pennsylvania, New York, and elsewhere. I agree with Lugones when she writes: "The reason I think that traveling to someone's 'world' is a way of identifying with them is that by traveling to their 'world' we can understand what it is to be them and what it is to be ourselves in their eyes."[27]

By traveling, walking, road-tripping, playing, reading, hanging out, working, listening to music, and dancing together we can also listen to each other's voices, and we can understand what we are being told and how we are being heard. I hope we remain inclined to listen and to respond with love and care.

Brooklyn, New York
2017

NOTES

1. Recall that John McDermott calls "glass without feet" the tall buildings of lifeless downtowns in western and southwestern US cities in order to indicate that they are not grounded in the lives and vital practices of local communities. See John McDermott, "Glass without Feet," in *The Drama of Possibility: Experience as Philosophy of Culture*, ed. Douglas Anderson (New York: Fordham University Press, 2007), 204–218. However, I think that being "glass without heart"—symbols of financial power that tramples upon the oppressed—makes buildings like the Trump Tower in Manhattan even less admirable.

2. Micky Huidobro, Paco Ayala, and Randy Ebright, "Frijolero" in Molotov, *Dance and Dense Denso* (Universal Music Latino, 2003), compact disc.

3. Henry David Thoreau, "Life without Principle," in *Political Writings*, ed. Nancy Rosenblum (Cambridge, UK: Cambridge University Press, 1996), 116.

4. Ibid., 115.

5. See Epicurus, "Letter to Menoeceus," in *The Art of Happiness*, ed. G.K. Strodach (New York: Penguin, 2012), 155–172.

6. I find helpful J. S. Russell's philosophical analysis of the general concept of human psychological resilience in "Resilience," *Journal of the Philosophy of Sport* 42, no. 2 (2015): 159–183. He defines resilience as "a virtue that is expressed in the ability to adapt positively to significant adversity" (164). His related philosophical analysis of resilience as an Aristotelian virtue is illuminating. I similarly conceive of human resilience as a belief-habit or disposition that generally guides conduct so that a person can adapt and thrive in the face of significant adversity. As a complement to Russell's analysis, I would opt for a pragmatic clarification of resilience as the sum of its effects with conceivable practical bearings. My description of my attempts at practicing resilient love, then, contribute to a partial pragmatic clarification of resilience as a belief-habit. For the pragmatic maxim to clarify the meaning of concepts, see Charles S. Peirce, "How to Make Our Ideas Clear," in *The Essential Peirce: Selected Philosophical Writings*, eds. N. Houser and C. Kloesel, vol. 1 (Bloomington: Indiana University Press, 1992), 124–141.

7. José Martí, "Our America," in *Latin American Philosophy: An Introduction with Readings,* eds. Susana Nuccetelli and Gary Seay (Upper Saddle River, New Jersey: Pearson Prentice Hall, 2003), 232–238.

8. Ibid., 238.

9. Ibid.

10. Charles S. Peirce, "Evolutionary Love," in *The Essential Peirce: Selected Philosophical Writings*, vol. 1 (Bloomington: Indiana University Press, 1992), 352–371.

11. Douglas Anderson and Michael Ventimiglia, "Learning and Teaching: Gambling, Love, and Growth," in Douglas R. Anderson, *Philosophy Americana: Making Philosophy at Home in American Culture* (New York: Fordham University Press, 2006), 170–173.

12. Peirce, "Evolutionary Love," 354.

13. Charles S. Peirce, "The Fixation of Belief," in *The Essential Peirce: Selected Philosophical Writings*, vol. 1 (Bloomington: Indiana University Press, 1992), 109–123.

14. Anderson, *Philosophy Americana*, 7.

15. Ibid., 9–10.

16. María Lugones, "Playfulness, 'World'-Traveling, and Loving Perception," in *Pilgrimages/*Peregrinajes*: Theorizing Coalition against Multiple Oppressions* (Lanham, MD: Rowman and Littlefield, 2003), 77–100.

17. Ibid., 89.

18. Ibid.

19. Ibid., 87.

20. Ibid., 77.

21. Ibid., 77–78.

22. I wrote of her sense of playfulness in the "Philosophical Prelude." For Lugones' full account, see *Pilgrimages/Peregrinajes*, 93–96.

23. Ibid., 29.

24. Ibid., 8–12.

25. Ibid., 96.

26. Ibid., 97.

27. Ibid.

Bibliography

Addams, J. *Twenty Years at Hull-House*, edited by V. B. Brown. Boston: Bedford St. Martin's, 1999.

Alcoff, L. Martín. "Toward a Phenomenology of Racial Embodiment." In *Race*, edited by R. Bernasconi, 267–283. Oxford: Blackwell, 2001.

Anderson, D. R. "Peirce's Common Sense Marriage of Religion and Science." In *The Cambridge Companion to Peirce*, edited by C. Misak, 175–192. Cambridge: Cambridge University Press, 2004.

———. *Philosophy Americana: Making Philosophy at Home in American Culture*. New York: Fordham University Press, 2006.

Anderson, D. R, and M. Ventimiglia. "Learning and Teaching: Gambling, Love, and Growth." In *Philosophy Americana: Making Philosophy at Home in American Culture*, 167–187. New York: Fordham University Press, 2006.

Anzaldúa, G. *Borderlands*/La Frontera: *The New Mestiza*. 4th ed. San Francisco, CA: Aunt Lute Books, 2012.

Baldwin, J. *Go Tell It on the Mountain*. New York: Bantam Dell, 1980.

———. "Sonny's Blues." In *Going to Meet the Man: Stories*, 101–142. New York: Vintage, 1995.

Berry, B, P. Buck, M. Mills, and M. Stipe. "Losing My Religion." In R.E.M., *Out of Time* 1991. Warner Brothers. (CD).

Black, C. "Flowers." In Casey Black, *Lay You in the Loam*. 2013. Catbeach Music. (CD).

Buck, R, and N. Merchant. "Hey Jack Kerouac." In 10,000 Maniacs, *In My Tribe*. 1987. Elektra. (CD).

Bugbee, H. *The Inward Morning*. Athens, GA: The University of Georgia Press, 1999.

Campos, D. G. "On Poetry and Authentic Philosophical Reflection: The American Philosophy of Octavio Paz." *Cognitio* 8, no. 2 (2007): 179–195.

———. "The Role of Diagrammatic Reasoning in Ethical Deliberation." *Transactions of the Charles S. Peirce Society* 51, no. 3 (2015): 338–357.

259

———. "Understanding Immigration as Lived Personal Experience." In *Pragmatism in the Americas*, edited by G. Pappas, 245–261. New York: Fordham University Press, 2011.

Chapman, T. "Fast Car." In *Tracy Chapman*. 1988. Elektra. (CD).

Chavez, C. *An Organizer's Tale: Speeches*, edited by I. Stavans. New York: Penguin Classics, 1988.

Cherkasova, E. *Dostoevsky and Kant: Dialogues on Ethics*. New York: Rodopi, 2009.

Cobain, K. "Breed." In Nirvana, *Nevermind*. 1991. DGC Records. (CD).

Connolly, N. "Calling Out for Rain." In Niall Connolly, *The Future Tense*. 2007. c.u. records. (CD).

Daniel, V. "La Vida Es Un Carnaval." In Celia Cruz, *Mi Vida Es Cantar*. 1998. National Own / Universal. (CD).

Debravo, J. *Antología Mayor*. San José, Costa Rica: Editorial Costa Rica, 1986.

Dewey, J. "Nature, Life and Body-Mind." In *Experience and Nature*, 248–297. New York: Dover, 1958.

———. "The Need for a Recovery of Philosophy." In *John Dewey: The Middle Works, 1899–1924*, edited by J. A. Boydston. Vol. 10, 3–48. Carbondale and Edwardsville, Illinois: Southern Illinois University Press, 1980.

Douglass, F. "Oration, Delivered in Corinthian Hall, Rochester, July 5, 1852." In *American Philosophies: An Anthology*, edited by L. Harris, S. Pratt and A. Harris, 337–346. Oxford: Blackwell, 2002.

Du Bois, W. E. B. *The Souls of Black Folk*, edited by B. H. Edwards. Oxford: Oxford University Press, 2007.

Eleta Almarán, C. "Historia De Un Amor." In Trío Los Panchos and E. Gorme, *Personalidad*. 1996. Sony Discos. (CD).

Epicurus. "Letter to Menoeceus." In *The Art of Happiness*, edited by G. K. Strodach, 155–172. New York: Penguin, 2012.

Fallas, C. L. *Mamita Yunai*. 2nd ed. San José, Costa Rica: Editorial Costa Rica, 1986.

Faulkner, W. "Red Leaves." In *The Portable Faulkner*, edited by M. Cowley. Rev. exp. ed., 57–84. New York: Penguin, 1977.

———. "That Evening Sun." In *The Portable Faulkner*, edited by M. Cowley. Rev. exp. ed., 391–410. New York: Penguin, 1977.

Figueres Ferrer, J. *El Espíritu del 48*. San José, Costa Rica: Editorial Costa Rica, 1987.

Frost, R. "The Road Not Taken." In *The Norton Anthology of American Literature*. 3rd ed. Vol. 2, 1099. New York: W.W. Norton & Company, 1989.

García Márquez, G. *Love in the Times of Cholera* . Translated by E. Grossman. New York: Vintage, 2007.

Gavaldón, R. *Historia De Un Amor*. Film. México: Internacional Cinematográfica, 1956.

Gibran, K. *The Procession*. New York: Philosophical Library, 1958.

———. "The Prophet." In *The Collected Works*, 93–162. New York: Everyman's Library, 2007.

Guevara, E. *Motorcycle Diaries: Notes on a Latin American Journey*. New York: Ocean Press, 2003.

Haya de la Torre, V. R. "Is Latin America Ready for Democracy?" In *Latin America Philosophy: An Introduction with Readings*, edited by S. Nuccetelli and G. Seay, 138–142. Upper Saddle River, New Jersey: Pearson Prentice Hall, 2003.

Held, V. *The Ethics of Care*. New York: Oxford University Press, 2006.

Hemingway, E. *The Sun Also Rises*. New York: Scribner, 2006.

Hopper, D. *Easy Rider*. Film. Los Angeles: Columbia Pictures, 1969.

Huidobro, M, P. Ayala, and R. Ebright. "Frijolero." In Molotov, *Dance and Dense Denso*. 2003. Universal Music Latino. (CD).

James, W. "The Moral Philosopher and the Moral Life." In *Pragmatism and Other Writings*, 242–263. New York: Penguin, 2000.

———. "A World of Pure Experience." In *The Works of William James-Essays in Radical Empriricism*, edited by F. Burkhart, 21–44. Cambridge, MA: Harvard University Press, 1976 [1904].

Jiménez, F. *The Circuit: Stories from the Life of a Migrant Child*. Albuquerque: University of New Mexico Press, 1997.

Jiménez, J. R. "A Luis Cernuda." In *La Corriente Infinita*, edited by F. Garfias, 171–178. Madrid, España: Editorial Aguilar, 1961.

Kerouac, J. *On the Road*. New York: Penguin, 1976.

Lancaster, K. "Travelin' Shoes." In Acappella, *Travelin' Shoes*. 1985. Clifty Records. (Audiocassette).

Larkin, P. "Church Going." In *The Less Deceived*, 28–29. New York: St. Martin's Press, 1965.

López Velásquez, S. "Indocumentado." Yotoco. 2016. (Live Performance).

Lowell, R. "No Hearing 3." In *Collected Poems*, edited by F. Bidart and D. Gewanter, 638. New York: Farrar, Straus and Giroux, 2003.

Lugones, M. *Pilgrimages/*Peregrinajes*: Theorizing Coalition against Multiple Oppressions*. Lanham, Maryland: Rowman and Littlefield, 2003.

Majdoubeh, A. "Gibran's *The Procession* in the Transcendentalist Context." *Arabica* 49, no. 4 (2002): 477–493.

Manzanero, A. "Esta Tarde Vi Llover." Armando Manzanero. 1967. RCA Victor. (45 rpm).

Mariátegui, J. C. *Seven Interpretive Essays on Peruvian Reality*. Translated by M. Urquidi. Austin, TX.: University of Texas Press, 1988.

Martí, J. "Our America." In *Latin American Philosophy: An Introduction with Readings*, edited by S. Nuccetelli and G. Seay, 232–238. Upper Saddle River, New Jersey: Pearson Prentice Hall, 2003.

McDermott, J. "Glass without Feet." In *The Drama of Possibility: Experience as Philosophy of Culture*, edited by D. R. Anderson, 204–218. New York: Fordham University Press, 2007.

McGuinn, R. "Ballad of the Easy Rider." In Roger McGuinn, *Easy Rider*. 1969. Dunhill. (33 1/3 rpm).

Mellencamp, J. "Jack and Diane." In John Mellencamp, *American Fool*. 1982. Riva. (33 1/3 rpm).

Morganfield, McKinley. "Louisiana Blues." In Muddy Waters, *Best of Muddy Waters*. 1967. Chess. (33 1/3 rpm).

Morrison, T. *Beloved*. New York: Vintage, 2004.

Neruda, P. *Canto General*. Translated by J. Schmitt. Berkeley: University of California Press, 1991.

O'Connor, F. "The Artificial Nigger." In *A Good Man is Hard to Find and Other Stories*, 98–126. New York: Hardcourt, Brace, Jovanovich, 1992.

———. "Good Country People." In *A Good Man is Hard to Find and Other Stories*, 167–195. New York: Harcourt Brace Jovanovich, 1992.

Paz, O. *In Search of the Present: Nobel Lecture*. Translated by A. Staton. New York: Harvard/HBJ, 1991.

———. *El Laberinto de la Soledad y Otras Obras*. New York: Penguin, 1997.

———. *The Labyrinth of Solitude*. Translated by L. Kemp. New York: Grove Press, 1985.

Peirce, C. S. "Evolutionary Love." In *The Essential Peirce: Selected Philosophical Writings*, edited by N. Houser and C. Kloesel. Vol. 1, 352–371. Bloomington: Indiana University Press, 1992.

———. "The Fixation of Belief." In *The Essential Peirce: Selected Philosophical Writings*, edited by N. Houser and C. Kloesel. Vol. 1, 109–123. Bloomington: Indiana University Press, 1992.

———. "How to make our Ideas Clear." In *The Essential Peirce: Selected Philosophical Writings*, edited by N. Houser and C. Kloesel. Vol. 1, 124–141. Bloomington: Indiana University Press, 1992.

———. "The Law of Mind." In *The Essential Peirce: Selected Philosophical Writings*, edited by N. Houser and C. Kloesel. Vol. 1, 312–333. Bloomington: Indiana University Press, 1992.

———. "Philosophy and the Conduct of Life." In *The Essential Peirce: Selected Philosophical Writings*, edited by Peirce Edition Project. Vol. 2, 27–41. Bloomington: Indiana University Press, 1998.

Petty, T. E. "Mary Jane's Last Dance." In Tom Petty and the Heartbreakers, *Greatest Hits*. 1993. MCA. (CD).

Richards, K, and M. Jagger. "Paint it Black." In The Rolling Stones, *Aftermath*. 1966. London Records. (33 1/3 rpm).

Russell, J. S. "Resilience." *Journal of the Philosophy of Sport* 42, no. 2 (2015): 159–183.

Salcedo, C. "El Año Viejo." In Tony Camargo, *El Año Viejo*. 1996. RCA Records. (CD).

Sattelmeyer, R. "The Remaking of Walden." In *Walden and Resistance to Civil Government*, edited by W. Rossi. 2nd ed., 428–444. New York: W.W. Norton & Company, 1992.

Sophocles. *Antigone, Oedipus the King and Electra*. Translated by H. D. F. Kitto. Oxford: Oxford University Press, 2008.

Springsteen, B. "Racing in the Street." In Bruce Springsteen, *Darkness on the Edge of Town*. 1978. Columbia. (33 1/3 rpm).

Steinbeck, J. *The Grapes of Wrath*. New York: Viking, 1986.

Stiller, B. *Reality Bites*. Film. Los Angeles: Universal Pictures, 1994.

Styron, W. *Lie Down in Darkness*. New York: Vintage, 1992.

Thoreau, H. D. "Life without Principle." In *Political Writings*, edited by N. Rosenblum, 103–122. Cambridge, UK: Cambridge University Press, 1996.

———. *Walden and Resistance to Civil Government*, edited by W. Rossi. 2nd ed. New York: W.W. Norton & Company, 1992.

———. "Walking." In *The Portable Thoreau*, edited by C. Bode, 592–630. New York: Penguin, 1982.

Trout, L. *The Politics of Survival: Peirce, Affectivity, and Social Criticism*. New York: Fordham University Press, 2010.

Twain, M. "Ghost Life in the Mississippi." In *Early Tales and Sketches:* 1851–1864, edited by E. M. Branch and R. H. Hirst. Vol. 1, 147–151. Berkeley: University of California Press, 1979.

———. *Life on the Mississippi*. New York: Oxford University Press, 1996.

Vallejo, C. "Los Heraldos Negros." In *The Black Heralds*. Translated by R. Schaaf and K. Ross, 16–17. Pittsburg, PA: Latin American Literary Review Press, 1990.

Virgil. *The Aeneid*. Translated by D. West. New York: Penguin Books, 1991.

Warren, R. P. *All the King's Men*. New York: Harcourt, 2002.

Weir, P. *Dead Poets Society*. Film. USA: Touchstone Pictures, 1989.

White, E. B. "Walden—1954." In *Walden and Resistance to Civil Government*, edited by W. Rossi. 2nd ed., 359–366. New York: W.W. Norton & Company, 1992.

Whitman, W. "O Captain! My Captain!" In *Leaves of Grass*, 337–338. New York: Norton, 1973.

Zúñiga, H. "Amor De Temporada." In *Lo Que Se Canta En Costa Rica*, edited by J. D. Zúñiga, 12th ed., 129–130. San José, Costa Rica: Imprenta Universal, 1980.

Index

About the Author

Daniel G. Campos is Associate Professor of Philosophy at Brooklyn College of the City University of New York. He specializes in American Philosophy, understood to encompass work from the Americas at large and to have intricate connections not only with mathematics and science but also with fiction, poetry, song lyrics, and popular culture. His academic writing has appeared in journals such as *The Pluralist, Transactions of the Charles S. Peirce Society, Inter-American Journal of Philosophy, Cognitio, Synthese, Perspectives on Science, Perspectives in Biology and Medicine, Journal of Evaluation in Clinical Practice, Studies in Philosophy and Education, Journal of the Philosophy of Sport*, and *Fair Play*. Other writing on ethics, culture, and travel has appeared in newspapers and magazines such as *The Philadelphia Inquirer, New Republic* (blog), *Elementos: Ciencia y cultura* (Mexico), *La Nación* (Costa Rica), and *Semanario Universidad* (Costa Rica). A native of Costa Rica, one of his passions is to cultivate his personal relations to people, places, local cultures, and languages across the Americas, including the United States, Brazil, and his country of origin.